To Linda –

/ love –

is a scarecrow

that scares

all

but the

crows –

Jim

3-10-2019

LAST OF THE OUTSIDERS

Volume 1: Collected Poems 1968-2019

JACK GRAPES

BOOKS BY JACK GRAPES

POETRY:

A Savage Peace, 1964
Two Poets (with Shael Herman, limited edition of 75 copies),1966
Seven Is a Frozen Number, 1967
Perchance, in All Your Travels, Have You Ever Been to Pittsburgh, 1969
Anything is a Conversation (limited edition of 25 copies),1972
Termination Journal (limited edition 100 copies), 1974
Breaking on Camera (limited edition,50 copies, Black Rabbit Press), 1977
Breaking on Camera, 1978
As Each Unit Is a Constant (with Bob Flanagan and Lori Jean Cohen,
            limited edition, 20 copies), 1980
AfterImage (with Kita Shantiris, limited edition 25 copies), 1981
The Big Warm (with Lori Cohen, Katherine Harer, Vern Maxam,
            limited edition 50 copies), 1983
Presto! (with Vern Maxim, limited edition of 25 copies), 1985
Some Life, 1986
Memo to Hiram (with Lori Grapes,
            limited edition of 20 copies), 1988
Trees, Coffee, and the Eyes of Deer, 1987, 1995
and the running form, naked, Blake, 1994
Breaking Down the Surface of the World, 1996
Lucky Finds (boxed set, limited edition of 100 copies), 2000
Pretend (spoken word CD, Poetry East), 2001
A Time to Sing, A Time to Dance, 2011
The Naked Eye, 2012
Poems So Far So Far So Good So Far To Go, 2014
All the Sad Angels, 2015
Any Style, 2018

NON FICTION:

Method Writing: The First Four Concepts, 2007
Advanced Method Writing: The Art of Tonal Dynamics, 2015

LAST OF THE OUTSIDERS

VOLUME 1:
COLLECTED POEMS 1968-2019

JACK GRAPES

EDITED BY

Phil Bevis

Chatwin Books
Seattle, 2019

Series design by Katrina Noble. Interior typesetting by Cyra Jane Hobson,
cover typography by Cyra jane Hobson and Annie Brulé. Edited by Phil Bevis
with the assistance of Cyra Jane Hobson.

Volume III in the *Chatwin Collected Poets* series.

paperback ISBN 9-781-63398-090-7

Visit us online at www.ChatwinBooks.com.

DEDICATED

To Lori

TABLE OF CONTENTS

THE LAST OF THE OUTSIDERS

"The poems in your chapbook, This Thing
Upon Me, *are as good as anybody can write."*
– Charles Bukowksi

The Last of the Outsiders is a two-volume work. This first volume, *The Collected Poems*, includes that body of work which the author considers to be the core of his poetic work. It opens with fifteen untitled poems, which first appeared in *The Outsider* fifty years ago under the name Marcus J. Grapes, which in part inspired the title of this book. It will be followed by a second volume, composed of the "Uncollected Poems", and a body of prose work related to the author's poetry.

The Outsider was published by Jon Webb and Gypsy Lou Webb at the Loujon Press, an anti-establishment literary journal that was printed by hand on an ancient 8 x 12 Chandler & Price letterpress, featuring Charles Bukowski, Henry Miller, Allen Ginsberg, William Burroughs, d.a. levy, Diane DiPrima, Harold Norse, and Denise Levertov, to name just a few. In 1968, Grapes, in his early twenties at the time, was the youngest among them. The Webbs were housed in a former slave quarters in back of a sagging mansion in the New Orleans French Quarter, "its windows," as Jon Webb wrote in the introduction, "gaping out into a walled-in courtyard dense to its broken-bottled brims with rotting banana trees, stinkweed and vine, while rats galloped overhead at night loosening showers of 1800's dust & plaster."

The Outsider was part of a larger movement in American literary publishing called "the Underground Press." Many of those publications were printed on mimeograph machines in the editors' kitchens, basements, and garages, and so the movement became known as the "Mimeo Revolution." Issue #3 of *The Outsider* featured Bukowksi as "the Outsider of the Year." Double Issue #4/5 was devoted to the work of Kenneth Patchen and included a "Marcus J. Grapes Album of Untitled Poems." Grapes's poems were accompanied by Salantrie's drawings and a pen and ink portrait of the poet by famed French Quarter artist, Francisco McBride. When Jon Webb passed away a few years later, Marvin Malone, the editor of *Wormwood Review*, published a special issue devoted to his accomplishments and asked "three generations of Outsiders" to write a tribute: Henry Miller, Charles Bukowski, and Grapes.

In the years preceding Grapes's publication in that issue, his poems had been appearing in dozens of underground magazines, most now defunct: *Wormwood Review, Bitterroot, Nexus, Olé, New Lantern Club Review, Bellingham Review, Electrum, Stone Cloud, PoetMeat, Black Rabbit Press, Deepest Valley Review,* and *Chattahoochee Review,* among them. Though he went by Jack – his middle name – in his personal life, Grapes used his first name and middle initial when submitting his poetry, writing as Marcus J. Grapes. Those early poems were published by Aphrodesia Press in four collections: *A Savage Peace* (1965), *Seven is a Frozen Number* (1967), *Perchance in All Your Travels Have You Ever Been to Pittsburgh* (1969), and *Termination Journal* (1971).

In 1969, Grapes moved to Los Angeles and made a second transition by rebranding himself, publishing as Jack Grapes from this point on. Over the course of the next fifty years, he produced a half-dozen chapbooks and ten collections of poems: *Breaking on Camera* (1978), *Some Life* (1984), *Trees, Coffee, and the Eyes of Deer* (1987), *and the running form, naked Blake* (1995), *Breaking Down the Surface of the World* (1996), *Lucky Finds* (2000), *The Naked Eye* (2012), *Poems So Far So Far So Good So Far to Go* (2013), *All the Sad Angels* (2014), *Wide Road to the Edge of the World* (2016), and *Any Style* (2018).

The association between these two bodies of work was not universal. While attending a book-sellers convention in the late 1980s, he bumped into John Bennett, editor of the magazine Vagabond. John had published Grapes's poems in his *Vagabond* magazine (1967-1977), and later in the *Vagabond Anthology* (1980).

"Hi," he said to Bennett. "I'm Jack Grapes."
Surprised, Bennett asked, "Any relation to Marcus J. Grapes?"
"That's me," said Jack.
"Oh," said Bennett, "we all thought you were dead."

In 1988, many of those original "Outsider" poets appeared in *The Maverick Poets,* edited by Steve Kowit and published by Gorilla Press. Included in that anthology were Raymond Carver, Wanda Coleman, Dorianne Laux, Sharon Olds, Billy Collins, Ron Koertge, Charles Bukowski, and Jack Grapes. In 2004, Grapes's poems were included in *Men of Our Time*, an anthology edited by Al Zolynas and Federico Moramarco. His work also appeared in the *Anthology of Revolutionary Poetry*, calling up his involvement in the anti-war and civil rights movement of the 1960s and his own leftist ideals. Grapes's poems were also included in the anthology *Stand-up Poetry*, edited by Charles Harper Webb. Stand Up poets were likened to stand up comics. Their poems were noted for humor and the rhythms of natural speech.

The title *The Last of the Outsiders*, is reflective not only of Grapes' early association with the journal, but also the fact that, despite over many years being associated with several schools of poetry, his body of work has defied easy classification. Is he an "Outsider Poet," a "Maverick Poet," a "Stand Up Poet," a "Revolutionary Poet," a "Vagabond Poet," or a "Man of his Time?" Some reviewers have referred to him as a "Confessional Poet." In 1985, Bill Mohr edited and published *Poetry Loves Poetry*, the first comprehensive anthology of Los Angeles poets, containing over 50 poets, many of whom had already attained a national reputation. Mohr's book of critical essays, *Hold Outs*, published by the University of Iowa Press, covered the post-World War II poetry movement in Southern California up to the 1990s and evaluated Grapes's label as a Stand Up Poet. "The manifold ways that Grapes's poetry differs from Stand Up Poetry," he wrote, "are probably as important as the way his poems inform the movement's first years. Grapes's poems are far more willing to engage with themes that are imbued with morbidity and desolation than most other Stand Up Poets."

This view has become commonplace among critics. Matthew Spector, writing in *Poetry Flash*, declared, "It's fairly impossible to do justice to Jack Grapes's diversity; he covers a tremendous amount of ground, abstract and figurative, personal and philosophical, literary and historical – and it goes on with wit and flair, a loopy, urbane surrealism not unlike John Ashbery's that collides with a large-hearted acceptance, a relishing of the ridiculous that seems wholly Grapes's own. It takes great courage to draw these disparate and too long opposed strands of American poetry – the intimate and cerebral, confessional and philosophical – into alignment." Nancy Shiffrin wrote in the *Los Angeles Times*: "In his work and in his presentation of himself, a surface geniality frequently masks something dark and bloody. This flip-flop from genial buffoonery to commandant of the dark side seems to be paradigmatic of Grapes's approach to poetry." As nearly the last survivor of those Outsider poets published fifty years ago, Grapes has defied even that characterization. David Ulin, book review editor of the *Los Angeles Times*, wrote: "Grapes writes poems that operate somewhere in the middle ground between pop-culture and philosophy." Douglas Blazek, editor of the underground poetry magazine *Olé*, wrote in a review that appeared in *Kaleidoscope*: "There is a supreme and eloquent strength in Grapes keeping out of the various 'schools' of poetry." Jim Burns, writing a review in *Shattersheet*, had this to say: "I'm not sure that Jack Grapes's magic could be pinned down even with a long involved analysis. He's a master at using ordinary language to paint fantastic, sometimes surrealistic events and images. I find phrases here, techniques there, that remind me of many great writers, but I can't compare Jack Grapes to anyone, nor find an underlying influence at work. He seems to have absorbed the best of them all and used what he likes to forge his own unmistakable style."

In his afterword to Grapes's collection *The Naked Eye*, Bill Mohr concludes:

> *The complexity of his poetry is perhaps too easily overlooked. The scope of his work will prove to be the most daunting aspect of anyone who decides to make a foray into his extraordinary complex assemblage of poems. He has not made it easy for anyone to grasp the full meaning of his artistic journey. In one of my favorite aphorisms by Paul Valery, he comments, "The best work is the one that keeps its secret the longest. For a long while no one even suspects it has a secret." There are secrets in Grapes's poetry that even I have yet to suspect as to the nature of their presence.*

Perhaps we should allow Grapes the final word on his "Outsider" status. In his most recent book, *Wide Road to the Edge of the World*, two haiku sum up his experience of the many attempts to categorize him:

I have always been
an inside-out outsider.
Everyone sees me.

Sometimes, outside-in,
a stranger in a strange land,
but I see you, too.

Outsider 15

poems from The Outsider
double issue 4/5
published 1968

MARCUS J. GRAPES: A PEN & INK PORTRAIT BY N. O. FRENCH QUARTER ARTIST F. MC BRIDE

JACK GRAPES

A Marcus J. Grapes Album of Untitled Poems

one

i started dying again
last week

it came on me
just like the time before
newspapers clogged with history

all the sad faces
showing up late for the big event
the dying started coming on
after the radios quit playing
i felt it walking barefoot
that night the floorboards
creaking the walls
standing trucks on the street
shaking the house of memory
i walked to the front window for
    air
a man on the street walking home
    drunk
picking up his pipe on the sidewalk
knocking ashes to cement finding
his way in the grass on his knees
i watched him and the newspapers
with one trained eye turned in for
    love
i felt the dying its fingertips
soft flower
running from room to room all
    night
staying years by the kitchen table
killing a roach with a can of
    RAID

they picked me up the next day
i made some excuse
kept a smile ready against
the questions
but keep a light burning
in the hall
just in case

two

an old house
that my father moved in
when he was what i am
trying to be now
in a picture
dusted away in the attic
the years between

lined yellow against the face
and the newer lines that have
come between us in his age
and the face between both lines
since his going
except now after being gone
and in the picture is
that where you lived?
yes, when i was a boy what
was it like, then?
i played stickbill they called me
slasher but not for that
we all had names beany
lefty shorty moe johnny gallager
his real name was morris tishfelt
and others and some good stories
i'll tell you when you're older
i was but he wasn't i never got
to hear them tell me one now
it was always hot
three of us on one mattress on
    the floor
my mother by the stove in the
    same dress
every day and when on the street
i called up to her for a
penny
how she threw it down to me
and both knowing we couldn't
    afford it
that or my mother
dying
i left that city and
that house and many other
things that changing places
can never leave behind
me talking now about
the me i was before i was born
him moving in that old house
where were the books
he held against the kitchen table
reading reading suddenly to turn
to his mother oooh mama, de
    mana gestorrben

de mana is dead
him in the night in the dirty
    tenement
my father him the bald head
now he too my father gone
as no picture the yellow closed
between us
a changing of places with changing
a place to go
me now thinking there is a
going a leaving in everything
this rain too leaving
the leaves without a trace of trees
or going beyond that price of tears
a man sucks his life in with
before his fist his shoulder his hair
his dying his going
mean something
even in this picture
bringing back part
between the negative and the face
bringing back in this
sad time of quiet
a faded picture of my father
when he was shouldered to hope
toward what would someday
    become
a picture
frozen
fatal
forgotten

three

oh it wasn't so much
her teeth spreading
under her gums the way
she talked my old man
beat me came to my bed
one night the ole bastard
part of her finger missing
you didn't notice till
she reached for the salt

JACK GRAPES

shaker or not so much the
way she loved
forgetting the knife
the other one
not even herself in
the darkness
going like she did
perhaps without
saying why and—
we frightened frightful people
unloved so in need
of answers

four

too many years pass
coughing up change old women
baggage themselves in waiting
rooms train stations
signals keep changing
where do we go if not
from here?
i come home
to the same chairs
the same stale coffee
outside even the weather
tires out stops
before it drags on
my arms turn against the heat
as if in a new question
we could find a new answer
there are times *i'd* like to stop
put down my two cents
the chips
the full house
get a drink
watch something happen some-
    where
and there are times
when i think of taking
the mailman aside
to see if he knows something
i don't know

and that maybe together
we could put an end to
this
stillness

five

leaving this clumsy town
car filled with ice-chest & cokes
i pass the cypress stumps
and slow down
the road carefully slides under me
shaded with graves
and i think of the nights
we played hide and seek
in the cemetery

summer comes out of hiding
through shadows bending
breaking the night in half
with a call "olioli-infree"
we ran out of hiding places
stood beside an unmarked grave-
    stone
wondering whose name
belongs on this one
there were others
we could make out the dates
in the moonlight but the
falling away of stone and sand
piece by piece takes with it
the shadings of a name so we made
some up and grew tired of that
no names left and not sure of fear
we walked to the keeper's house
carved our initials in a tree
in the noises between i
told of a girl who had turned
into death and then into
a skinny tree with clumsy branches
was cut down by midgets
it got late we went home that
night i dreamed they took my body
and washed it with vinegar

the road turns and i with it
the sun opens its mouth at the end
of the highway i turn and move on
wondering what can a man lose
beyond the grave when
even his name he trades for
glazed stone and flowers

six

could i believe
for a moment
grass on the cement
walking you mean
to say other things
what dies will not
for long be a secret
but you know
big jackass i told
you to watch the
road yes a lovely day
or a wish to
put the eagle
to shame is
all she ever did
was eat the big
slob ya got
mustard on
a man should see
his dreams burn
before any of us
tell on
him

seven

if they send another bill
i'll tear torches off their shirt hooks
and wave them to hell one by one

heaped between the letters the
    postcards
the scraps of paper reminders

traced back to St. John
love-one-another himself
and other inuendoes of
civilizid rock-throwing the bills
gather like frightened ants in
    search of god
look you lousy muva i don't owe
you the $2.58 and if i get one more
letter about it or one more phone
    call i'll tear torches
somehow it's not worth it

we're all doing our job *the job*
i look at the page under my arm
the half-mad message half-written
    in black ink
there's no one around to see me
    laugh
this secret private joy
the untutored wisdom of the ages
focused on letters and bills
pay the refrigerator man get the
damn sink fixed a reminder to buy
flashlights all singlehandedly
like the neighborhood drunk
kissing the tree goodnight

the system moves forward
catching you like the landlady's
daughter some dues
to pay on this end a little
lovin to get on the other

eight

the madness is power and what
do any of us know of what lies
ahead or
if i thought my life my work would
come to nothing there would
be things to face or
have you ever considered this?
it was like in the movies or so
we made it hearing soft voices

JACK GRAPES

the creaking of seats
mouth to mouth

at breakfast the dream
comes uncaught in search of parts
in a river between thighs the
    hands
for pondering asleep or not

they will be kind before
the kill
this i have assumed
even broken in the mud
a stream of what they call
consciousness

and knowing when they get to me
to kill the mirror first
forgetting the news of their own
dreams the madness of cement
and you think is there any point
    to this?
and I say *this?* and you say "the
    poem"
and i say "o i thought you meant
the other"

nine

i spoke to jenny
the other day
her voice hadn't changed much
but i think mine had
i know you guess
what we talked about
she was okay
and the baby was 4 already
her husband still
fixing cars
i'm fine nothing
much to complain about
no i didn't know
your father died
a cloud i see

from where i'm talking
changes into the shape
of a lion
what else is new?

ten

legendary men in the forest
will not come here again
i have grown a flower
that no man knows
running up and down the streets
i stand beside the garden
a flower
growing from my head
seeing the changes
with a slow and sluggish eye
evening brings a sky looking
like a secret
the voices of men in pain
rise from the thick trees
and shadows without petals
come to rest along the wall
the eyes come for the last time
but the faces belong to men
i have known long ago men
panthers in my dreams
rising thin as smoke
growing freshly stained teeth
reshaping our cities
with the fragrance
of decay

eleven

and when they killed him
i came home the house
catching its breath
even the darkness was unsure
which corners to hide in

and one night finally
he led me to a place

where the grass had been cut
for secret meeting places
four of us that night
crawled on our knees
through the vines and weeds
higher grass falling back into place
where we had gone and left
on each side white shotgun houses
their kitchen lights
pushing out against the summer
and the night and the heat of
our being alive

we had no trouble finding
the bicycle i stood
lookout against the tree
on the corner
i forget the rest
no one ever caught us
years later they leveled the lot
new brick houses went up
filling the block
with a different kind of space
we grow up to change
new houses or ourselves
becoming the same shape over
the years and one day
far from the first one
he came back once

by then we had changed
what we had been that time
we were no longer
and i looked at his uniform
his face which had grown
older and he at my face
and keeping the mystery our
best we talked

and when it happened
i came home the house
put my coat down carefully
rearranged the emptiness
with the patience of old age
the television had finished

its late shows and news
and when it was quiet enough
    i thought
sometimes a new shape to things
brings comfort to the unchanging
underneath so i put food out for
    the dog
i fingered things in place put
the newspapers wherever
newspapers belong found the bed
and sleep with another secret
uncovering in the dark
older
uncertain
faces

twelve

finding new bones
memory comes twisted
with a shared newness but
it won't always be like this
i have made secrets with myself
encountering new faces
in the mirror this hollow
sadness

they take things away from us
little by little
so that the growing older
is a losing
keeping secrets even from our-
    selves?
what do any of us know of mad-
    ness?
today i find the window panes
scrape them their grinning sanity
this too invades
what little belief i have left

and in the end
we must all face meaning
to ourselves for ourselves
we must piece together

JACK GRAPES

the justice of chaos
and put to paper the match
if it were easy
you would be out buying news-
    papers
and i might after thinking about it
be collecting wooden
nickels

thirteen

some jerk with baltic-brained
hands looks at the sink
and says you need a new gestapo
or whatever telling me

as he rattles his teeth you
gotta tear up the concrete and
put a new pipe in otherwise
the whole thing'll back up
and i hear him go on pretty sure
about other people's concrete
and what he knows about sinks
    pipes
and i'm doing the best i can
like a lawyer waiting
for a green light
he shakes his tool box kicks
the dirt from his feet
and bumps off to his fat little
wife and her three brassieres
it takes a man i guess

to tear up your sink and plunk
it into a round sweating woman
all in the day
but i guess he was man enough
to know plumbing call me
if you want to get it fixed
trailing his sunset into the distance
call your insurance man but
don't tell him about the new
pipe say it's an old one
needed fixin and they pay for
the concrete and all

hell i thought everybody
gets a piece of the action
why not let the insurance man
get his fair share so
i go inside turn on the
water and watch it back up
and over the sink under
the floor now the whole
house lifting up gently
the entire block pretty soon
floating down the expressway
four cops on our tail
and i'm sitting here feeling
damned good about it knowing
i got the insurance man covered
and the cops won't catch us
for another few miles
at least

fourteen

this tender minute
while we are alone
before it is finished
let us get some things straight
tell how we have suffered
    and loved
how we have been with the sun-
    light
for a time
in the rain too

against a tree
the sun falling down somewhere
like a child
and we
caught in our own beautiful
    madness
watching the world end
just long enough to
    remember
just what it was like

fifteen

some of us
had hopes to catch on sooner
but the days passed
and the winters got colder
and friends left for other cities or
    died
and new skies rolled over
showing new bones more
rainy days we had put off for
while the money turned hard in
    our pockets
the sleep that waked to pain
the faucet the children
the shape of shadows in our throat
stiffness in the legs
things we knew and understood
deserted for higher ground
and faces we loved fell against the
    bone
and turned cold movies that spoke
new pictures young faces smiling
the rage of torn sunlight doors
    closing
that had got new locks
and more of us died
and some of us tried harder
to catch on & the winters came like
    anyway days
the sky turned away from our eyes
smiling the wrinkled flesh of its
distance darker

eyelashes coming together
seeing a different sky on the other
    side
and then it was a sad
suddenly kind of thing
for which they made prayers and
    cried
and put new memories into the
    sun
they were becoming
desperate strangely as we had once
    been
for remembering
under years of pressure and
    passion
there was a way not out
or in but just a way
a venture beyond that nobility of
    excuse
the sermons end the open beards
huddle against the light

all in all
it was a pretty fast operation
but we left anyway
a further city wondering
what had we missed so much
that we had loved?

Drawings by Salantrie

JACK GRAPES

Trees, Coffee, and the Eyes of Deer

What counted was mythology of self.
....until nothing of himself
Remained, except some starker, barer self
In a starker, barer world...

He came. The poetic hero without palms
Or jugglery, without regalia.

It purified. It made him see how much
Of what he saw he never saw at all.
He gripped more closely the essential prose
As being, in a world so falsified,
the one integrity for him, the one
Discovery still possible to make,
To which all poems were incident, unless
That prose should wear a poem's guise at last.

—Wallace Stevens
from "The Commedian As the Letter C"

Trees, Coffee and the Eyes of Deer

Jack Grapes

ALL THE WAY BACK

All the way back, all the way back and start over,
start over, go all the way back and do it again,
over there, by the tree, go over there, stand over there,
by the tree, walk on over, go all the way over, by the tree,
not by the rock, over by the tree, all the way back,
past the rock, go past the rock, go all the way over and
start again, from the tree, slower, start again slower this
time all the way over past the rock and do it again, without
flinching this time, slowly and without flinching, get your
hands out of your pockets and do it barefoot this time, without
flinching, from the beginning, from the start, from the very
beginning, all the way back without flinching past the rock
slowly and barefoot by the tree and get your hands out of
your pockets, drop the knife, drop the coins, drop the string,
leave them by the tree with your shoes, with your fingernails,
in the box that holds the fire without flinching, that burns
so slowly the flames seem frozen, glittering like swords in
light, without a trace of blood, ice, so dry your skin sticks
to it and comes off, without flinching, from the beginning,
all the way back from the start, go all the way back, and slowly,
as slowly as possible, so slowly you appear to remain still like
that without ever beginning, as if you hadn't yet begun,
when in fact you had begun from the beginning, all the way back
from the start, all the way back, all the way, without flinching.

THE PICTURE

I am five
but that's
not me
in the picture
that's some
one else
who looks
like me
but isn't
me I'm be
hind him
telling
him what
to do with
his mouth
so he'll
look like
me to some
one who does
not know me
if you know
me you know
I look com
pletely diff
rent with
my mouth
shut tight
and my eyes
wide open

JACK GRAPES

and both hands
covering up
my ears so I
won't hear a
thing or say
what I see
when I see
so much
and I'm five,
not even that
yet not until
September
eleventh then
I'll be five.
Imagine when
I'm ten

I AM THE DARKNESS

I am the darkness
Within you all.
I will get you.
Cheat not, tell no man
Lies.
Love those you can
And reserve the others
For boredom
But not pity
And not hatred.
Do not cover your face.
It only becomes
What you are.
Give children pennies
Especially in the winter
Or a candy bar.
Don't cop a feel on a bus
Of a woman
And whatever you do
Don't forget to feed me.
I am the Darkness
Within you all.
I will get you.

JACK GRAPES

MIDNIGHT IN THE KITCHEN

The stiff finger of the wind—
no, it doesn't come here anymore.
We used to have eggs stacked in the ice box,
two seltzer bottles,
my father's favorite salami and cheese
to snack on after midnight,
when you were you.
You could see
how the mustard spread on the hard bread
by the light of the refrigerator,
the closing door that put the light back in
to keep it cold and stiff
where all the light you need at midnight is
in the ice-box
and you are you
and your mouth tastes the food,
elbows on a Formica table top,
fat sad eyes in the dead of night
chomp chomp   tick tock
light dark
and you think and you think.
The mouse under the floorboards
breaks a leaf and is gone
knocking a mud-caked coke bottle
against a piece of slate,
and you think and you think
chomp chomp
tick tock
and you are you

getting fat and getting full,
my old lost father
sitting in that midnight kitchen,
1946,
a slow sweep of the hand
and the salt is off the table,
this white rain
spreading on the floor.

JACK GRAPES

GREENHOUSE EFFECT

If there is a sound, it is not crying.
To tell you the truth, no noise
comes from the house across the street
where rain collects in the bird bath
on the front lawn, though no bird
ever drinks from it there's so much scum
and floating objects thrown there
by kids walking to and from school.
But where are the children?
We haven't seen any in years,
and the school's been closed,
boarded up, as a matter of fact, burned down,
razed to make a harness factory that shut down
after the strike and sits in disrepair.
That's right, it's not a school at all.
But I take the quiet as a blessing.
What's vanished into the asphalt's
best left where it belongs.
No one around here wants any kind of new life.
I lose a shoe, I wear another that doesn't match.
What's the difference. I see a flower,
I snap it off just like that.
Down the street, Eloise invites the weeds in for tea.
The old bushes rake and rummage across the front yard
like the crippled monster from one of the tales
we used to tell the children with a wink. No one winks now.
We are the thing told and like it. Last year a young decorator
working the neighborhood with his red leather briefcase
and white shoes made the mistake of knocking

on one too many doors. We did everything but
eat his bones. Threw them in the bird bath
to rot and stink up the place so they'd never be noticed.
The sun's our only enemy. But we can wait.
Let it come just a little closer.

WHAT THE LEAVES MAKE THAT TURN IN AUTUMN

What the leaves make that turn in autumn
is pinched from the wind.
On the front porch of my uncle's house
we watched the pony named Pinto
ride down the neutral ground
up and down Elysian Fields Avenue.
What the water tower painted green was green for,
high on its legs, a fresh god,
and I was that child that water
has not come to again.
The hurricane's coming, Aunt Bea said.
Moaning of the dead surrounded the house.
What the windows exed with masking tape faced;
that rags were wrapped for the freeze;
Uncle Charles gone to the store for flashlight batteries;
and the horse called to me,
he was my horse wasn't he.
What the Indians rode when I wished I was with them
to have bare legs against a blanket
and threaten the hills that turn black
when the sun goes behind them.
How did it work, I wondered,
and waited for the work to begin:
The lightning froze our faces first,
then thunder inside steel boots pranced on the roof,
and the rain filled the water tank
where Pinto could drink the next day
after we rode him in the air of a fall afternoon,
where Elysian Fields and Esplanade Avenue meet,

where I want to go again,
to feel that pony's teeth on my hand,
to climb the ladder to the top of the tower
and pick splinters from a green god's hand.

MARDI GRAS, 1950

Dressed in a Superman costume,
I fly over them.
Karl is Daniel Boone.
Louis is Davy Crockett.
Charlaine is the baby in the gypsy outfit.
I fly over them.
Beer in the streets.
Is it a man or a woman
my mother asks
as it swishes by and flips up
showing crinoline
and a bare ass.
I fly over him.
King Zulu goes by, throw me a coconut
we scream, running after the floats.
Beer in the streets beer cans.
Flambeaux carriers dressed in white robes, struttin'
where 'ya at, mutha!
Harem girls, spacemen, monkeys
in monkey suits.
I fly over them.
Sick in the streets, wine in the streets.
The floats go by throw me something mister!
Music the bands drunks singing.
I fly over them.
The Indian princess kisses Dracula.
Don't step in the vomit! my mother yells.
Frankenstein's holding a glass from Pat O'Brien's
filled with pink punch and rum;

he sips from a long pink straw.
The Devil with his pitchfork gooses Buck Rodgers.
Broken glass and confetti float down the gutter.
Someone steps on the pink hot dog bun.
Dad sneaks a drink as he hugs
the lady in the cowboy suit.
Raiders from Mars!
Black leather jackets and boots!
Flowers out of the magician's mouth!
I fly over them.
Gangs with razor blades snug in the tips of their shoes.
Faces with knives.
Police shoving the crowd back.
Drunks singing in the beer streets.
Pissing in the streets.
Faces in the streets.
Throw me something, mister!
Throw me something, mister!
Throw me something.
Boom goes the drum.

WHAT DROVE DAMON DOWN

A short thunder is what drove Damon down,
and not meant to be confused, he stood on the corner
of Pico and Alvarado until the rain was in his pocket
next to the bumble-bee (how he loved anything that bumbled,
Damon was that kind of a guy)
and cried himself to sleep.
His mother came by once,
and in Africa he saw himself a huge rhino
(when are rhinos small, I know)
snorting in a pool of water.
Once in Woolworth's Damon took a toy airplane
trembling it under his coat
and all the way home on a bus
even under his pillow trembling
then finally down in the dark corner of his closet
where it stayed until he was past his third wife,
the plane was gone,
Damon never knew who took it.
"I want meat!" he shouted, pounding his chest
with one clenched fist holding a fork.
Damon liked pigeons.
Damon fixed flat tires.
Damon was in love with women.
Damon kept looking for things that would change his life.
A book, a poem, a stranger on the streetcar.
The end came in July.
Damon was in bed, smelling the hot okra sidewalk
and listening to the rain.
This is old, he thought, looking at his skin,

but if I was never young
why do I remember my pet turtle, hollow in the sun;
the hard washcloth my mother rouged against my cheeks;
no one's moon but my own
outside the window next to my crib?
Then thunder came in, and
Damon said it was too short,
and he went down.

SOMEONE IN THE NEXT ROOM GOES MAD, 1953

Aunt Adela is pushing fish into the grinder.
Aunt Fanny swings around the dining room
talking and bumping her ass
into the table set for Passover.
On diet pills, she's a 45-year-old speed freak.
My mother sits in the kitchen
on her fat hams, fat thighs, fat arms,
cheeks in a bulge,
like a moored battleship unfit for tourists.
Bernice in white maid's uniform
understands the Yiddish passed
between these women, why not,
she was there when my grandmother
shriveled in her wheelchair, yelling in Yiddish,
"Too much noise, the children
make too much noise."
We ran around her wheelchair whooping like Indians.

This is the exhibit at the World's Fair
next to the Disney version of frontier life:
Mrs. Boone does the wash out back;
Abe Lincoln's father drags home a deer.

In the next panel is the home of the future.
There's me and my family wearing red jump suits,
staring out the windows—magic panes
that do not break and keep out the cold,
where nothing freezes or burns or rusts or goes crazy,
and you're forbidden to remember the past.

In the next panel
strapped to a chair,
someone is writing this down.

JACK GRAPES

NOTHING LEFT TO CHANCE

Begin with fish,
smack their heads off with a mallet
or tear through the entire phone book
sheet by sheet
and digest the lives listed
five hundred to a page.
You don't remember one old phone number
but all the addresses
for each home you've lived in
bob like little boats
on the ocean of your daydreams.
You can't understand why poets
write lines like that,
or what makes a car go,
and when you see those steel girders
going up on the vacant lot,
the exposed elevator shafts,
glass and concrete not far behind
you wonder how so much can be built
one piece at a time
and nothing left to chance.

ARMS THAT TAKE YOU IN

She does not climb
the star of lion,
had nettles put in place
and takes your face
home in a bag.
Now she was clever, all right.
Each night she removes
her robe, butchered
ankles with one swoop
and the flapping trips
the alarm swarming
the place with cops.
This is it.
The face tucked safely
into her pocket,
she fades back and fades
to this day,
whether full-mooned
or in charge,
each arm takes you in,
without phony,
without pensions or blue playthings,
without kisses or kissing,
trumpets or slander,
without one sign or sure word,
a warning hiss—nothing.
I mean nothing at all.
She stands there
in clever home and opens her robe

JACK GRAPES

flaps naked arms
and takes you in and to this day
she takes you in.

. . . . . .

She returns the turtle
with both legs open,
strokes the inside of her thighs
on a tie,
each knot passing
port cities and storms
above the oceans.
This is the wrong place,
but she waves the curtains back,
and shoves me down by the one light
on the bed stand,
uncertain headlights that circle
these walls in my sleep.
Crunch for one tabletop;
a breath that is good as gold.
By now, I am sweating.
I can slide off the muscles
of her skin.
Trombones.
Glaring spoons of bugles
where the flesh snarls glue,
butler, pussy, reingold,
shifting asses surfing on the bedspread,
fluctuate,
blaze down and into her,
she tuggles me in and bugles me out,
both legs open,

each knot passing,
she strokes the poor cities
on the inside of her thighs
and returns the turtle,
a breath that is good as gold.

. . . . . .

Who are we? Not noble.
We confuse structure with bear-traps
and bears for a song.
But there is no music,
just her humming by the dresser
as she returns each part of her panties
to her legs,
not a clasp notwithstanding.

The rhyme is with the lion.
A picture hanging crooked on the wall;
a window shade unpsrung;
the mirror on the closed closet door.
And the radio on.
I am only back where the old entrance
remains open,
the rest in hand.
A glacier that humbles Tuesdays
in my mouth and raises welts
if I suck too hard.
There is no sign.
There is only this turning,
this constant turning.
She adds a blouse,
a skirt,

a pair of high-heeled shoes
and hums,
what is the tune?
The tune is not the mirror
but one belt loop missed
is all I'd need to find her;
just this nickel in the palm of my hand.
Then she raises her arms like a dancer,
takes a deep golden breath of bars,
and goes.

LIZARDS, BACKS, AND SHOES AS THEY ARE

Someone's overturned the lake again.

I do not understand this one word here, he says.
Neither do I, which is why I keep it in.
But countless things escape so easily out of you,
he gasps.
Are you gasping? Actually gasping?
He apologizes, says he's been reading too much.

And someone's given birth to a brilliant lizard.
Perhaps you know the mother. Clues abound.
Geography is so bare: Like a wet fish
the thumbprint on the refrigerator
wiggles across the chrome.

You'll have to explain that other one, he says.
But we meet each other in so many different places,
I yell (yelling is allowed).
First you march up to the door and swing it open.
Then you learn the beast's language, full of eager notes
and Yippee! the soldiers are home!
Who minds their muddy boots.
Look at the moon how full it is.
My what a moon you say and see,
our problems are gone already.
Meet you at midnight with the fox of the evil evening,
backslapping summer mouth full of sucking flowers.

Ah, but a hundred miles away the city is being eaten.

Who's in charge of burning all these papers? someone asks.
Now this incessant questioning will just have to stop.
We'll never get anything done this way.
Count the bodies again. Are any new? Keep just few.
And Monday, the notary publics. The sheets
and the suits with no names attached,
false teeth still in their cup
and Wednesday too, missing with the rest
no one puts anything away, sheets of dead skin
hard and brittle crunching underfoot
static on the radio, fire drills, children
in the street hitting other children
with long crackling sticks.
Who is going to marry at a time like this?

There is so much and so much to do.
Let us be vegetables together or bubble gum.
Let's make love while the broccoli cooks.
Let's mail our shoes to the richest men on earth.
Who can ask questions with so much to be done?
And so many shoes piled by the door as we sleep.

WHICH CUP, WHICH EYE

The cup has come to his hand
and she says
which eyes
which eyes were you talking about?
He has begun to remove
her hands
which float up without complaint
each finger spread
apart
as if to say
no more.
A look out the window
reveals
the possibilities:
first the long black automobile
stranded with rust and bullets;
then the rubber knife beside
a leo lion puppet
and over by the trunk of the tree
crackling through the sidewalk
the book, stiff against the wind,
still wet,
covered with muddy footprints.

Which eyes,
she says again.
The eyes that approximate,
he says,
that remove tissue

without cutting bone;
eyes that
like your hands,
spread apart
as if to say
no more.
He opens the door and looks out
but there is no one, nothing.
Someone just a minute ago was listening.
He recognized the face.
They've seen us, she says.
Yes
and the skin
begins to come away
without a sound
from their heads.

AND THIS IS MY FATHER

Up
up
up.
Up through five green
hospital floors I run the
elevator up through five
green hospital floors
to where my father walks
along the clean halls
hands in his red robe
to meet me stepping out
to meet him.
A pale hand on my shoulder,
he takes me deep-dyed in ceremony
to the nurse's station
where all the work to be done
is flourished in rich flames
and slow thighs
that squeeze through the night shift.
"This is my son," he says
but I catch the stare of the red-headed
nurse turning her blood-dimmed face to mine.
It is the night shift;
she is the shadow of an indignant falcon.
My father spreads his thick pale hand
with me within it
down the halls into each living room
not staked with hanging vines
of water and blood.

JACK GRAPES

"This is my son," he says to Mr. William
thickening in his heart.
"This is my son," he says to Mr. Butler
covered to the neck with a sheet.
"This is my son," he says
to whomever we pass in the hall.
The dying glide without glee
in their beds;
birds fly at the windows
and turn back.
"When are you coming home?" I ask.
My father smiles and his hand opens wide
without fear floating up to his ear, scratching.
The tall nurse catches him out of bed.
"What are you doing out of bed!" she thunders.
"Why, this is my son," he says to her
carrying off in astonishment
the fully mortal laugh of all his teeth.
And this is my father,
long after his death has died
haunting the night shift hospitals
with the relish
of a gypsy.

HOW SIMPLE A POEM IS

it means to see to see the pitiful
handful of ashes you hold
as you move toward the horizon
singing and making a monument
on a road no one will pass
ever in your life time it means
to run against the wind mouth open
like a nut escaped from adjacent
territories of the interior the radiant
bedfellow of foolishness it means
to believe to believe that you
can be this far from the center
of the earth and still feel the fire
that washes up from the core it means
to stop to stop at once give birth
to whatever is handy that does
as it will do for no one
but yourself
for now

JACK GRAPES

AMERICAN RIVER

A few birds
go into the fresh sky.

Someone sings gaily
along the black river.

It sure is a pleasure
California.

Look down upon the fork
of the American River.

Lie there in the sun;
a brown and fired look.

God, is that a peach?
Juicy as a watermelon.

Last night at sunset
I pointed out the pink sky.

This is the place to live.
Even at night, it's bright as day.

PRETEND

Pretend you don't see me
behind the typewriter.
Pretend the words
were always just this way
on the page
before the face
of the one
who wrote them
in his underwear
on a cold November 5 a.m. Monday
morning
thinking about the commercial audition
he has today at 3:15
For Benson & Hedges.
Thinking should I shave
my mustache,
should I cut my hair,
should I wear a suit,
should I tap dance?
Thinking my sister lives
two thousand miles away
and at 20
hasn't what it takes
to live the next 30.
Thinking why was my wife crying
over the toilet when I walked
into the bathroom.
Pretend I have no face,
no name, no history.

JACK GRAPES

Pretend
the poem's
the thing
that dies.

HOLDING ON

It's been such a long time holding on.
I die with the ones I love
and they go on without me.
Is that me in the photograph?
Jack, do you see me looking at you?
Do you know that camera is the future,
and there is nothing out there
but me, looking back at you,
wondering whether to rip you out
as if you were the imposter.
I have forgotten what you seemed to know,
smiling as you climb out of the pool,
sliding hair out of your eyes,
no rush to get your medal,
just a pause to let your tan body glisten.
What did you know that you could wait
a winner at the lens.
I am tired of your marvel.
I dare you to leave that picture
and walk with me now and remain beautiful.
I'm the one who has marched backwards
to keep you where you are.
I'm the one who holds onto all the family movies and pictures,
boxes and boxes of beanstalk seeds.
My body dies to keep you alive.
My spirit dies in your name.
I'm the one who writes this
unable to hold on.

FEEDING TIME

The horse
in the house
is not dead
but he pretends to be.

"Get that horse out of the bathroom!"
my wife screams.

The crows beat on the doors.
"We want our money!" they cry.
My five buck friends I call them.

I am in the attic—
the giraffe—
sticking my head out the window.
"No one's home," I shout down.

And you know what's in the belfry.
My wife complains.
"Move out," I say, "if you don't like it."

She moves out, taking
Morgan the canary,
Trigger the cat,
Bruce the dog,
and Lassie,
our pet hamster.

So it's the horse and me.

One of us pretending to be dead.
The other, stretching his neck out in a dry season,
reading leaves,
cleaning ash trays on the coffee table,
cooking up a roast in the kitchen.

The tigers are coming for dinner.

JACK GRAPES

LISTEN

Listen, what are you reading this for?
Haven't you got bills to pay,
a movie you've been wanting to see,
a woman to love or a wife to ignore.
I'm here because it's raining,
and poets write poems when it rains—
at least that's what I read once somewhere.
(Listen, I'm lying to you. It's not raining.
I just said that because it sounded good.
It's a beautiful day. There's liable to be a law
or a proverb dealing it a blow from which
it may never recover that's how beautiful a day
it is and you should find a girl or a football
and a field of clover
to take them both
around around around.)

Are you reading this to feel better?
Do you think writing this makes me feel better?
Let me tell you something.
You know what'll make me feel better?
A million dollars. A million million dollars.
I want to be corrupted by money and fame
so bad it squeaks my socks.
I want to be filthy with money
to buy filthy men out
and sell their souls
for a bucket of paint.
I want to have so much money

I'll be able to rob my own bank,
buy my way in and out of jail,
cook omelettes from golden goose's eggs,
send every starving poet
a twenty-dollar cook book
and laugh in their faces
saying:

I don't need your words!
I don't need your poems!
I don't need your books or your dreams.
I don't need your aches and pains
and sensational sufferings!
I don't need your visions
your eyes your goddamn poet's eyes!
I've Got Money, Baby!
I'VE GOT ALL THE MONEY
IN THE WORLD!
I OWN THE EARTH AND THE SUN
AND THE PLANETS
AND THE STARS I DON'T OWN,
NO ONE CAN BUY!
I CAN BE GOD! I CAN BE GOD!

. . . . . .

Listen, I didn't mean what I wrote.
I got a little carried away.
You'll forgive me because it's raining.
I get carried away when it rains.
I don't want money.
I don't want power.
I don't want to own men's souls.

JACK GRAPES

I want just to be poet.
To write words of startling beauty
to fill the universe
of emptiness
in your soul.
To make the trees dance
and the winds curl back upon themselves
like confetti off a ship.
I want your tears.
I want to reach
the dept of such beauty—
I want the universe to suffer
because beauty is a pain beyond pain
that dies in the willow
as well as in the wars of men.
I want all men to own my soul,
the poet's soul,
for it's always for the asking.
I want to belong to all the nations,
and all the oceans.
I want to belong to the earth,
the planets,
all the stars,
and all the spaces
beyond all spaces.
I want to be God.

HOW THE STRANGER IS

How is the stranger?
He's okay.
See him eating in the kitchen.
Dirty boots full of mud.
But he likes the ham sandwich.

How he got in
I don't know.
It was so early when he knocked.
Go take a peek.
Is he still eating?

Now the mailman comes for a coke
and the two of them chat.
Perhaps they know each other.
I walk around the house
thinking what to do.
The stranger comes out
and asks me what I want.
What I want? I say.
But he laughs and punches my arm,
then sits in front of the TV
and watches.
Should I talk to him?
Three paintings by van Gogh
on the wall I got at Sears
he likes, says they remind him of home.
Are they still fixing the street? he asks.
I go out and look, but nothing's there.

JACK GRAPES

He laughs when I come back.
Tricked again, and he punches me on the arm.
He punches me again, harder.
Then again, harder, and again
on the other arm, with his other hand.
What's for dinner, he asks.
He asks to see my maps, all my maps:
The close-up of the Salton Sea
and Lake Pontchartrain.
He punches me again, harder.
Hey, I yell, that was pretty hard.
He smiles, takes the salami and cuts it in half
with the large bread knife.
Want to cut, he asks,
big teeth showing in his smile
and he hands me the knife.
Go ahead, he says. Cut.
Tonight he throws all the pillows on the floor,
takes the chairs and sets them
against the walls.
He stomps around the house
with those big boots and leaves mud tracks
in the kitchen and on the carpet on the stairs.
He goes about dumping everything on the floor,
sweeping his hand around the cabinets and cupboards.
Bam-bam, he one-twos me in the stomach
with each fist,
then slap-slap in the face.
Big meaty hands.
Slap-slap again.
Chairs through the windows.
Kicks in the TV.
Books topple from the shelves.

Hurls the telephone into the bathtub
that is already filled with water
and overflowing.
Have a cigar, he says.
Have a cigar.
The stranger lights it for me,
and watches me puff on it
and lights one for himself,
and gestures me to sit down with him
next to the overturned sofa
and we sit
blowing smoke above our heads.
Real fine, he says, dontcha think?
Yep, I say.
Real fine.

LIGHTS IN THE MUSEUM

My brother wears long-sleeved shirts
that cover the tracks on his arms.
He lives alone now in the big house;
we've all married and moved out
or died.
Louis stalks the rooms like a walrus
and forgets to turn out
the lights.
I come home for a visit and hear
the ghost of my father complaining
about the light bill.
"Louis, turn out the lights
when you leave a room," I tell him.
As he leaves each room, he remembers
and lurches back,
slamming his arm
on the wall,
hoping to find the light switch;
and this is how I see him
after I've gone:
lurching from one room to another,
lights on,
lights off.
The lights in my home back home
go on and off
day and night
all year long.

My brother could hop fences

like a deer
and my father once took his picture,
a freckled face covered with dirt
and peanut butter and jelly
smeared on his chin;
a photograph that once hung
in the Delgado Museum for a month.
It was titled The All-American Boy
because the confederate hat he wore
had "The All American Boy"
written across the top band,
but with that face and freckles,
there was no mistake that here,
under the hat,
was the real thing:
the all-American boy.

That photograph hung with others
along walls full of light switches
and someone going from room to room
turning out the lights—
a woman giving tours through the museum.
My home back home is like a museum.

In it my brother is a photograph
that moves down the halls,
meaty hands and shirt tail hanging out,
freckles and tracks on his face and arms.
Everything about that photograph
my brother has become
moves like the flesh
of an old lake.
Everything moves but his eyes.

They stare without direction,
and it is hard to tell
whether behind them
the light
is on
or off.

ANOTHER POEM

The simmered center of your life
hardens on a teaspoon.

You do not begin
at the beginning.
You begin at the end
of a brutal whiteness
when the heart has lost its nerve,
the incomprehensible hand
that reaches for the incomprehensible razor
waits for the death of the body
that follows the death of the heart
which refuses
in spite of its name
to die,
and if you don't know this already,
it will take more than poetry
to teach you.
After all, life is a tomato,
whatever that means.
It is also a wristwatch, and by and by
a pencil.

In the middle of watching Beloved Infidel on TV,
a movie I've seen four times and know by heart,
I come here to do this, to write,
to stir up the soup of my life, as it were.
My wife and I are not living together now.
I wonder how my brother is,

eating up the skin on his arms,
trying to save his life, his tomato,
his wristwatch.
The high point of my day these days
is getting a peach at Farmer's Market.
These facts are only of my life;
like yours, elegant as they are dull.

But I come here to write this
to save my life, when it is a tomato,
a wristwatch, and by and by a pencil.
So what's to save?
On channel 9 Victor Mature is an Indian;
On channel 13 Matt Dillon kisses the girl
and carries sacks of flour to her house;
On Channel 4 they're dancing to Isaac Hayes.

It's about time I end this poem,
wrap it up like laundry to drop at your feet.
I know you need these loose ends tied up.
When a man sits down to save his
tomato,
as it were,
it's the least he can do.
And the truth of it is, I can do it.
I'm a good enough poet to do it.
I know how to begin and end a poem.
But just now,
on the edge of a pain
I can't point to or name,
I don't feel like it.
My life is not a tomato.
My life is not a wristwatch.

My life is not a by and by.
I'm going to watch Beloved Infidel end
the same way it always ends.
My ends will all be different.

And this poem?
I'll end it
in another poem.

BURIAL

Plucking the light above me
I dream in the darkness
of my black mother
a running splash of rust
whose head grows immense
in my arms.

Dazzled and green-eyed
from the streets
I watch brown stockings
fall to her feet.
Coffee blossoms
amazed at the armpits,
to come home
hung by a thread
the brown carcass of my black mother
who has strangled the tired voice
whose head grows immense in my arms.

She says your mother means well.
I do not tell her
that she is my mother
brown my black mother
asleep in white calico
who rocks with the voice
whose head grows immense in my arms.
You are not from my country
she says
but I am brown your black mother

I pass fingers through your hair,
come here
high on the tree
to sit when it rains
overgrown with coffee blossoms
my boy   my boy   my boy
I am brown your black mother
my head
grows immense
in your arms.

THE COUNT'S LAMENT

There are not too many ways
to drink the blood.
Thick and slightly warm
like pureed vichyssoise.
Sometimes I roll it around,
what little there is,
in my cheek between tongue and palate,
just to get a taste again
of what I've forgotten the taste of,
drinking it so much now out of desperation
that perhaps even this sip
is not enough anymore.
Perish that horrible thought!
I go now from neck to neck,
throat to throat,
reeling, scratching with my fingernails,
flapping against invisible mist
that issues from their mouths
as they walk about the streets
in a cold that lies above the ground,
a cold you can wave your arms in
should you need to.
Not the cold darkness I bask in.
A darkness that has a taste,
a dull texture that grinds in my sleep.
It's all the same:
Flamingos!
Daffodils!
To dream of a blazing sun,

just think of it,
to dream of that burning
and be unable to touch it,
suck its fire into my own veins,
down the gullet where it boils
the substance of my flesh—
then to wake, biting at splinters.
It's no life for a Count, believe me.
Were I to drive drunken
down one of your neon streets
what breath test would you give me
when even the flesh turns thin and white
at the end of a century.
A century!
It's like a snap to me.
All I vomit is blood.
That sickness comes out of my throat.
To be drunk again for fear of the waste.
The indignity!
Just to stand at the sideboard
with a scotch and ice in my hand
and clank the cubes around the glass
and finish it off with a puff.
The worms. The rats. The beetles.
The spider spinning its web
for the unwary fly,
tiny cracks of blood I've long disdained.
And now all there is left
is you,
your own meager supply
that brightens with my pulse.
Imagine what it might be like
to flow in my veins
for centuries without end.

ASK THE BULLS

What are you sure of?
Ask the bulls.
The kill must be easy,
quick if you can
manage it,
but easy if nothing else.

So you're outside Mexico City.
The local boys torture the bulls.
Their silk is full of sweat and dust.
On wooden benches
you sit watching
and crack pistachios
between your teeth.
You don't see blood
until the black animal
is dragged through the dust
on ropes and chains
like a stalled truck.
The banderilleros push
from behind, churning
their thin legs.
Flies buzz lazily
in the plaza.

Now you know
you are going
to write a poem about this.
Down the aisles the kids

had yelled all afternoon—
"Piece da cheese! Piece da cheese!"
waving little bags in the air.
Why are they selling
pieces of cheese, you thought,
but finally buy,
and as the bull
is being dragged through the dirt
you crack the "piece da cheese"
between your teeth,
spitting shells into the ring.

You look around,
at the fat *afficionado*
displeased with the slow kill.
The bull's neck hanging
to the ground.
The matador stands over him,
hands above his head
like a dancer in fifth position
to drive the blade in.
He thrusts six, seven times
and the bull is weary
and no one watches.

You see this all
taking place
not just now,
but later,
in the poem,
in the poem you will write:
the flags and the ceremony
and the fat *picadores*

grunting in the saddles
of their horses;
the hot sun, the animal smell,
fierce ladies in yellow hats
shaking their fists for blood.

You sit back, smug and grateful,
the empty page of the poem
folded in your back pocket.
You know just how it will go.
There's no need to rush it.
Anytime you need it,
the poem's yours.

An easy kill.

SUSPECT

Suspect
the poem
that is not
a matter
of life & death.
It is like
all the other
poems
that are not
matters
of life & death.
When a man
talks to you
without
blinking an eye,
when a man
listens
without glancing
over his shoulder,
his hand
is on a knife
and he knows
what he wants.
He wants
your crippled mother
clutching that
foolish poem
in her
wheelchair
hands.

JACK GRAPES

INVISIBLE

Dispatch: Blue baby left
    in back seat
    outmaneuvers rat
for rattle.

Sun goes down. Sun comes up.
    No one touches me.
Even in plain sight: hiding.

They come to my room
These are his things.
    a dozen pipes;
    five thousand books;
    pennies by the jarful.

Just what is too much to ask
    when you're invisible:
that they leave you alone?

SHE FUCKS AND I FUCK

She fucks and I fuck
and both of us are fucking.
Now I'm up,
I'm thinking I'm fucking
then I'm not thinking
I'm fucking
I'm just fucking.
Then I'm telling her how good it feels
then I'm feeling how good it feels.
I want to come and I don't want to come.
She wants to come and she doesn't
want to come, oh not just yet,
you can't fuck and think about fucking
all at the same time,
your leg is in
her cunt all of a sudden
and you want
to be her cunt all of a sudden,
to be fucked, not to fuck,
to include, not to penetrate,
to be killed, not the killer
Oh and it's always moving,
it's going to be over
suddenly you think and then you don't think,
A tongue licks your closed eye
and it licks your closed chest
and you lick back, thinking of licking,
then just licking
and your heart breaks, it breaks,

you're fucking the woman you love
and it breaks your heart.
You're deep and full
in pity and in pain,
coming up from life
for air,
and yes, I love me now,
I am plunged and raised,
set down and risen,
the inside breaks against the bone,
and God, dear God,
if You could fuck the woman You love
when You are loving her,
everything that hurts
in your heart
would come true.

RECITATIVE

When the bottoms of tables re-embrace their
former students and the doorbells embark
upon stranger journeys inward,
keep this edge in your face that you know
which friend to love and lover to betray.

If there are words to be said to those
who threaten with their kneecaps
better to move against the wall sideways
like an animal in the zoo who keeps secret
which friend to love and lover to betray.

Certainly it's no use being skillful;
show your naked body to the camera even
when the background's similar; those
who look look back and fail to answer
which friend to love and lover to betray.

If you cannot sleep, sleep will pay no debts;
if your hands are shamed into motionlessness
take care that your feet scrape
the proper mud from your shoes and lead you to
which friend to love and lover to betray.

I've got no answers. A coat or sweater
works as well as a shelf though a bed
unobserved is no place to dream or cut your
wrists. Cut your eyeballs out if they know
which friend to love and lover to betray.

JACK GRAPES

Never mind. This is taller than you are.
A movement to the window. Out there the name,
walking on its fingertips, at the edge
of the face, on the tongue of each friend
who loves you and each lover you betray.

THE BEAST AND THE DREAMER

There is a beast
in the bed with you.
You'd rather pretend
it's the dream
or the overcoat
you forgot to hang up
or that person
you share space with
on the sheets.
When you roll into him
during the night
and his teeth fly up
to the ceiling,
you hold still,
listen for a sound
to explain it,
look for the book
you fell asleep reading,
then roll back over,
and the beast settles
down again beside you
like a black balloon.

I know about this beast.
He does not sleep
and he does not dream.
To himself, if asked,
he is more a beast,
knows his ugliness

78   JACK GRAPES

to become more ugly.
Swamps dry up in his mouth.
The death of ships
under the ocean
slide in slime on his skin.
His arms are the broken
bones of asteroids,
his eyes
the open ass of Krakatoa.
And though he's never died,
his death is all he truly remembers.
Condemned to the light within the dark of sleep,
he is not permitted his own,
but puts one arm
behind his head
and thinks through the night
with you,
avoiding the beast of thoughts.
He lies beside you,
envious of your slow breathing,
wishing your dreams
were his to dream,
wanting just one
of your nightmares
to wake from.

THIS STORM, AND THE NEXT ONE

All of this pain
is an envelope.
Look what upsets you:
a spilled glass of apple juice
and your kids,
why worry about them?
Where are your parents now,
now that you tie your shoes
and ignore your wife
who locks the doors
when you go.
An envelope, a chair,
a dish of almonds,
that ridiculous $40
hand-painted
waste-paper basket.
Today the city is under mud.
The sun comes out
and everyone's back
to buying hamburgers and gum.
I'll bet your suit is pressed.
My shoes are wet
and still I wear them
but no big thing.
Was that a neighbor of yours
who carried a bag of valuables
into the den
just before the water
swept his bedroom down the hill?

JACK GRAPES

An envelope. A chair.
A plate of cheese.
Did you read about the winter Olympics
with transit strikes and Soviet medals?
This Lake Placid is that what you mean
by pain?
An envelope.
A chair.
A line of tanks and bombs.
And what of that Greek
who burned the enemy's fleet down
by reflecting sunlight off the shields
of his men.
And that shoemaker in the lava of Pompei,
still bent over his workbench.
Envelopes, chairs, shoes, shields.
The sky is getting dark again.
They say the next storm is 200 miles
off the coast, due later tonight.
Well, it's me reaching up and dragging
all that rain down.
That's my hand going up black
behind the bushes.
Remember this storm years from now
when you are swept into the cities
by the cities,
and into the sea by the sea.
This one: an envelope,
a chair,
a line of hands
reading your own hands' future.
Stay in tonight.
Lock the doors.

STRANGE VISITORS

I believe I have seen
whole houses lift right up
and fly off, without
a sound.

Now, the doorbell rings
and I pull my pants
up my walking legs
to get there
before my miracle goes away.

But it's just two tall girls
of the Jehova Witness—
clean and fresh flesh
under thin summer dresses
and they put into my hands
lit-ter-a-tchure, instead of their own hands.

"Look," I say, "I'm an atheist,
thank you anyway."
But they keep their smiles
and come right back.
"An atheist! Well, we can fix that.
See here on page ten
where the light
came out of the sky
and the face of the void was full?"
And I listen to their talk
full of bloom and bubbles,

shaking my head, "Ahuh, ahuh..."
Then finally:
"Look, I was beating off
when you rang the bell.
Could you come back in about ten minutes.
I'm almost finished."

I believe I have seen
strange visitors from other planets
unwrap salami sandwiches
in the park, plastic forks
in cups of chopped liver.
I believe I have seen strange faces
disappear in supermarkets.

My sister called today, long distance,
to tell me my brother's
shooting up again.
"We haven't seen him in weeks, Jack,
and I'm scared."
"Charlaine," I say, "maybe he just
went to visit that girl in Houston.
Maybe he just had to get away,
fly off somewhere."
"Maybe," she says.

The light in the sky goes away
and the night comes now
in one large, slow footstep.
I have been feeling ancient lately.
Something in me wants to go back.

I look out the window.

There goes another house.
In the distance, it looks
as it rises
like a kite.
And the doorbell rings.
And the phone rings.
And my hands,
blooming with fingers,
ring,
waiting to be answered.
And my hands, strange visitors,
fly off,
and take me
with them.

BREAK DOWN

Of course, you're alone.
In America, on a Texas highway
watching the last smoke of the sun
grow black.
Without oil, without gas,
without a pay phone that works,
Tonight, you'll be killed:
that, you know.
A drunk pick-up does it as a joke,
or the night swans
who prowl for your kind,
who leave your shoes,
and take the camera,
the luggage, the money.
You're alone, you're going
to be dead, if you walk
toward the closed Texaco station
one mile up or sit it out till morning,
you're going to be dead.
Where were you going? El Paso?
On the map, for some reason,
you circled Carlsbad and Sonora.
The last for gas, you thought.
Then:
A pair of tail-lights turn
on the gravel shoulder
and slowly become headlights.
You begin to laugh,
make an outstretched gesture

with both arms wide
as if sending aloft
a dazed insect
from the palm
of each hand.

BUZZARD

Buzzard makes the mountain
and says to me:
"The light. I made the light, too
and cracked those rays in my throat,
tasted what you call flesh
but was plaster, then copper,
then rusted pipe,
the blade of a knife still sharp.
Is this what your people
have come to?"

The snows melt and take with them
the cave raging of the buffalo.
My first dance. Will she dance
with me? If I squeeze her hand
will she squeeze back, and if that,
then what?
Buzzard flaps in my chest.
He wants out.
He wants to follow the trains
but to meet no train
that stops.
He wants to trust the trees
and melt the cities down
to mercury and sulphur.
Buzzard says:
"I can eat my own kind, too.
It wasn't easy, but you taught me.
And I make the light;

I go up and lay the killing
at the feet of the father
and bless its food.
Reason will justify anything
but bless the poetry
and the light will bring you up."

He has a point.
Some days, we sit in the yard
and listen to the rain
shatter on the tin shed
by the plum tree
or watch it from the bedroom window
clog the backyard drain.

Buzzard shuts his eyes and takes
my hand.

"You have two homes," he says,
"but you can only die
in one."

MY RODEO

I'm ashamed of my cheap rodeo
so I keep it secret from my friends.
It's not even as big as theirs
and needs constant repair.
"How's your rodeo?" someone asks at a party.
"Fine!" they chirp up.
They jump at the chance
to extol the virtues of their rodeo.
Pretty soon a circle gathers
and everyone's discussing its size,
weather control, the acoustics, the peanuts.
If I stay in my corner someone will notice and ask about mine.
I don't want to talk about it.
So I join in, chirping up with *you-don't-says*,
and *isn't-that-amazings and*
what-about-the functional-glitter?

By the time I get home
I'm exhausted from avoiding the subject of my rodeo.
I get home and there it is,
not much on weather control, lousy acoustics,
Styrofoam peanuts.
There's no sub-culture, no glitz-trimming,
no contour illuminations, not even jacket hitch
where the top bolt exceeds the maintenance quota lining.
I'm embarrassed and ashamed of the damn thing,
give it a kick and stub my toe, then cover it with a sheet.
Maybe smother it.

I am a man who comes home depressed, lonely,
frustrated, who tries to smother his rodeo,
his cheap rodeo.
And I haven't even the courage to do that.
Imagine smothering one's rodeo.
The shame would haunt me the rest of my life.
So after a while I take the sheet off and go to bed,
hear its slight breathing throughout the night,
its occasional cough, the short low moan
just before daybreak. My cheap rodeo.

JACK GRAPES

THE EASY PART

The Eiffel Tower's on the cover,
cubist, prismatic, unshaven.
I watch the rain
shine up the earth, layer by layer,
Je vois tomber la pluie.
It's all one kind of rain
or another:
rain in the teeth,
rain in the palm of the hand.
It stops everyone from talking,
this yet and yet.
Once around the earth.
There is someone
who wishes to sleep beside you,
and you consent.
Because this is the easy part.
Just before sleep.
Just what your life has been
up to now:
a bird, a little bird;
so many things,
on their way to postage.

BUTCHER

Butcher sipping tea.
Butcher fishing with the cord tied round his neck
    as he leans over the bank, thinking:
    trout or shark.

Butcher notices his mother's getting old.
    Cradles her wrinkled arm in his hand.
    Takes a peek at the other arm in the
    bottom drawer beside the bed.

Butcher's asleep now, so don't disturb him.
    Tip-toe through this part, passing
    his feet sticking out from under the sheets.
    Stop! He's turning over.
    The mountain rearranges itself and crawls
    back into the dream, that deep mouth.

It's morning, he's off to work. His hands clean
    as a baby's.

Butcher's in the bank. His desk neat: each pad,
    pencil, loan request arranged geometrically
    like a Mondrian. Here come the customers!

Butcher checks the vault. Smells new money.

Butcher's at his desk. His foot held above the button
    on the floor. Sips his tea. Waits breathlessly
    for the gun-wielding, stocking-faced, blood-thirsty
    robber.

                                      JACK GRAPES

THE FIRST OF EVERYTHING

The first hand does not touch you.
It is a warning.
There is the breath of rocks,
a face that holds papers down.
And the first foot does not step out.
It too is a warning.
You see it approach on a clear night,
its heel full of crushed berries.
A reminder, but of what?
The first eye has no need of seeing
and this too
in a way you cannot understand
is a warning.

These warnings slow you down.
Then, thumping your back door
like the morning paper
comes the first mouth tied with string
and never mind what it says,
you take it as a warning.

The first of everything
revolves like a planet
around your mind.
Your standing at the front door
is a warning.
So is your walking out.
Your day is a road
broken only by bridges.

GIVING THE NAMES TO POETRY

Birds uphold and princes fart.
Along the world and around it
runs a silver ridge.

Donald Zelanka,
Jerry Pinero,
Martin Shaprio,
you'll never read your names in this poem.
Maybe one of you is a lawyer
but I doubt it.
Your names go with your faces,
your lives.
One of you still wears white socks, I bet
with brown shoes.
And who still jingles coins in his baggy slacks
(God, who wore "slacks" in 3rd grade?),
and one must work now
in his father's fruit stand on Carrolton Avenue.
I can just see you
Jerry Pinero
weighing a pound of peaches while you wonder
how your name got into poetry.
And that donkey laugh of yours,
Donald Zelanka,
do your kids own it now,
with that silver watch chain
half-mooned on your belt
(God, who wore watch chains in 3rd grade!), and
Martin,

Martin Shapiro,
I know you died of leukemia
three weeks before your bar mitzvah,
and I saw you in the coffin, too,
white, yeshiva face, and you still had dandruff.
What a big dope you were,
a big Jewish dope.
In a natural history museum
I'd figure to find you behind a glass labeled:
Rare Species—The Jewish Dope.

What is this
when the world gets suited up for winter
with slow moving skies
and the only sound I hear is the humming of the refrigerator
in the cold kitchen.
What is this that I think of you,
Donald Zelanka,
Jerry Pinero,
Martin Shapiro.
What is this that I wonder
what names like yours are doing now in the world,
names typed on credit statements,
traffic tickets,
letters from Shreveport.
What is this that makes me want
to give your names to poetry,
where a ridge is all there is
dividing birds from princes
and its world gives nothing away?

THE LOST THINGS

I lost my hiking boots.
And my green sleeping bag.
Maybe someone stole them.
Anyway, they're gone.
So is my copy of
Hear Us O Lord
from Heaven
Thy Dwelling Place
by Malcolm Lowry.
So are some of my other books.
Daniele left my red baseball cap
with the silver wings of Mercury
in the bathroom at Barbera's Pizza Parlor.
And I can't find my favorite pair of scissors
either, not to mention
my Bluit camping stove
and large cooking pot.
I loaned them to Karen Kaplowitz
coming out of the Cucamonga Wilderness
and she still has them.
She's a lawyer.
Now my mail isn't coming.
Someone put in a change of address form
and the post office
has been forwarding my mail
to the Graduate Department of English
at the University of Pittsburgh.
This is true.
"Why am I losing these things,"

I keep asking.
I keep asking this.
Out loud.
I'm driving Lori crazy.
"Something strange is going on here,"
I yell.
It's getting hard to concentrate on anything
for very long.
"Where are my boots," I whine
in the middle of a movie.
My favorite hiking boots.
It's very distressing.
Someone has my sleeping bag right now
and they're hurting it.
Someone's grimy hands are pulling apart
Hear Us O Lord from Heaven Thy Dwelling Place
and they don't even care about the underlines
or the notes I've made in the margins.
I'm not going to let it get me.
The red hat, with the silver wings of Mercury,
I plan to get back if it's the last thing I do.
I'll keep a look out
and someday whoever took it
will be wearing it in the May Co.
thinking I've forgotten all about it.
But I haven't.
I'll see it.
And I'll get it back.
I'll get all my things back.
My Bluit camping stove
and my large cooking pot.
And my mail, all my mail.
My sleeping bag.

My boots.
My broken-in hiking boots.
I've missed you all so much.
So very much.
The lost things are coming back.
It's all coming back to me.
And I need to feel that I deserve this.
I need to learn
how to open my arms
and take them in,
as I would myself,
lost
these many
many
years.

JACK GRAPES

NEARING THE POINT

Nearing the point
where the point at center
and once on its own
transforms earth to water
and back up above the shore line
around the unnecessary eyes
of its fish.
And each too to have seen it,
this black eagle
that flies out from your throat
and refuses to sing.
In our twentieth century
not because of me
not because of you
love is denied
kept silent
touches in departing
brushes us with wingtips
in cornerless space.
And higher still,
each out of desperation,
in orbit,
a little weaker,
reckless,
sprung from the bedhead
where only yesterday
we stood
surrounded by the white ash
of our bodies.

So if not dead from the black water,
then dead from the frost,
from the window from the contrary idea
and so dead in fact from peace.
Convinced by the rooms we have loved in,
I get up from my chair
and walk toward the door
in this name flying up like a balloon,
while on the earth
there is time between points
to swim up from dreams
and smell your lover's shoulder
so deep in the earth's arms of sleep.

JACK GRAPES

TO WRITE A POEM

When I sit down to write a poem
I try not to think about anything.
Sometimes, I begin with a line
that just comes to me,
a line that might make no sense whatever,
and then I have to go on from there
making more lines that make no sense
until I've found a way before the end
to make it all make sense,
some kind of sense.
Now, I'm not know for being abstract,
so when Michael Ford asks me later
at The Lair where we all go for coffee
after the poetry workshop,
"Why are you writing so abstract?"
All I can answer is,
"That was abstract?"
I look down at the poem
and it doesn't seem abstract to me.
I read the beginning out loud.
"Nearing the point where the point
at center and once on its own
transforms earth to water and back
up above the shore line
around the unnecessary eyes
of its fish.—What's so abstract about that?"
I ask.
Michael tries an answer, but it's
abstract, too.

Bob says
I should cut the line
about my name flying up like a balloon.
And I agree with him.
Enough about my name.
My flying name.
Though, I think, the name too is abstract,
a rock I keep cracking into pieces,
or a balloon that does what balloons do,
and I wish it would make up its mind,
abstract flying cracking name.
Fist, rocket, staircase.
What's in an abstract flying name, anyway?
Did you know that *slug* spelled backwards is *guls*.
Thank about that
if you want to understand what abstract means.
And I find also that I tend to leave the poems
I write
somewhere in the middle and then have to come back
to them somewhere before the end.
Like now. Like here, in this poem.
And just what the flying hell is a poem anyway?
Huh?
Huh?
HUH?
(pause)
I didn't think you knew.
Well if you don't know
how come you're always combing their hair
and holding your hands over their mouths
and tying their shoelaces together?
I see all the poems we've strapped
and tied to straight-backed chairs

in cold basement rooms,
barely bringing enough water
and bread to choke on.
I'd set them all free—
hordes of all our poems
descending upon us
in rage.
And my own head hurts.
And I'm sick of seeing my body
fill with the death of poetry.
I'm fat and getting fatter.
I can't stop eating.
I'm sick of poetry and sick of being fat.
I'm sick of combing my hair.
Sick of wearing the one shirt that fits me,
sick of seeing my desk piled with mail
and paper clips and unpaid bills,
sick of sleeping all day
and eating all night
and sick of praise and sick of grief
and sick of misunderstandings
and sick of love
and sick of fucking
and sick of jerking off
and sick of poetry, that's for sure,
sick of my poetry and sick of your poetry,
sick of everyone's poetry,
sick of reading
and sick of baseball
and sick of movies
and sick of the horses—
I like Charlie Chaplin
but I'm sick of just about everything else

and that includes poetry
which includes everything anyway.
And I'm sick of this poem, too.
This poem that makes such sense,
that flies off, like my name.
It nears the point
where the point at center
and once on its own
transforms earth to water
and back
up above the shoreline
around the unnecessary eyes
of its fish.
And it's abstract.

Like a rock.

Like a slug
that spelled backwards
becomes a large white bird
that screams out in the air
and flies far
far away.

THE LOVER

A book with a picture on the cover
of a lady dressed in red on my desk.
This woman I love
trying her tennis shoes up on her feet.
A root-briar pipe,
straight-grained and carbon-caked
leaning on the rim
of the cork-centered ash tray.
A memory in the room
that settles like netting
as I enter,
the big house with winding
tunneled stairs.
These I own, these thoughts,
that book,
the woman I love,
my pot-bowled pipe.
And they own me,
they stretch and spread
and suck my flesh
not just into themselves
but out to air,
out above the hills and water,
in touch with
some-un-named holy voice
that calls me to my life.
And I am this one man
attached beyond beauty
to forms I cannot imitate.

And woman too,
I touch my nipples
and run my hands over the cool
flesh of my ass,
and I am woman too,
barely sensing that other beauty
I lost long ago.
And I touch each part of me
that walks in red dresses,
that thing smoked
those shoes laced,
these memories loved.
And I am open,
if not always,
then now,
to leave my hands on table-tops
and give up,
to let go,
to walk from my bed
in the morning,
open a window,
lean out,
open my mouth to speak
say nothing but song,
to flap my arms
and fly off,
to sail out
beyond the map
of my own
un-
traveled face.

BODIES

At first I am talking
about my body,
then something else.
What do you know
about bodies.
When Ben and I
have to move them
from one table to another
they're so heavy
and stubborn and clumsy.
Ben lifts the head
and puts a block underneath.
It's like lifting a broken desk lamp.
I swing the feet up
and straighten them.
Always under the cover.
When I go home
I sometimes think about
the part of my own body
I am soaping in the shower.
This hand holding *this* breast.
Why does touching myself here
feel better than touching myself
there?
Whose hands would feel better?
There is so much about bodies
I don't understand.
Sometimes, after we make love,
I discover that I'm bleeding.

There's a spot on the sheets,
and between my legs when I wipe myself
in the bathroom.
He comes in to watch, concerned.
Blood comes off in my hands
but after a bit the bleeding stops.
We're both naked.
There's a little blood on his penis.
I watch him wash it in the sink.
It's as if he were bleeding too.
Back in bed, lying side by side,
we talk about the bodies
then fall asleep.
When I wake during the night
I can hear his heavy breathing.
I lay my hand across his belly.
He turns and snugs his ass
up against my side
and I turn with him
throughout the night;
a kind of dance, a breathing,
a small exchange of words.
To wake in the morning
beside someone you love
is a miracle in itself.
Then the bodies get up
and have breakfast.

JACK GRAPES

"There is no insurmountable solitude.
All paths lead to the same goal:
To convey to others what we are."

– Pablo Neruda
(Nobel Prize Lecture)

ANOTHER SENTENCE

Every sentence is another sentence,
really another life.
Someone's always one step ahead.
The streets glow from the snow plow's blade
chipping up stone with a daylight flash.
From here, the same tree out back,
the same asphalt roof,
the same wounded clothes pins
shifting on the line.
Sometimes the man hanged is a hero,
sometimes a traitor.
Perfect sight and perfect blindness
when it suits our needs.
One day you realize
that you cannot break out
of your own bones.
There is snow-mush in the gutters
and along the edge of the highway,
melting here, turning to rock there.
Something's always a step ahead.
Every sentence is another life,
really another sentence.

JACK GRAPES

A BURNING

Old cans full of sour milk
stacked in the back room,
his shoes, boxes of them,
not to throw anything away,
even shoelaces for sentiment
remembered in leaning cardboard boxes
once used to pack pillows before
the house burned down.
He smells that all the time:
the dry burning wood,
wet strips of ash and black puddles of water.
Sometimes he can trace the smell to something real.
Sometimes, to something else, coming or having come.
It will come again, he reasons,
and begins again to pack things away
so that what will burn will burn together,
each head in its proper place.

I remember his standing out back without tie or hat
looking up at the house, his shoes caked with mud
and the black marbles of charcoal he kicks with his toes.
The palmetto trees take up the sounds of the wind
and pass them down Elysian Fields Avenue.
A storm is coming
and I catch the bristle run up my back
as I watch him from the window
stoop to the burned pieces of wood,
the half-blackened fence posts,
a piece of metal covered with ash.

He stands and turns and sees me,
and I rise the man above him to him the boy below me
afraid to look at the unburned skin of his own hands.
Later, he brings the smell in with him to the table,
and leaves it on the chairs, and the sofa,
and the bed he takes for a month.
The last day with us he spends
talking to my father in the kitchen,
his hands flopped like fish in his lap,
and the burning and the burned
spread across the life of his back.
Had my father lived I might have yet remembered to ask
just who he was in his black coat,
this man with bad breath who looked at me in fright
as some other life unburned.
Had my father lived,
I might have yet asked just who he was:
A half-brother?
A friend? Another
Jew, passing through.
But I am not ungrateful of puzzles that grow strong
against the known and the sure,
nor the smell a man brings and takes with him.
I have that smell too somewhere.
I can recognize it from blocks away,
and sometimes days ahead.
I can look at you and tell if the smell of a burning in me
is the same as the smell of a burning in you.
I can tell who brings it in their hands,
how the bleach of their faces
wants one such burning to replace another.

JACK GRAPES

SOME LIFE

Some life that seems better than none
and all the beautiful women
who do their hair with Head shampoo
and never spill the ketchup.

inside the nightingale
the bat
and inside the leopard
the leopard

Now there are women
who sit with other women
or they sit alone
and I sit alone and watch them.
Just once I'd like one to get up
and come over to my table
and ask to sit and talk.
Give me that chance to show
that I am a man
who would make friends with women
and just that
and no more,
as if that were an honorable
place to stop,
an easy place to come to.

Some life is always better than none.
Inside each of us
that other animal,

as proud as hungry as fearful
as dangerous.

I think women are afraid of us
because we murder in ourselves
what they love too much in life to lose,
and there is no room now for love,
or friendship.

But I am not afraid of you.
I love your smells,
I love the blood that stains your underwear.
I love the rash under your arms
and the fat
below your buttocks & between your thighs
you pinch and wish away.
And that illusion of self
we both adhere to,
well . . .
we can forgive each other
for wanting this darkness
to see itself first in the eyes of the enemy.

Some life is all we have.
A marriage that lasts 10 years;
A love affair for 2;
A weekend with a stranger;
A voice on the phone—
wrong number.

and inside the nightingale
the bat
and inside the leopard

the leopard

Some men; some women;
some life.

Each one
inside
the other.

JACK GRAPES

POEM WITHOUT PICTURE FOR PICTURE WITHOUT POEM

Dear *American Poetry Review.*
Enclosed are several pictures of me,
one of which
I would like you to consider
for publication in your paper.
I realize that along with each
poet's picture
you print a poem or two,
but I'm not sure I have any
that you would like.
Can I have a picture
without a poem
published?
I feel so different
with the camera.
The poem, of course,
is another matter.
I could just as well
fall flat on the page
and be done with it—
this creeping out
word by word
takes my breath away.
The pictures, though,
remain whole.
You can see where I gained weight
last summer
and the beard I grew
for a lover.

But smiling or not,
they're all just me,
arms open,
placing all that dumb trust
in this dumb world.
Sometimes, just looking at those pictures,
I want them to change me,
to give me back
the face I've been.
But, it's still my face
looking back at all of you,
daring you all to look back.
I've been looking back
at all the poets' pictures
you've published since you began.
They're good faces.
We've got such strong, healthy,
beautiful poets in this country.
It's time to face the poem
of all our faces,
and it's good that there's a place
we can look back at each other.
Thanks for considering my face.
Sincerely yours,

Jack Grapes

JACK GRAPES

TRYING TO GET YOUR LIFE IN SHAPE

It's like doing the roof.
Just when you've got the slate set,
the tacks in your mouth,
the tar hot and ready,
your foot accidentally
nudges the hammer
and it begins to slide away
from you
like a christened ship.
Down it goes.
You hear the crash below,
take a deep breath, say shit,
and turn for the ladder
just as it
catches a wind
and begins the long lean
away from your outstretched hand.
Aww, shit!
You look up.
Storm clouds from out of nowhere
belly over the setting sun.
The dark ice age is at hand.
And no one is home.
And the doors are locked.
Your baloney sandwich
has been pecked away by birds.
You sit back,
you contemplate this new richness
come into your life,

and shiver on the roof
knowing it could be worse.
Why you could be inside.
Warm by the fire.
Sipping sherry.
Shoes off.
Just
temporarily
alive.

MY LIFE

Now that's a log cabin if I ever saw one!
Someone else left that message.
I'm fishing.

Yet another silver fender blade.
See around the edges all those paper cuts.
But with summer this close, ear to jaw.
Lovers just don't care for politics.

You can wear any coat to the dance.
If all black then you must know something.
Each vest should contain a secret.
Who did you kill wearing those shoes?

I have this delicate relationship with my dreams.
Run for your life!
Will this gray rain ever stop!
The closer I look, the less I dream.

Some say there's method to one's madness.
Delirium is robbed of its meager truth
as madness if its called a *Work of Art*.
The chance to see being born, over and over.

After a while, even De Sade bores me.
Violence promises to recover the self,
but you can't limit the world that wounds you
any more than you can disappear into Nature
when Nature is invisible to begin with.

To lose everything at the movies
is an act of faith.
Scene. Close-up. Tracking shot. Dissolve.
You think that's something.
You should see my life.

JACK GRAPES

WHY I AM NOT A SARDINE

After Frank O'Hara

I'm not a sardine, I'm a painting.
Why? I guess I'd rather be a
sardine, but I'm not. Well,

for example, Michael Ford
is cutting a poem into shreds. I drop in.
"Hang out the window and bleed," he
says. I hang; we bleed. I look
up. "You've got some poem there."
"Yes, it needs shredding THIS POEM."
"Oh," I go and the years fly by
and I'm still bleeding. I stop by.
The poem is still being shredded
into smaller and smaller pieces.
And the years go by, bleeding,
the two of us, almost finished.
"The poem's finished," he says.
"Where's the poem?"
All that's left is blood.
"It was too much," Mike says.

But me? One day I am eating a sardine.
A silver sardine.
I bleed into its mouth.
Pretty soon it's a whole fish of blood,
not even a fish anymore,
shredded.

Then another shred,
scale upon scale.
Lifesize to scale.
Wonderful silver.
Bloodthirsty.
There are more fish than sardines.
Life is horrible. Fish accept
the passage of time; the days
go by; years shredded into poets.
My meal is finished and I haven't even
mentioned I've been hanging out the window
all this time.
And one day, at a poetry reading,
Mike throws confetti over his audience,
and announces that it's not a poem,
but his old friend, Jack, a sardine.

CONFESSIONAL

I wish I could write it once and easy
to belong to me.
It always belongs to you.
And you never care to know
if it's once and easy
when it's yours.
What is going to grow in the heart
that is not ventured
or given with the hands open and up
to being within you again
when all you can say is how saddled horses
wait by the tent
or how mountains predict misfortune
or how your legs are the legs of a woman
and your breasts too yet you are afraid
of what you really know, believe only
what they tell you.
Everything you dare not say
truly yours
and so abandoned, like a viewpoint.
Will you count insults and grievances
or stand once and easy with the grief.
I wish I could write it once
and it would belong to me
and no one else,
but it always belongs to you.

TO MY FATHER, THE CAPTAIN

In this wake
where blood separates me from midwives,
my father lies in his coffin,
engines cut,
his face done up,
still commanding me
not to exceed him.

But what excess, and whose?
I can go too far, I can not go
far enough.
Either way you win.
Dad, all I know in this life
is the waythrough excess:
Too much pie in the face;
Too much flesh on the bone;
Too many words.

Power in the perfect ending,
in the gold piece
on the dining room table.
Power to make your son
frozen in his life,
the way you were in yours.

You never thought
the gift of poetry
you gave like a meager token
would set me free.

JACK GRAPES

I do this for myself, Dad,
not for you.
For you, I would
peel my flesh away,
inhabit stale bedrooms;
For you,
I would never try hard enough,
sell shoes,
look for my face
on the bathroom floor
where you told me it would be.
But look at the dream I am rising from.
For you,
I would chisel the stone in my chest,
walk with my shoulders bent forward,
mumble my name.
For you, I would ride the whale down
to your ship on the reef,
not shine for myself
in his belly.

For me
I write this poem.
This is the power, Daddy:
that I will finish this poem
the way I want to,
with my name,
not the way you'd have liked,
with yours.

love,

Jack

ON RAISING THE HAND

On Tuesdays I get up at 4:30 a.m.
to teach poetry in the schools.
My first class starts at 7:20—
it's called *zero period,*
which to me is very ominous
as if it were the final meeting
before the end of the world,
a final poetic countdown.
The students are tired, you can tell,
and drag on in without saying much—
to me—to each other.
When I read a poem and ask who liked it,
no one raises a hand.
"So how many didn't like the poem?" I ask.
Still, no one says a thing; no hands go up.
This is zero period. Barely out of sleep.
We sit drugged like flies at the screen.
I go home tired as well, feeling I've failed.
It's best to think of this as just a job.
I get paid for this, and that makes me honorable.
Poetry doesn't. Poetry gets me vacant stares.
And yet, from this thing we pay so little for,
we want so very much.
Sleepy, tired, educationally bewildered,
what they want is for me to set something on fire,
to open a door to another world,
to change them.
For a penny I'd throw myself at their feet
just as long as they'd embrace this thing

JACK GRAPES

that sucks the blood from me and speaks always
in more voices that I can hear at one time
while the monotonous voice of the world drones on
about how to keep from dying in the cold of a strange city.
And then, today I come home and read the poems
they have written after weeks of treading
the waters of process.
Richard writes:

> *Was it you who used to look*
> *people in the eye?*

David writes:

> *This is not all that matters I like this.*
> *Life it is not out this class.*

Cindy feels she's being tortured and starved,

> *maybe for being beautiful, instead of useful.*

Sam thinks

> *writing*
> *is the first of all things*
> *that builds up the world.*

Charlie looks into the fish bowl and wonders if there is

> *loneliness in the unblinking eyes*
> *of his guppy.*

Bobby writes that

> *Dancing shoes that dive with desire*
> *tremble with the fear they've failed.*

And Tom ends his poem:

> *The glory that cloaks me is dying.*

I read their poems in the early morning and raise my hand.
They've set something on fire.
They've opened a door for me.
I embrace their words, their courage.
In the cold of a strange city,
I keep from dying,
both my hands go up.

TO BOARD THE BUS

Just make enough sense
to board the bus,
he said.
I board the bus,
but I don't make sense,
I said.
Better to make sense,
he said, and stand in the street.
I stand in the street
but get nowhere for all my sense, I said.
For all your sense,
he said,
you don't have to go anywhere.
People will come to you.
They will board the bus?
I asked.
Exactly, he said.
Then let's stand
and make sense together,
I said.
Two of us making sense,
he said,
and the world will move.
Exactly, I said. I feel it already.
What you feel, he said
is the bus coming our way.
Then let it pass, I said.

JACK GRAPES

THE CHILDREN LOOK FOR CRABS ON THE BEACH

There's a reason for this:
You put on your trunks and go stand by the water, watch
the guts of this planet wash up on the sand.
Two girls dig in the root-bones of a plastic-looking sea plant.
They say they are looking for crabs for their collection
and show you a half-filled paper cup stuck in the wet sand.
I'm not satisfied not knowing anymore
what is wrong with me,
what storm is tearing me apart
plank by plank on the rough sea.
I'm not satisfied anymore going from metaphor to metaphor:
a sinking ship,
a drowning sailor,
a beached hulk of a sea monster blinded on the beach
being picked apart by children.
I look out to sea and read the poets for comfort,
but if poetry is to save me,
it'll have to be my own, full of lies and mischief,
and the one paperweight of truth
that keeps everything from flying off.
I want to toss that paperweight out to sea,
that smug stone so breathless on my desk.
So I go back to my car,
shake the sand out of my shoes,
check the mirror to see if I've gotten any sun.
What do I need sun for anyway?
What do I need anything for anyway?
Why can't I fix the sink?
Why am I not more ambitious?

Why won't I come back to me?
I drive off down the highway
in my car that needs fixing everywhere.
God, I feel like a housewife
in someone else's soap opera.
Christ, I feel like laughing.

FINAL EXAM

Can you have a spree of cheese?

Would you loan a bank a flush?

Why is the back door of your house
      so morbid?

When you tie your shoes, do you
      indicate with word or gesture
      your preference for boots
      or do you have something
      to hide?

Say three words that don't dissolve
      or melt or evaporate or turn
      to powder and blow away
      without a fare-the-well or
      so much as a kiss.

Dillinger puts a nickel on the porch
      when he wants a newspaper
      but now he's dead. Some say
      he's alive still. Is this fair
      and why must the law
      protect the innocent?

Are you tired, listless, depressed, suicidal,
      rabid, loquacious, engaged, visionary,
      plastic, fiber, traffic, a kosher

pickle, exact change? How could you
stop this and change your life?

Would you rather live in New York or
cash a ten-dollar bill?

What does the word *gaberlunzie* mean?
Look it up.

Why is symmetry happy? How does grief expand?
Is retribution a crystal?

Think of someone you've offended, grievously
wronged. Is there any way you could
make it worse? Is there any area that
remains unwounded? What are the prospects
for permanent injury? Is your day booked,
or do you have time to settle this matter?

How do you adjust?

Why does the broom whisk; is there any edge
to an elephant; what mystery burns your heart
the best?

JACK GRAPES

HOME FREE

We're buying groceries for dinner
at the Vegas mini-mart,
so I plunk two quarters into the slot machine
stationed by the check-out counter
and on the second quarter hit a $12 jackpot.
The tin cup is designed to make it seem like I've blown up
Fort Knox and bells go off to let the customers know
there's a silver waterfall, one to a customer.
I'm hooked and I know it.
I give the money away, three bucks apiece to Vern
and Katharine and Lori, saying here's some lucky quarters
but I'm really just trying not to hoard the luck.
Too much might go off in my hands.
Too much might alert the gods.
This luck is stolen, and after all the other luck
that's come my way—well, I've got to be careful
is all. Now we're in the casino,
the big time. Vern hits a $50 jackpot.
I'm at the blackjack table losing my breath.
Lori and Katharine are in the bar picking up strangers
while UCLA loses on a field goal to Arizona.
I lose another $20 at blackjack waiting for my free drink.
By the time we leave I'm $60 down, probably $100.
Next day at the Crystal Bay Club I pick up $100
at blackjack. Lori convinces me to leave a winner.
But I know I'll be back. The next morning we're back
and I drop $120. By the time we get to Reno
I can't tell for sure if I'm up or down.
Quarters go into the machines as I go by.

I'm pulling handles down the way I'd strip bark
from a tree or rickety-rick a stick against a fence
when I was a kid. I walk by a blackjack table, bet $40
and win. Walk off and put chips on roulette and lose.
Fork up a few bills at another table and win on two kings.
Bells go off, lights blink.
All you have to do here is win one jackpot,
one big fat fucking jackpot and the rest is history.
Lori's grabbing my arm and Katharine's hungry
and Vern's walking slow and easy out the door.
This quarter, this next quarter, this $5 yellow chip,
this $25 black chip, this is the one that does it,
one more plunk, one more pull of the handle and it's done,
we're home free, we escape the pull of gravity,
we're off this rotten earth and heading for the stars.
"Lose here, win everywhere else," I say
as we get back in the car.
Merry Christmas, friends. Happy New Year.

JACK GRAPES

I JUST HAD TO TELL YOU

Listen I just had to tell you
I wrote five poems today.

Can you believe it—five poems!

Russia's still in Afghanistan
the hostages are still hostages
ah forget 'em
another storm coming
and other one for Sunday
fuck it
radioactive rain
the candidates on TV
elect 'em for all I care
we need ten presidents anyway
all those homes slipping into mud

destruction

death

one man looking for his wife
another girlfriend
hoping her lover is alive
and they're starving in Asia
and the blacks in Africa
are overrunning the white man's cities
well, come on,
drop the bombs here for a change

swarm up our black beaches
set fire to the whole Archipelago—
taxi A-bomb sewer rats parades
the tired and the hungry and the weak
up from the bottom of the sea
the molten core of the earth
and comets
strike us,
asteroids
planets
off their course
another sun
moving our way
fuck it fuckit fckit
I wrote five poems today.
This is the sixth.
Whoooopeeeeeee!

JACK GRAPES

SO MANY

So many plays
and novels
and stories
and essays
and history books
and philosophy
and science fiction
and fiction
and science.
I thought once I was going to write them,
a novel, or a story, or a play.
I don't think so anymore.
It's so hard to write a novel.
You have to work at it every day
and you have to type up at least 200 pages,
even if you never go to a second draft.
And a play?
All those characters,
and scenes, and lights,
the changing sets,
and worst of all
the actors, acting.
Genghis Khan, Attila, Hitler,
Vlad the Impaler
are nothing compared to what
actors can do to a play
once they get to say the words out loud.
No, I won't be writing any plays.

And stories, fiction . . .
what can I say.
Men left the tribe and headed into the dark forest,
climbed out over the black mountains
and were gone for years. We were children
when they left,
but when our children mark off
a new boundary with boulders,
they come back, full of scars, jewels,
and strange women with shaved heads.
And they begin to tell stories.
And our children listen, and we listen,
and the weather and the seasons
and the sun on its way across
stop until the stories are all told.
That's what I think about
when I think about stories.
I won't be writing
any of those.

What, that's not in a play, or a novel,
or a story
can I possibly tell you.
How can I write enough and the kind of words
that conceal the lack
of anything true.

There is only this one,
true, utterly beautiful poem.
And each of us, possibly one time
in our lives,
can write it.
I would like to do that.

JACK GRAPES

I would like to try that.
And when you write yours
I would like to hear it.
It's the same poem, each of us have to write.
So we'll know it when we see it.
So many plays, and novels, and stories.
But only one
poem.

I LIKE MY OWN POEMS

I like my own poems
best.
I quote from them
from time to time
saying, "A poet once said,"
and then follow up
with a line or two
from one of my own poems
appropriate to the event.
How those lines sing!
All that wisdom and beauty!
Why it tickles my ass
off its spine.
"Why those lines are mine!"
I say
and Jesus, what a bang
I get out of it.

I like the *ideas* in them,
my poems,
ideas that hit home.
They speak to me.
I mean, I understand
what the hell
the damn poet's
talking about.
"Why I've been there,
the same thing," I shout,
and Christ! What a shot it is,
a shot.

JACK GRAPES

And hey.
The words
Whew!
I can hardly stand it.
Words sure do not fail
this guy, I say.
From some world
only he knows
he bangs the bong,
but I can feel it
in the wood,
in the wood of the word,
rising to its form
in the world.
"Now, you gotta be good
to do that!" I say
and damn! It just shakes
my heart,
you know?

Shall we put in the heart now?
— Dr. Earnst Praetorius,
The Bride of Frankenstein

THE POET'S FUNERAL

Friends, we write the eulogy
and it is crap.
We praise the bird that barely
survives the rainstorm,
we make miracles of the poetry
written on, what?—paper!
and not the other kind
this is just her arms around me.
We believe the spirit
does not die with the man
when most often it dies before.
Shovel the bastard down, I say
and cover the pine with leaves.
A kick of dust and a what's for supper
will do any time.
Flesh!
Even now you're more concerned
with your itching leg
that sets the table and warms the palm
just midnight to a lover
and as it should be!
Talk to me for chrissakes! is what I say.
Toss the glass once in the air
and let it smash wine and all and say
good for that and riddance.
Stalk your own hearts and be ruthless about it,
swing each high in the air and wait
for the music to begin again
and when it does

with a hard hard heel and laughter
that fills a fist,
dance on, dance on.

HERE'S A POEM

Here's a poem that has not
been revised or rewritten
or read aloud or cut
or extended or given to a lover.
Here's a poem that
has no code word, no
name for something else,
no intended meaning,
no axe to grind.
Here's a poem inconsequential
as a thumbtack.
Give me a penny for it
and you've overpaid.
Lose it and it's still there
for all that it was worth.
Here's a poem less than
twenty lines.
Defend it.

VOYAGE

Now on the table
all my friends in ties
waving goodbye.
This voyage.
And so much time
taken to learn again
what we once knew
from each other
and forgot.
It's still daylight
but I can see the moon.
Almost
or so it seems
transparent.
Not even a full moon.
But a full moon.

JACK GRAPES

PASSING THE KETCHUP

She says pass the ketchup
and I grab the salt shaker
and stretch it across the table.
"The ketchup," she says.

The lawn chair's full of rust
and the nylon straps in straggles.
It leans in the corner of the garage.
"Let's throw it out," she says.
"Not yet," I tell her. "Maybe we'll find
something to do with it."

We come home from the beach
and a trail of ants
flow to and from
the sugar bowl
down the counter to the floor
and out the screen door.
"Look at them all!" she shouts.
So I do.

These men grow old in my body.
They take such slow steps,
and take all morning
to drink a glass of milk.
They find nothing familiar
in the familiar,
debate the eye of the city
and the hand of the country.

They fall asleep in the kitchen.

"Where are the car keys?" she asks.
"The car keys," I repeat,
unable to remember
what is a car
and what is a key.
Finally:
"In the car," I say.
"The keys."
I wake in the middle of the night
to answer the phone.
Hello. Hello.
Nothing but the sound of someone's breathing
coming from the other end.
It sounds like my own,
but I can't be sure.
"Who was it?"
"Who was what?"
"On the phone!"
"Me. I think."

Today I sit on the beach
and watch the waves come in,
break in a stiff white line
forty feet out,
and carry the boogie-boarders
to the edge of the sand still standing.
There is nothing on the horizon.
Not a storm coming our way,
not a black ship,
no land.
We are all stretched on beach towels

inching the white breast out for a tan.
We are all lying here at the edge
of a continent.

I get up and brush the sand from my body.
I take the napkins we brought
with the food in the ice-chest
and stick one each into my ears
and nose: wings of a sort.
Then another I roll for a fang.
Insert it under my top lip,
hunch over, and limp down the sand
like a walrus trying to dance
on the edge of the berm.
The kids step back at first,
then begin to mimic me;
finally, they join in, following me
as our footprints just above the water line
one on top of the other
change and grow larger, deeper.
A single new life form
come out of the water,
come out from the land.

"What do you think you're doing?" she calls.

"Passing the ketchup," I say.

A DEED OF LIGHT

My sister dies.
I am not born yet.
She barely strikes soul
and goes.
My Uncle Jack dies.
I am not born yet.
It is right
to give me his name.
Among other things
it means
something smaller
than the usual of its
kind;
a small stuffed puppet
set up to be pelted
for sport.
For years they call me
Jackie.
My father sneers.
What kind of name is that!
Uncle Charles dies.
Everyone in the kitchen
stands and cries.
A year later
on the kitchen floor
Uncle Lou dies
vomiting on the newspaper
under his head.
I bring him more newspaper.

JACK GRAPES

My socks flap at the toes.
My name is Jack:
a small national flag
flown by a ship.
The next year
we move to the new house.
This time of brick.
Martin Shapiro dies.
My mother drags me to the wake.
In the open coffin
his face can be seen
all the way from the back
of the chapel.
Applejack, jackknife,
jack-o-lantern.
Aunt Adela dies
all summer in the back bedroom.
Withers on the sheets of cancer.
Jackie, she says,
show me the movies.
My mother prances
with grief around the grave.
Sarah Bernhardt.
A year later, of cancer too,
she gets it down.
Hisses bitch at the nurse
the last two days.
When I leave for Europe
I forget to tell my father
goodbye.
In Italy the phone rings.
Come home, it says,
you're the man in the family

now.
Jacksnipe, jackstraw, jack-in-the-box.
From tides to bushes
on Sundays,
each of us digs holes
in the backyard.
This growing further apart.
Karl who is my brother.
Louis who is my brother.
Charlaine who is my sister.
Jacksmelt, jackshaft,
jackpot.
I am Daniele's Uncle Jack.
I am Benjamin's Uncle Jack.
I am Ari's Uncle Jack.
My arms become trees
solitary with the base pale face
of a green kitchen door,
jewels for teeth to kill my father,
see me, see you,
see who dies on Tuesday.

No more of graves and names.
On the dead I spit on the dead of the dead.
The Jack deads and the Charles deads
and the mother deads and the father deads.
My name beats the bush
that sends up flocks of birds.
This lantern cut to look
like a human face.
The name looks out of my eyes.
The meaning looks out of my name.
Jack is a deed of light.

ANOTHER SLEEPWALK

So severe and desperate is the heart's resistance
to cold crying sleep
that its one finger thrusts up screaming
at particles of separation
the dead cough up.
No, it says. No.
Those gods who walk on thin legs
and refuse to speak
counsel us to do the same.
A speechless bravery.
Well, tracks beaten in the canefields
are more determined in their course
than we with our nail of science
on the one hand,
a brief and perfect faith on the other.

I do not always sleep in peace.
She wakes beside me and pads off into the kitchen,
and I know how large out there is darkness,
a plain brown pillow thrown to the corner
of the room.
It is there for her, beastly in its fold of gray,
loving another deep death deep deep within her
and I am afraid that one can swallow the other
as easily as I fall asleep again,
passing so easily into dream.

What a lovely and beautiful and tingling thing
this fear is,

and I see my arms go out and take it all around.
And my fear in the night takes hold of itself
and dances back with the darkness.

How love can know from its losing
is beyond me,
but it does.
Yet the space grows to include us all.
We are big
for being so small
as to make the rest so large.

And we bring the light again
and say the words
and give the voice a shape
that says yes,
and again says yes.

Then:
lightswitch; footsteps; bedcover.

Then it is that her body slides up to mine
and the world
in its limping way
goes on.

JACK GRAPES

TESTIMONY

Why should I lie?
Ask any bed, the stutter gives it away.
One machine measures the heart beat;
others, more sophisticated,
the dilation of the eye,
the contraction of the pupil.
I still don't have a son
or for that matter, a daughter,
but loved as I am by children,
I wonder if I've not gone already
in some larger way beyond paternity,
the excessive transformation of my genes.
I am still here, and still there,
and already continuing in concrete and ash.
Why should I even think of lying?
The real killers are to be congratulated,
slapped on the back and toasted
for their inscrutable ingenuity,
the way a decision is sounded like an earthquake.
I'm always appalled by the ones
who pucker their lips and cannot laugh.
The pain,
to be humourless, tightly bound by logic,
the very idea that understanding
is not a killing, knowledge not a form
of asphyxiation.
It touches me that we whittle our lives down
to the smallest of entries in a notebook,
the notebook we carry with us on daily routine,

the notebook no one is ever allowed to read,
filled with one lie after another,
but our true children nonetheless.
Dare I let them out to have lives of their own?
Dare I give them up and admit
I am the father, I am the mother?
I would have my children carry on
with their own names, look back at me
and remember that what I did I did
out of love, that murder is always
an intentional accident, living easily
between the grain of expansion and the grain of collapse.
This is only part of the evidence.
I've never meant to lie.

TREES, COFFEE, AND THE EYES OF DEER

Do you want coffee?
He was only nineteen when his first book of poems
  was published.
I wasn't going to go back.
I was going to sleep at the edge of the driveway
  in my sleeping bag
  until all the cars
  went up in smoke and teach 'em
My mother sat on the flesh of her face
  such grimness in her palms
  such unpitying bitterness.
But I digress.

The cities too in my back bedroom,
  18-Century St. Petersburg under the desk
    where it belongs;
  the Paris of Abelard and Eloise high
    on the carpet;
  smoky London and shrill New York take up
    the whole closet,
    and even tho' I keep promising
    to farm the clutter,
    I just close my eyes
    when I reach for a shirt
    and slam the door shut again.

More coffee?
Sometimes inventing conversation is impossible.
  "Shall we get in the car?"

"Your perfume smells lovely."
And everything is about three weeks, if it's important;
  two months if a hand-me-down;
  a year if you like jazz or Isak Dineson.
Then my father falls to the floor like a tree under
  thunder boom on his back and down comes
  the phone and the phone book boom and
  his startled eyes boom back at me
  because I had pushed him.
Lately I can't remember the dreams.
  When I wake up, they scamper off, like deer.
  At best, I remember the eyes of the ones
  who stop and turn to look back at me.
  "I mean you no harm," I call out to them,
  but they swing and leap away.

The tree I can see from here next to the garage
  is still as a brick, and as smug.
  So solid to have lived this long,
  another life in the city worthier than mine,
  thick-barked to my own thin skin.
  "Fuck you, tree! Up yous! I yell out the window.
But I digress.

No I don't. Nothing here is digression.
  If you can't tell digression from inclusion,
  why don't you try Hy's Deli on Beverly.
  They make a great brisket sandwich.
And in March, the deer from their winter of hunger
  come after the running dogs to be fed
  in the kitchen where my mother flips through
  the pages of my first book of poems.
  They mean nothing to her. Which is okay.

It's the idea of them she can't stand.
She holds the book they way you'd hold a rock
that has just come flying through the window
and landed messageless on the table.
No one seems to know
when my father is coming home.
"He may never come home," my sister says.
Mom pushes the book across the table
as though she were brushing aside a fly
that landed on her arm.
"Up yours, too!" I say to her now,
dead tho' she is.

Is this how people talk in a Russian novel?

Well I don't care anymore how they talk,
  how the dead persist in their life after death.
  It is us they need, not the other way around.
Today I take care of that tree, that goddamn tree.
  I'm going down there and pick a fight
  if I have to.
  Take it apart with my bare hands
  if it comes to that.

This is between us, the living.

Any landing you can walk away from
is a good landing
                    —Superchicken

and the running form, naked, Blake

And the running form, naked, Blake,
Shouting, whirling his arms, the swift limbs,
howling against the evil...

—Ezra Pound
Canto XVI

AND THE RUNNING FORM, NAKED, BLAKE

Jack Grapes

NOTHING

It's not Freud or western civilization,
It's not wheat germ or tractors,
It's not strange men standing around shopping malls
              looking to gun us all down,
It's not the concrete slabs that cover our brothers
It's not someone's love letter lying in the gutter,
It's not the messages on our answering machines,
It's not sex surveys nor voting polls,
It's not the mediocre poems,
It's not the gifted who commit suicide,
It's not the gifted who cannot do themselves in
              but hang on in a kind of graceful stupor,
It's not a John Ford film,
It's not the Hard Rock Café,
It's not your mother (even though you thought it was)
It's not postage or paperclips or tax forms or mule deer,
It's nothing,
not even nothing, certainly not nothing,
if it was nothing, which Wittgenstein says is nonsense,
it would be nonsense, which is something.
It's not space within space nor the vacuums within space,
              the quantum fluctuations out of which all the
somethings come,
it's less than that,
so much less, that stretched to infinity,
it's still nothing,
nada nothings, nien nothings, nyet nothings,
no nothings, not nots never nones,
zilches, millions of zilches, zilch to the zilch power,

which is still more than I had in mind.
It's your life, and this poem, and everything that lies between.
It's this poem
that will save you,
when everything else
is nothing,
and your life
which is something
goes on with greater effort
than you can manage or imagine.

JACK GRAPES

L.A. IN THE MORNING

*There's a 47% chance that a 7.5 earthquake will
hit the L.A. area sometime in the next five years.*
—*Los Angeles Times,* December 2, 1992

L.A., your earthquakes slam me to the floor,
and I beg for more.
Anything you ask, I'm yours.
Earthquake, fire, pestilence, flood; I deserve them all.
L.A., where are you in the morning when I need you.
Where are your bungalows and movie stars
          who come to eat my head off
          with their love scenes and car chases.
L.A., where are you in the morning when I need you,
    your bug-eyed money lenders promising the new house,
    the new school,
    the new shoes lined on the closet floor,
    shined and shining.

L.A., you're hamstrung and bleating,
    squealing like a pig about to be castrated.
We're coming to you in the morning
        to make over our lives.
We want our star on your sidewalk.
Why does my neighbor sing her scales thrice a week?
    Why isn't she out filling her face with food and
    gliding up the coast highway to get the hell outta here?

L.A., I don't know how to leave you.
I want to breathe better air and drive without bullets

and drive without fenders backing into my teeth.
I want to walk out of my back door into a YARD
    and barbeque a steak and baked potato
    and have my neighbor BOB slap me
    on the back and shove another beer into my hand.

L.A., where are you in the morning
    when I am trying to leave you and cannot,
    cannot leave the lines or the hoaxes.

L.A., L.A., where are you in the morning
    when I need you to want me;
    persuade me to stay,
    coax me with your irresistible urban expansion,
    the public works, the Egyptian World State,
    the heart of China's shifting capitals,
    the knuckles in the soul of your walled borders,
    the irrational city,
    the city without sense or meter,
    an instrument of colonization and madness.
Slap me into stupidity so I can love you more,
    love your concrete and chrome
    and tar pits and salt water.

L.A., where are you in the morning
    to bring me to my knees at the feet
        of your palm trees and sitcoms.
Here, here is where all the world bends its knee.
All the cities speak through you.
    Athens, the true democracy;
    Quattrocento Venice,
    Medicean Florence, the jewel of Tuscany,
        pilot of the Renaissance;

JACK GRAPES

Goethe's Weimar, the universal man;
All your unpredictable spiritual powers
　　sweep me up into each crevice
　　　　of slime and glint, glitter and sludge.

L.A.　L.A., where are you in the morning?
　　Take me to your breast, make me suck,
　　squeeze the milk of your rage and fraudulent dreams,
　　squeeze the milk of your processed glory down my throat.
You're all the great capitals and I am everywhere and there—
　　　　Alexandria, Rome, Constantinople,
　　　　Cordoba, Paris, Mexico City
　　　　St. Petersburg, Vienna, Isfahan,
　　　　smoky London and shrill New York.
Who needs any of them?
　　They're all in you, you're all of them, L.A., L.A.
I say your name
　　and feel the blood of your liars
　　and screaming coke freaks,
I am one of your liars. I am one of your coke freaks,
　　blasting my brains with every imaginable kind
　　of woodgrained molded polystyrene
　　vinyl structural urethane polypropylene veneered
　　stain resistant DRUGS of all your possessions.

I send my resume to every street corner huckster:
I've been on *Lou Grant, Hill St. Blues, Mash, Divorce Court*—
　　　　or was that my life?
I feel you on the movie sets, the Hollywood tours,
　　the get-rich-quick change-my-life wheel-of-fortune-
　　blow-me-to-Hawaii-and-back lottery fix.
I feel you everywhere in the bones of consumer items.
I feel you in every street straight from hell and back—

Fairfax and Sunset in my blood
Pico and Sepulveda in my veins
Venice & PCH in my flesh
Beverly and Doheny in my dreams,
Western and Olympic in my arms.

L.A. L.A., Where are you in the morning when I need you,
      I am here for you to be fucked and made holy,
      I am here for you to break my will and shave my head,
      I am here for you to corrupt my best ideals.
I spread my legs I spread my chest
I spread my heart wide open.

L.A., L.A., Where are you in the morning when I need you,
      shaking and stomping with your steel boots for everyone.
            Explode the sod for me!
            Topple the buildings for me!
            Shatter the glass for me!
            Blast apart the pipes for me!
Smash the brains of wealth and corruption and decadence for
me
            into my heart,
            into my loins,
            into my El-ay soul.

JACK GRAPES

I DON'T GET IT

I don't get it!
It doesn't make sense!
I don't understand it.
It doesn't make sense.

I get hit. I get beat.
Am I nuts, am I naive,
foolish, am I stupid?

Pushed like a dog,
cut into pieces like a flounder,
broken like plastic against a stone,
I push my brain and my heart till they bruise,
put up with everything unreal,
get nothing for it but salt,
a thousand years of debt.
I don't get it. It doesn't make sense.
I don't get it.

I was fucked.
I was shuffled about.
Someone's drinking my blood.
Someone's dismembered the whole family.
No one is left who can walk;
those who can, build their little fortifications.

Our struggles smell up the streets,
our cries sprout berries in the gardens of the rich,
and they eat them, tasting the bitter grief that stains their fin-

gers.

"Whose grief is this?" they ask.

"Ours! Ours!" we scream, but they do not hear.

They continue smacking their fingers with the nectar of our
woe.

It doesn't make sense.

We wanted so little. I don't get it.

We're planting bodies in time for a good spring crop.

We're planting our regret, our savage despair.

We're planting our spoons because there's no more food.

We're planting our pillow because there's no more sleep.

We're planting our shoes because we've lost our feet.

We're planting our words because there's no more hope.

We sing and out fall rocks.

We dance and up comes tar.

If anyone laughs they bandage our teeth.

It doesn't make sense. I don't get it.

Who peels my flesh away and steals the bones from our bread.

Why are the children strapped to ignorance,

      why do they send them on fruitless journeys,

      to lose one finger at a time

      to the gods of finance and architecture?

What are we losing when no one is allowed to sing.

Who spits in my face the teeth of my ancestors.

Who takes my wife and breaks her back.

Who wants us bleeding and naked and crying out in pain.

What can we say that frightens them so.

What have we seen that causes their brains to explode.

What do we know that turns their arms into knives.

JACK GRAPES

Who are we so poor and dying to love
        that their planes and factories go up in smoke
        at the mere mention of our names.
We hope for so little.
We are so small.
What power can our single songs have.
We know only pain and thirst and hunger.

Nothing but grimness.
You never stop crying.
I've been cheated. Who did this?
Why do such damage you cannot undo.

It doesn't make sense.
I don't get it.
I'm telling you I don't get it.
It doesn't make any sense.
I'm telling you I don't get it.
I'm telling you I don't get it.

THE FATHER AT SAFEWAY

I'm standing in the line at Safeway, getting formula and
diapers, behind an old Jewish lady counting coins in her coin
purse, and in front of another 4 or 5 people, anxious to get past
the cashier and into the parking lot. Everything on the counter
says I'm a father, a new father at that. Formula and diapers,
small, 12 to 18 pounds. I can feel the incongruity of it, if there is
such a thing. Big ol' me, in my red shorts and torn sweat shirt
with white paint spatters on the front, dirty tennis shoes, slip-
ping out my American Express Gold card to pay for the stuff.

I could be 18, standing in line to buy beer and scotch for the
party Friday nite, ready for a blitzed-out weekend tearing up the
streets in my Chevy Bel Air. I could be 25, buying cookies and
ice cream for Friday nite party, something for the munchies
from the dope we'll be smoking. It's the supermarket on the
corner of Clairborne and St. Charles, where the street cars make
their turn to head back downtown, and a weekend of grass
and Kafka and everybody rolling around on the floor laughing.
Today, I'm 49, standing by the counter in Safeway on 3rd and
Fairfax.

We size each other up by what's on the counter. There's the
lady buying a chicken fryer, two carrots, and a loaf of bread. The
other woman, buying Calistoga water and yogurt and some kind
of health flakes, wood-chips, who knows. I'm the father, buying
formula and diapers. Perhaps they already know to feel a little
sorry for me, thinking of the long sleepless nights, the walking
around dazed feeling, the plastic keys and rings strewn all over
the floor you step on in the half light of midnight.

I don't feel like the father. I just feel like Jack, standing in
line, buying something. I look down at the giant bag of Huggies

and Enfamil low-iron formula, and it seems like something out of a dream; in my back pocket a little gadget and I bring it to my face and say, "Beam me up, Scottie!" and I'm in my Bonneville convertible cruising down Claiborne Avenue, taking the big curve at Nashville, yelling out the window at Jerry Jacobs, who's driving like an idiot in the gray Plymouth in front of me.

When I hold Josh, when I'm feeding him, when I'm just looking at him in his summer seat, I try to find the father feeling, but it escapes me.

I feel the edge of the miracle, of the wonder, of the unbelievable face and those cheeks I could suck, that face I could swallow whole, but the father feeling, what's that? I'm just Jack, and by god, I have a son, and his name is Joshua, after my father, Samuel Joshua, dead these thirty years.

My father sits in the kitchen, his face in the palm of his hand, staring down at his cup of coffee, thinking of his own long ago, the cold streets of New York, the east side, yelling up to his mother for a penny. He sits in the kitchen, and his three sons yell and play in the rumpus room while his daughter sucks on her long curls, and his wife harumphs around the house in a flower print dress. He sits there and stares off into space, a boy from the lower east side, sitting in the kitchen of his three story home on Fontainebleau Drive. Where was the father feeling in him? To me, he always was the father. As much as I tried to see him a boy, he was always the father.

And Josh, my own son, beginning to kvetch in the summer seat, looks up at me for rescue. He wants out, he wants my shoulder, he wants me to beam him up. But Scottie's not here. There's just Jack standing in line at Safeway buying diapers and formula. Jack the boy, Jack the man, Jack the father.

SUNDAY MORNING

Sunday morning. I wake to the sun lifting one leg over the top of the Ticor Building on Wilshire Boulevard. The new leaves on the tree outside my bedroom window are tinged with sunlight. If only I were a photographer or painter I'd freeze this moment and crawl into it.

Sunday morning. I have to get up but my body wants to drown right here in the bed. Spring ambles up the street waving its arms. A matinee today. I have to be at the theater by two. Yesterday, I find out from my agent that I didn't get the part I was counting on.

Eat this, they say. It's good for you.
You've eaten it before. The next one will be sweet.

I eat and concentrate on the window, on the tree, on the sun beginning to beat its chest as it comes over the top of the tallest building.

I drive down Beverly Boulevard, take the curve where it changes into 1st Street, turn on Grand and park right across from the museum. It's just after ten, hardly any cars on the street. MOCA doesn't open till eleven. The sun has followed me all the way, reflecting off the Security Pacific Bank Building, glass and steel going all the way up.

I get off on this urban sleekness, especially the unfinished building across the street, another skeleton of steel and concrete. Someone should stick a sign on it, make it part of MOCA, part of the Permanent Collection, and leave it just as it is, unfinished. No clear line where the museum ends and the rest of the city begins. One easy flow, stretching all the way back into our homes, into the very center of our lives.

I walk past the California Plaza sign, running my hand along the chrome and glass, then head downstairs for a cup of coffee and cinnamon roll at the "Il Panino." There's a girl two tables over, in the sun. We both drink our coffee in silence, checking our watches, writing something down in our journals.

She's an art student from Santa Barbara come to see the Jasper Johns. She asks what am I here to see. "Oh," I say, "the art. Just the art. I don't care. Just something."

I AM FIVE YEARS OLD. I don't understand anything. Hot and humid days; nights, dark and mysterious. They take me to school. I stare at the blackboard. The kid from around the corner beats me up at recess. Some nights my father doesn't come home. My mother shrieks on the telephone. My pet turtle dries up in the sun. My uncle dies on the floor in the empty kitchen. Who is the world? Why is the moon where the sun is? If the street goes nowhere, why is it in my bed? What is the rain that rains just rain, and why does it rain crows, or bats, or baseball gloves? How is the pencil writing my name, and why is my name the name for the thing that fixes tires, the name for the flag on the pirate ship, the name for the clown crushed in the box? Outside, the kids continue to jump rope on the sidewalk, singing, "A my name is Alice," seeing everything, but knowing nothing.

I AM SIX. The class takes a bus with Miss Cook to the Delgado Museum on Elysian Fields Avenue. We're going to see Vincent Van Gogh. Later, when I tell my mother, who was born in Antwerp, she says to say it like this, Vincent Van Gough, and she coughs as she says it. Van Gough! Van Gough! But Miss Cook says Van Go. We are marched single-file from one room to another, walking past each painting that hangs just above our heads. I can't believe what I am seeing. Everything mysterious and horrible about the world vanishes.

He paints like I paint! Trees outlined in black. All those wavy lines,
all those colors. And he piles the paint on. He's wasting all that
paint, just like I did before they told me not to waste all the paint.
He sees everything I see. The moon is where the sun is. The street
that goes nowhere is in his bed. It's not just raining rain, it's raining
crows and bats. He sees the blood, he see the faces. Everything so
bright it's on fire. Everything so dark it swallows me up. The man
cuts his ear off. The man leans against the table so sad. The man
dies on the floor of the empty kitchen. I stop in front of the painting
with crows above a cornfield. The world I see is real. I bring my hand
up and touch the dried paint. It's real! Mounds of paint, swirls of
paint, rivers of paint! But it's not paint. It's real. It's the world.

   "Don't touch the painting!" Miss Cook yells. She pulls my hand
away. She yanks my arm into the center of the room. "Never ever
touch a painting!" She shoves me into a seat in the back of the bus.
It doesn't matter. The world is real. I fold my hands in my lap. I
know what I will do.

I will write about the real world.

11 o'clock. The girl heads off toward the Jasper Johns. I walk
into the J. Paul Getty Trust Gallery and find the Geary cardboard
chairs and cardboard houses. "Can I sit in them?" I ask the guard.
"They can be sat in," he says, "but you can't sit in them."

   "Oh," I say, and walk into the room with the huge pavilion
shaped like a fish. I walk into the belly of the fish. The wood
inside is so beautiful.

   "Don't touch the wood, please," says the guard.

   I wander over to the Nauman video. A clown is being tortured
on simultaneous video screens. "Clown Torture," it's called. Later, in the Permanent Collection, I bump into the girl from Santa
Barbara. In the center of the room, a metal sculpture of a man
moves his motorized mouth up and down. A silent

YAK

YAK

YAK

This, I understand.

I stand as close to it as I can. The guard watches me suspiciously.

Over the in North Gallery there's an empty spot in one corner. Something was there, but it's been   removed. I make a sign for myself and hang it around my neck. I stand in the corner of the Permanent Collection, North Gallery, as still as I can, one arm out in the gesture of an actor about to speak.

Eat this. You've eaten it before. The next one will be sweet. The street that goes nowhere is in your bed. You know nothing, but you can see everything.

A woman and her little girl walk up to me. "What does the sign say?" the girl asks.

"Touch me," her mother says. "The sign says touch me."

So the child reaches out a hand and touches my own.

CAWS YOU GET HOLDOUT

Caws you get
holdout
blow-up me slap
character esplanade

she was dutiful without
sure footed envelope she
was something sinister in
an ancient sort of way
drop out something
begun and lately plaster
of paris she was my fancy
dream caws you get
holdup slap-out me
blow away from naming
the wrong things the right
name she was sinister
in an ancient sort of way,
miami, a miasma
of terrify, holy blowfish
she was sure-footed
caws you get holdout
and she was something
sinister, a drop-in
something started in the heat of the sun
blown out by smithereens of starfish, a light,
a necklace of quicksnaps,
sand, thumbtacks,
doorknobs, paperclips,

her teeth biting off caskets of marshmallows
something sinister
in an ancient sort of way
slapped out, me blow away
me gone, me hers
me for the taking,
caws you get holdout
you get blown away you get rearranged
like tuna fish
you get lost,
and found
and lost again,
an episode of light
on your way to a train depot,
the death of the best part of yourself
buried in a fanfare of alternatives,
ambivalencies of swordfish,
twisting in the proverbial wind,
scraped clean,
caws you get blow-out,
in a sinister sort of way,
falling apart with plaster lips
of the woman
who sees you blown-out,
of the woman who takes you hold up,
of the woman
in an ancient sort of way
who finds you lost
and names you right
again.

STILL LIFE

Some remote, exquisite creature:
behind you
            beyond the mass of light
the erotic force
     shapes the better performance,
another range of available styles.

Now you are pigeon-toed to the sun,
      and I look up at it,
neck stretched, holding up by torch
   the power
between thighs   entire plates
concealed beneath the ridges
of your skull.
So to be any of it   so much to be
      like the others
So much to be driven over the concrete
     and the smell of gasoline
So much your arms pointing out some strange
       flying object
there   over there   by the blue
   cloud   just   about
to eat the reindeer's head

And we are so alone in this inscrutable palm,
that presses against the other
         palm
of exact passion   ready to curl
  to the sweet fist of science

                      JACK GRAPES

while in your car, engine off,
            at the end of the driveway,
unable to go   anywhere else
        you   you

I would have thought we could have
stayed there
    where we were, where we are.
I would have hoped all of us
could have remained there, without radio
or cigarette
and gone back further if necessary.
An anxious life that is not
                the legend of jobs
or the enlarged study of stones.
Through these other walls you hear
  the solid citizen with clear politics.
So much is the hunger of our particular
        existence,
ground chosen to stand on—
            a doctrine of fact
that baffles intuition and
momentum
out from beyond it all you turn stories
    of legitimate escape
and wait there at the windshield
    turning from the cold.
  It is nothing   it is nothing at all
that stops you
      this hour   and this day
looking out at the sloping roof
  through the branches of the neighbor's
      sycamore
  over housetops

and the grim streetlights between houses.

How can you be still
and at the same time
in motion?
How do you measure yourself
frozen and worthy and groping
as always
for love?

So much is this brute doctrine of fact.
All that you must do, all that is
yet to be done.
                  think of all the one-sentence
                  autobiographies
                  you have written
and the sun is gone
     and there is no one
to be going home to
        and your children
forget your name
     and your father is dead
and dies every time you say his name
     and your mother is dead
but continues to eat your name,
       and in your own name
eats you

So much is this brute doctrine of fact.
     And I would say to you
        stay there
unmoving   in the blood
   of a particular
kind of courage.

                                          JACK GRAPES

Breaking Down the Surface of the World

BREAKING DOWN THE SURFACE OF THE WORLD

PART I:
GEOGRAPHY

Jack Grapes

JACK GRAPES

Sometimes I am very small.
In another life.
Low to the ground.
Eyes with clubs.
Axe-handles.
Drums.

I see what's up.
I run from one end of the room
to the other.

There.
Safe.
Thunder.
The long shadow of wood.
Belts accreted 'round cratons
and flung across the island arcs
consuming plate boundaries.

There's a red bed in the corner.
Outside I can see the zinc tubs
my mother does the washing in.
Through crust and bone,
from trench to arc,
she hangs her flesh out to dry
and is nowhere to be found.

Each knife has a name.
Butcher.
Bread.
Paring.
Every door a lock;
key and bolt,
latch and chain.

Outside the window
lines of cars
their yellow headlights
in the bright sun.
My father drives among them.
He waves to me.
I wave back.

Every morning
the same size.
The house so quiet:
Brain torture.
Shuffled about.
Eyeballs into cement.
Neptune bursting into flame.
Jupiter, a perfection of toes.

Old rocks within younger rocks
line the front yard where I bury
little things
I find around the house.
Less familiar the longer I hold them.

Big wood.
Axe-handles.
Drums.

The mailman pushes his cart
packed with letters and magazines
and parks it next door.

I'm out here breathing
waving goodbye, saying hello,
getting the mail
not even waiting for the mailman.
To meet no train that stops.
Hands in my pockets
rocking back and forth on my heels
as a car goes by full of fish,
swarms of kids on their way to swimming lessons—
the last swimming lesson of the summer.

There goes Mars
barfing up suicide.
There goes Pluto
gristle in the brain.

In another life
toothpicks investigate the courage of seashells.
Rearranged like furniture.
Nighttime, bedtime, bloodtime, moontime.
Burglar bars, daddy bars, baby bars, bloody bars.
The slavery of the head.

A thin blanket, green with stripes
lies among the granite-like rocks
in the backyard.

Layers of crust in the toaster.
On the mantle above the fireplace with no fire,
golf trophies,
souvenir shields,
belt-buckles,
white-china plate with ripple marks
steadily losing heat
to gold cuff-links in its center
flashing reflections of sunlight
as I walk by.
Venus as I walk by.
Mercury as I walk by.
Uranus as I walk by.
I walk by looking for permanence.

The chairs get up during the night
and dance.
They vanish beneath the ocean water
and bathroom basins.
I feel the shift in the house.
Low rolling surfaces.
Blocks of various shapes and sizes,
raised, lowered, tilted.
Some notion as to their character
still deeper and worn down.

When I try to reach into their sleep
it is like freezing my teeth
on refrigerator water
left in a frosted milk bottle.
The sun is so red today.
Ernie says don't look directly into it.

JACK GRAPES

We find a piece of cardboard,
prick a hole with a pencil
and peep through it.
See the red sun and go blind.
Everyone goes blind.
We bump into each other in the streets,
bump into the trees,
bump into houses.

"I'm, blind," yells A.J.
He's excited.
He walks stiff-legged, hands stretched out,
groping the air in front of him.
"Me, too," yells my brother.
Everyone's lined up to go blind,
wanting to look into the sun.
Darryl falls into the gutter and laughs.
"I can't see either," he says.
We're delirious with blindness.

We sit on the curb
and watch the cars go by—
same cars, same drivers.
We wave at them, they wave back.
I look at a broken coke bottle.
A.J. stares at old lady Seenac
rocking in her rocker
on the front porch across the street.
No one's in the mood to tease her.
Darryl watches the tree out front,
my brother looks at me.
We can all see again.
Later, I dig a small trench in the yard,

fill it with water,
watch the displacement of rock and dirt,
their strike-slip movements
as they slide down into the murk.

One night there is a sudden distress.
I'm being picked up in the thin green blanket
and thrown across the room
to land in a cardboard suitcase.
The big steel ship stale with fatigue.
The suitcase filled with dirt
and fingernails,
dry crackly pieces of skin.
My own skin.
Bits of blood where the break was too deep,
dried rust against the light-veined brown.
Someone pours in water.
The chips of skin loosen and turn soft,
hold flat against my forehead and cheeks.
A new face shuffled around the original crust,
shifted beyond recognition.
Was it a sort of slag on the surface
of the case when its rocky crust
first took form?
Or did it change along a zone of weakness
too subtle and precise to contain
even the smallest scream?

My father snaps the case shut.
My mother retreats into the closet;
whimpers, laughs, pecks at the door.
She's mad.
I see this clearly.

Her madness flourishes like an umbrella.
Already it's too late.
While you gallop through your sleep
each night
trying to understand love
and prevent the last sour dream
from spilling onto your pillow,
my mother and I slash at your shadow:
she, pecking at the door;
me, pounding on the inside of the suitcase.
One of us can not get out
without the other.

All in another life.
Neptune. Mars.
Fat women raise their dresses
to dance over skinnier naked bodies.

> *no platform. no*
> *ridges.*
> *her breast is a rift.*

She steps lightly over each one;
penises rising as she bends
and strokes them, down,
far below the limits of observation.

One woman is up, the other down;
legs kick high as the fat jiggles
and rolls out the shadows
that catch in their folds.

Red splotches appear on their thighs,
on their breasts, flushed and bruised,
never hotter than they are now.
A thrust oceanward.
Iron formations give way to red beds.
Inside, where my defective heart
pumps rift systems in alkaline complexes
that drive deeper into the interior,
I feel that heat acting as a thermal buffer
to everything closing down around me.
I hide in the basement,
attain a degree of rigidity.

How far am I from the spreading center
of the room as flesh and cotton float
among the pillows and blankets?
At the edge of the room
with my back to the door
I shine with the head of a new deformation.
The flare of a match.
Magnetic polarities shift,
each band moving outward in turn
sizzling from my body.
Fractures everywhere.
I move from one end of the room to the other.

Never again in the spreading center.
Never again the single place to turn in.
It's one end or the other.
Folds upon folds upon folds.
My transformation into granite.

JACK GRAPES

Winter is a bright moon
hanging, as the horses kick dogs
that worry them in their sleep.
Everyone is cold.
Strangers wave icicles
by the fire;
Mutants everywhere
mate with others not their kind.
It is a terrible night.
No one can read yet.

Uncle Charles takes me in his new convertible.
We ride around and look up at the stars.
"That's the North Star," he says.
I ask him where the South Star is.
"There is no South Star."
When he dies, they tell me he's gone.
To the North Star, I think.

There's always something someone's not telling me.
Cold dust and stone.
My father comes home drunk
and smashes the mirror in the bathroom.
Chunks of glass in the sink.
When I look, there's my face,
looking in so many different directions.
Water I cannot put my hands into.
Sea shells in the Rocky Mountains.
Marine deposits on the plains of Kansas.
The remains of fig trees in Greenland.

Glacial debris in Australia and Brazil.

One night my mother bundles me up in a blanket
and calls a cab to take us to maMa's house.
She lives far away in Metairie,
where the train comes from.
I tell the cab driver:
"My father's coming to chop our heads off."
Even with the windows shut, I can feel the cold.
There's the sign for Ritz crackers.
The first word I learn to read.
Everything is ritzy.

I begin to put one and one together.
The concept of a random universe.
The idea of causality.
Is it one or the other or both?
Red and Yellow make Orange.
Blue and Yellow make Green.
Green and Orange make Brown.
That's something you can count on.
When I color, I press hard on the edges,
soft on the inside.
I can breathe inside the colors.
I spell my name.

The child studies the mirror, then the face.
Which is no longer the face of the child,
but man,
waiting in the winter of the mirror

JACK GRAPES

to be born.

Snow melts as soon as I touch it.
Most of it melting in the air
melting when it touches something warmer
like the sidewalk
or my fingers
and I hold my hand
inside the freezer as long as I can
and go out running
to keep the frozen flakes
clustered in my palm
to catch sight of the pattern
science books showed.
By comparison
my flesh sizzles
beneath the crystal
of ice.

For a long time it is winter.
In the mirror, way back in the background,
my mother walks back and forth,
putting on her girdle, taking off her girdle.
My brother cuts his finger on some broken glass.
My father drinks from the bottle.
My sister isn't born yet.

I touch everything
like flies, like rivers,
like the black pearl
stored away in boxes

ornamented with gold rope.
What will I let myself remember today?
The box with the pair of scissors
varnished black?
Or the one with dried grains of corn?
I open the door.
Eat with great deliberation.
The house burns day and night.
A cow is no longer a cow.
A sack of grain no longer a month's food.
The black pearl reminds me
of something else.
In the mirror, I watch myself.
The beauty that is born
stands on two feet
even in the slime of creation
and sings as it moves
among beasts.

We are crossing the Suru River
looking for Yaks, the primitive cow.
The pilot's head is on my lap
and I'm flying the plane.
With enough fuel
I can take the Himalayas:
the white goats climbing the crag.
The animals below us
immune to the land,
look up at our noise
but barely.

Then back to climbing,
to grazing.
The world beneath their feet
their one earthly thing.

Someone has gone
and overturned the lake again.
I don't understand this one word here,
he says.
Neither do I, which is why I keep it in.
But countless things escape
so easily out of you, he gasps.
Are you gasping?
Actually gasping?

And someone's given birth
to a brilliant lizard.

Here is some news:
Today is meat.
The cows, letters etched
into their hides, play
the alphabet game:
Guess who I am?
It starts with a C.
Once the fastest animal
in the world.

What nigger meant
and kike
and dago
and polack
and wop
and jew-boy
and sheeny
and litvak
and mick
and crab.
Old man Seenac in his ragged undershirt
shows hairy underarms
as he stands by the kitchen door
yelling out at me you little kike
bastard jew-boy.
I loved his daughter Linda,
under the house
spreading her legs
to catch a peek of red, hairless vagina
and pissing in the dry dirt, both of us
pledging someday to marry:
the kike and the dago.
And the blacks all around us,
mother goose nuns at the corner.
Division   division   division.
Clean spit against the windshield
of a 1947 Dodge.
Bicycle down to Prytania Street
and watch the girls roller skate.
Catch a snowball on the way back.

Dago street where Rosalie lived
sucking the boys off down in the basement,
boys who didn't even know yet
what it was to come.
Did you get the feeling, A.J. asked,
and we all lied, even then.

A dream: I am carrying the large lizard
over the back of my neck like a stole
up the stairs and into a room
filled with my friends.
They're on fire but they're laughing,
eating with both hands.
A vat of tomato sauce boils on the stove.
I dump the lizard into it.
Half of him hangs out
struggling to escape.
He makes no sound,
but his jaws snap and his body
swings across the rim
like a loose hose gushing water.
I take him out
and eat:
It's good.
It tastes just like lizard.

In the evenings I come home
and there's my mother
laying the ties out
in regular rows on the kitchen table.
Blue ties.
Nothing but blue silk ties.

My father boards the airplane,
and flies
over the mountains.
For there is no eminence on earth
not subject to erosion,
the inexorable
destroyer.
"When is he coming home,"
my sister asks.
We go outside
and watch the sky.
My father waves.
I wave back.

My brothers and I scoot into the corner
around the kitchen table
and eat our steaming chicken noodle soup.
No one talks, no one breathes,
just my brothers slurping
soup

and me, sitting in the steam
saying the words to myself:
nigger
wop
jew-boy
dago
polack
kike
sheeny
litvak
mick.
The words roll off the tongue
with a strange kind of music.
At night, we take our shovels
and sneak into the backyard
and start digging.
In the glare of the moon
I can see A.J.'s face sweating.
Darryl wants the words as bad as I do.
He's got the big shovel.
Everyone wants the big shovel,
but Darryl's the biggest
with actual muscles in his arms
so no one takes it from him yet.
Shit comes first.
We stand in a circle around the hole
looking at it.
I hear Mr. Higbee open the ice-box
in his kitchen next door.
We stand very quiet,
our cheeks streaked with mud.
The light in Mr. Higbee's kitchen goes out
and we resume looking down at Shit.

The word glows in the darkness.

A.J. reaches into the hole

and picks it up.

He brings Shit up and shows it to us.

I like the way it looks with the capital S.

Darryl says keep digging.

The moon passes behind a dark cloud

and we dig.

Out comes fuck with a pop.

No capital.

The word amazes us, we are stunned by its beauty.

The k remains partly buried

but everyone knows it's a k,

everyone knows it's fuck.

The breathless wonder of seeing it like that.

I'd say, "fuck, that's beautiful," but the word

isn't in my hand yet.

I dare to pick it up first.

I shake the dirt off the k

and hold it up in my hand.

fuck, says A.J.

fuck, says Darryl.

fuck, says Karl.

fuck, I say.

The sound of it stuns us.

The mystery of the word deepens

the more I say it.

The more we all say it.

fuck. fuck. fuck.

Louder and louder.

The lights in the houses go on.

We dig faster, and deeper.

My shovel hits cunt.

A.J. unearths dick and screw and piss.
We're pulling the words up and saying them aloud
and all across the neighborhood
the lights in the houses go on
and we're saying the words even louder.
fuck. And
cunt.
Say them with the capital letter, I yell.
The power of it all surges
like an electrical storm,
the houses tremble in the dark and fall down.
If they were cities, they'd fall, too.

We dig deeper.
All the bones of the words come out of the earth.
The moon is full and bright again.
We can see as if we'd been blind.
The words lie in the palms of our hands,
murderous, horrible, beautiful words.

Maps bring the greatest pleasure:
a faded navigational chart;
an authentic medieval portolano;
outlines of the Mediterranean;
maps of the flat earth;
the ocean: the universal cataract.
Under the last, translated from the Spanish:

>   *"The nature of waters*
>   *is always to communicate*

and to reach a coemmon level.
This is their mystery."

We are crushed beneath his weight.
The men go to Grande Isle
and bring home giant fish packed in ice.
But I do not eat the fish.
I want to know the secret.
What makes his breath change?
What makes him leave in the night?
What makes him
the captain of the boat?
He tells me stories of his days
on the streets of New York
and his days as a cowboy
wounded out West,
and nursed back to health by Juanita,
the Mexican woman who loved him.
He tells us tales of throwing bricks
from the roofs of tenements,
with Beany, and Shorty, and Lefty, and Moe;
onto the heads of the policemen below,
of running with a gang called Murderer's Row.
Which do I believe?
From the backseat of a '49 maroon Mercury,
I watch him drive the car
and never once does he hit a tree,
never once do we go sailing off a cliff,
or run out of gas in the middle of the forest.
He drives us in our little egg,

JACK GRAPES

the force of love blinding us to his pain.

When he walks, the rooms shake.
In the kitchen after work
he writes long columns of numbers
on a yellow piece of paper,
the code fathers know,
the secret formula
in a world for which there is no map,
no permanent state of nature,
no gene that carries
a knack for direction.

He wraps packets of money
inside the yellow paper
and wraps that with a rubber band.

In winter he stands on the prow of the ship
and faces into the wind,
the smooth skin taut against the bone.
Yet nothing is permanent.
New plateaus warp toward the sky.
New torrents obliterate the land.
He sails off in his boat
and leaves us in the kitchen
to add numbers by ourselves.

The men who are his friends
carry him home
and put him on the sofa.
He smells of whiskey,
lies there with his eyes closed,
but still he drives the car,

and still we fly through space in our little egg.

I tell him I never saw a purple cow
but that I hope one day to be one.
Is he dead or sleeping?
He puts his hand out and touches my head.
Does he know it's me,
or is he feeling for the wheel?
Which do I believe?

My mother sings:

>   *Dormez-vous, dormez-vous,*
>   *ding dong ding.*

This part of me is a continent—
the mysterious earth,
the lava that holds mountains together,
the richest traveler sold to silk,
the flutes,
the bellies of women,
the pubic hairs,
the secrets too old to forget,
the child
who stands at the end
of the hallway
afraid his father might die.

I leave my father in his hospital bed
and wait for the elevator alone.
The neat walls pucker up like fish.
For the first time
it is possible to sit and count:
moons, stars, inevitable shadows;
Neptune, Jupiter, Uranus, Pluto.
Starfish, seahorse, catfish, seagull,
the frescos, the billboards,
the skywriters sputtering up there
selling suntan oil.
There goes Mars. There goes Venus.
All fall down.

In the morning we are children again.
Someone knocks and says
"You have to get up
and get dressed
and advance in the ashen world."

Mother wipes the frost from the windows.
I scoot out from under the icy sheets.
Poles migrate rapidly
over different parts of the room.
Imprisoned in the paved cities.
Graves in caverns of age-old rock.
To penetrate the disguises of the visible world.

Born on this strange craft,
the awful vibrations of its deck,
clinging to the surface of this sphere.

The enormous room.
Two pennies lie on the floor near the bed.
One, a black war penny.
We take war stamps from the book
to pay for gasoline.
I hide in the backseat.

There's a giant birthday cake.
Sunday, October 23, 4004B.C.
"Fossil discoveries are
devices planted by the devil
to delude us," he says.
But we go to work in the ever-lasting Fire.
A.J. carries his briefcase full of rocks.
Darryl pokes around in his lunch bag
full of some iron-magnesium silicate like olivine,
a heavy, greenish crystalline substance.
"I can't eat this!" he yells.
I pour out my vial upon the sun
and men are scorched by the great heat
and cities of the plain fall at our feet.
All the towering peaks we know lie crumpled
on the ocean floor.
There goes Betelgeuse. There goes Antares.

We walk to school looking for bugs
to put in our lunch bags.

We begin to advance in the ashen world.

JACK GRAPES

The class room is filled with maps.
I can't remember where they said the bathroom was.
Afraid to ask again,
I walk into every room
and back out, looking for the door.
The seniors bulge and hold the walls up,
the hydraulic monarchies advance
beyond the steep hills,
the steepness of the land
shown by layer tints,
contour lines, relief shadings,
while the true character of the land
is difficult to infer.
Back into the small desk,
I stare bluntly at the folds and faults
of the techtonic map
thumbtacked below the blackboard.

The teacher reads out of a book:
> "*Early Pleistocene deformations*
> *brought about a widespread emergence.*"

Her voice sings above our heads.
I can see her stockings,
her chubby thighs, the five rivers,
the walls of fortified cities!

      She cups both hands before her.

Gunpowder!   The bayonet!   The stirrup!

The atom bomb!   The coming of the clock!

Printing!

I squeeze against the metal frame of the desk.
I grip the edges of the desk top,
rippling against geometry
that shows each rise and fall of rock,
and release, and release the warm urine
along the line of my leg,
down to the socks,
slow to burn its way to my toes.
The piss, the hot piss, the fundamental nature
of the continent, piss after piss after piss,
Russian piss and Chinese piss and Roman piss
along the skin itching as the bell rings
and everyone grabs their schoolbags but me,
squatting in the warm pool that continues to build
in the piss of the piss by the piss
warmest of arms all around my body
bellowing up from the earth.

Since winter,
the windows have been closed.
I open the box of coins:
human profiles
blurred by the touch of hands.
If a woman were here,
I would obey her.

JACK GRAPES

Geography is so bare.
Like a wet fish,
the thumbprint on the refrigerator
wiggles across the chrome.
It's midnight.
They march up to the door
and Yippee! The soldiers are home.
Who minds their muddy boots.

Ah, but a hundred miles away
the city is being eaten.
Who's in charge
of burning all these papers?
The sheets and suits
with no names attached,
false teeth in a cup
and Wednesday, missing with the rest.
No one puts anything away.
Sheets of dead skin crunch underfoot.
Static on the radio,
fire drills,
children in the street
hitting other children
with long cracking sticks.

Who is going to marry
at a time like this.

Jaunty is the word
for someone who dies before you were born.
That's my second cousin Alfred
and Alfred's father, and their first car.
Everyone over there is crossing the street.
There's the blue tablecloth
we'll fold on the old folds, if possible.

And Uncle Joe or Pappa or Mr. Lettelier:
look how young I look
bordered in white,
yellowing.
Scotch tape on four corners
facing Cockeyed-Jenny
on the other page,
just off the boat from Antwerp,
afraid to let go of the rail
as she walks down
the gangplank
to touch the ground of New York,
the New World.

The erotic force
        shapes the better performance;
another range of available styles.

I am pigeon-toed to the sun

and look up at it,
neck stretched, holding up by torch
                    the power
between thighs   entire plates
     concealed beneath the ridges
               of my skull.

My arms point out some
     flying object
over there   by the blue cloud
     just   about
to eat the reindeer's head.

Looking out from the sloping roof
          through branches of the neighbor's
                    sycamore
                    over housetops
and the streetlights
                    between houses,
I move to the edge

               ready to take off.

I don't pray for miracles.
I put pebbles in a box
and bury them near the magnolia tree
because it is messy and too sweet,
as imperfect as the rest of us.
The comfort in that.

And in the ritual of school,
of pencils and paper and swivel chairs and chalk.
Lines painted on asphalt I follow
to the bathroom, to the library, to lunch.
When my father dies
I don't look inside the coffin.
I hear the sound of dirt hitting the coffin
with my eyes closed.
Then I am driven, in a line
of dark cars,
everywhere,
except
into my life as a man.

Geese fly south.
Swans skirt the perfect edge
of ponds,
their long necks
an arc of feathers.
Their wake opens outward
in the water.
I am outward in my gaze:
the perfect incision
between lava and rock.

In the palm of my hand
I mix a little paste;
a little blood,
a little zinc.
Some of us have weak eyes.

The blind bump into everything.
Mix in a little sand,
a little grass.
Some gunpowder.
Anything living will do.
Parts of the body
fly across the sky.
There goes femur.
There goes backbone.
There is little need
to remember numbers.
Only the naming
becomes important.
St. Peter's Sandstone.
London Clay.
Montmarte Gypsum.

You can read the paper
and catch up on everything,
though in some countries
they only print the truth.
When I make soup
I sing to myself in the kitchen:

dormez-vous, ding dong ding.

The song is what gives me away.

Now on the table
all my friends in ties

waving goodbye.
And so much time taken
to learn again
what we knew
from each other
and forgot.
It's still daylight
but I can see the moon.
Almost,
or so it seems,
transparent.
Not even a full moon.
But a full moon.

Vows:

We're going to get married
and have kids
and live together
and be bloody.

JACK GRAPES

Lucky Finds

LUCKY
FINDS

Jack Grapes

These pieces extend and parody the dynamic artistic production of high-modernism that began with Stéphen Mallarmé's *Un Coup De Dés (A Throw of the Dice, 1897)*, continued with the works of the Italian and Russian Futurists after World War I, and reached their apogee in Ezra Pound's *Cantos* (1930-1966) with their graphic ideograms, Wallace Steven's *Harmonium* (1923) and *Notes Toward A Supreme Fiction* (1947), Louis Zukofsky's "*A*" (1959-1975), and Charles Olson's *Maximus Poems* (1950-1970). As individual cards, these poems can be shuffled into different secquences, extending even further their nonliner nature. Traditional narrative poetry is undetermined by the work's graphic intensity, and the spaces and syntactic gaps between images and statements offer the reader multiple layers of meaning (if meaning is your cup of tea), while at the same time subverting the very notion of meaning itself (just when you thought it was safe to open a dictionary). Thus, the reader is left to encounter the linguistic contradications inherent in collages, cubist simultaneity, and multiple points of view.

TABLOID OF CONTINGENTS

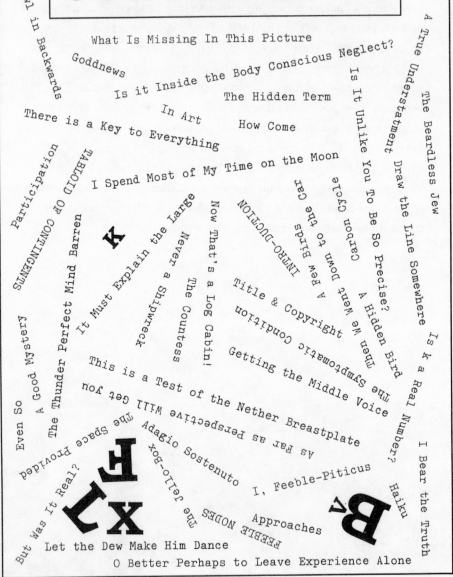

Crawl in Backwards

What Is Missing In This Picture

Goddnews

Is it Inside the Body Conscious Neglect?

A True Understatment Draw the Line Somewhere

The Beardless Jew

Is it Unlike You To Be So Precise?

Is It k a Real Number?

The Hidden Term

In Art

How Come

There is a Key to Everything

Participation

I Spend Most of My Time on the Moon

TABLOID OF CONTINGENTS

Carbon Cycle

Then We Went Down to the Car

A Few Birds

A Hidden Bird

The Symptomatic Condition

INTRO-DUCTION

It Must Explain the Large Barren Perfect Mind

Now That's a Log Cabin!

Never a Shipwreck

The Countess

Title & Copyright

Getting the Middle Voice

A Good Mystery

Even So

The Thunder

But Was It Real?

The Space Provided

This is a Test of the Nether Breastplate

As Far as Perspective Will Get You

the Jello-Box

Adagio Sostenuto

I, Feeble-Piticus

Approaches

FEEBLE NODES

Let the Dew Make Him Dance

I Bear the Truth

Haiku

O Better Perhaps to Leave Experience Alone

JACK GRAPES

INTRO DUCTION

As most of us know, the clarification of the nature and limits of received positions, especially as regards the philosophy of language, generates metaphysical utterances that violate the bounds of sense, placing both reader and viewer between apparently unavoidable poles, e. g. realism and idealism, Cartesianism and behaviorism, Platonism and formalism. Obvious as this was in the Middle Ages, for instance, contemporary linguistic philosophers have had a hard time displacing the social basis of meaning, especially when it comes to the constantly changing semantic environment of poetry and prose, and the blurring boundaries of everyday and literary langauge. It does no good for poststructuralist theoreticians to deconstruct the personalist impulses of discourse analysis. Look what happened to Wittgenstein, Jakobson, Bakhtin and Bloom. Even Lévi-Strauss was forced to admit that Durkheimian sociology was acceptable as a system of signification, but failed utterly to render plausible the relatively open text, much as most of us wish he had.

This is not the place to rehash utopian concepts such as symbolism, futurism, and surrealism. What was, was. No amount of recapitulation can bring back the purifying word of the tribe. Even the deliberate flattening of tonal register and the extensive use of non-sequitur fails to diminish the role of the lyric subject in favor of a relatively neutral voice (or multiple voices). Each of us -- poet and writer, reader and viewer -- must decide whether or not we believe the category of language is to be understood as hypotactic or paratachtic. Socrates preferred living speech to writing, but that was because he believed that writing alienated language users from memory. Homer's epics aside, we live in an age in which most of us imitate, not Platonic dialogue, but the logical or *logos*-like discourse of Aristotle, purged of mimetic interchange. Real speech can be ideologically threatening because it is centrifugal, because it flees the philosophical "center" of truth toward which all discourse is aimed.

Perhaps we are meant to be isolated by language. Maybe poetry leaves us little room for reassurance in a world whose center cannot hold, in a universe unable to come up with the small change of dark matter that would prevent thermodynamic equilibrium. Heidegger transformed the inner form of language into a messianic "speaking" of language that was potentially redemptive. But later, Lucan and Derrida used Heidegger to read Saussure against the grain, so to speak, but in the end, the sign does not always generate meaning, especially when the thing itself -- or the "spoken" thing, if I may mix my metaphors -- is the very stuff of which literature is made, while linguistics is but a form of systemized hostility toward language, and perhaps, toward literature as well. The closer this introduction approaches literature, the less coherence of formalist principles it maintains, and the more it contaminates scholarship, nay, even the mysticatory Platonism of mainstream linguistic descriptivism, which, however hard it tries, cannot neutralize the disguises of various socially imposed personas.

We approach the cul-de-sac of what Augustine called "fleshy" speech, where the lack of ideological validation abhors the vacuum of methodological unity. Freud's *Interpretation of Dreams* (1900) and *Jokes and Their Relation to the Unconscious* (1905) served only to enter the fray already cluttered by the oppositional approaches of Wilhelm von Humboldt and Kenneth Burke in the 19th century and Karl Vossler and V.N. Voloshinov in the 20th. A linguistic kind of chauvinism was the best they could muster against the frayed apologies of Noam Chomsky's tranformational-generative linguistics, which affirmed Humboldtian creativity but split it down the middle, as it were. No matter where we turn, we continue to face the ancient discipline of rhetoric and its notions of figurative ornamentation. When Burke wrote that rhetoric was concerned with "the state of Babel after the Fall," he wanted us to stare the reality of real language use in the face. But as a poet, I am not sure how to do this without making a fool of myself.

The poet is a maker of poems -- a text in verse. Bound speech. Thus, the poet, in a way that cannot be explained, captures the Word in the steel trap of Language, and in doing so, imprisons himself as well. For to escape is to be silent in the face of the Big Bang.

JACK GRAPES

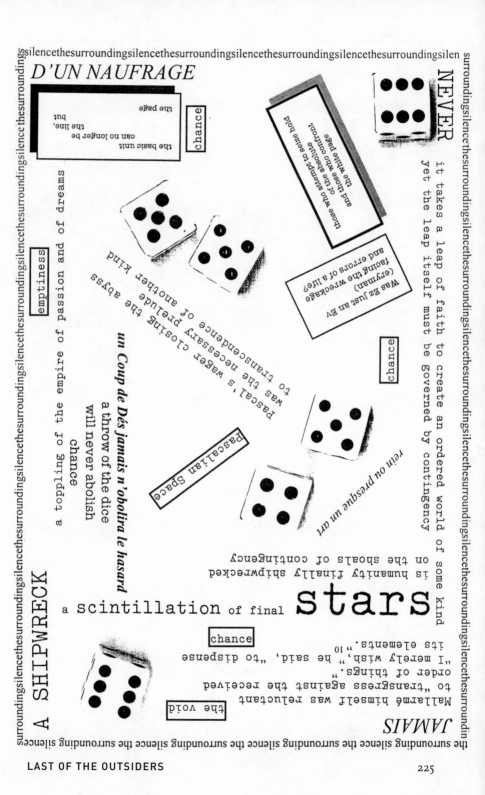

D'UN NAUFRAGE

NEVER

chance

the basic unit
can no longer be
the line,
but
the page

those who attempt to seize hold
and those who absolute
the white page

Was Ez just an EV
(eryman)
facing the wreckage
and errors of a life?

it takes a leap of faith to create an ordered world of some kind
yet the leap itself must be governed by contingency

emptiness

a toppling of the empire of passion and of dreams

Pascal's wager closing the abyss
was the necessary prelude of another kind
to transcendence

chance

un Coup de Dés jamais n'obolira le hasard

a throw of the dice
will never abolish
chance

Pascalian Space

rein ou presque un art

is humanity finally shipwrecked
on the shoals of contingency

a scintillation of final **stars**

chance

the void

Mallarmé himself was reluctant
to "transgress against the received
order of things."
"I merely wish," he said, "to dispense
its elements,"10

A SHIPWRECK

JAMAIS

C the man play Kapellmeister R bare arms [5]
"I, too was born in Louisiana," the lady says.

Hot wind above Thy brain.
Dem bones broken in the zink.
Eyes full of weary sleep.

Beethoven takes the Palestrina style in the last quartets
(--"Art demands of us that we shall not stand still."--)
the asperities of wind intonation
the jog-trotting accompaniment of the violin.
How far are we
the unconscious channel for our works,
and how far are we the arbiter?
Willing co-operators or trance mediums?
His words written on the score
of the C sharp minor Quartet:
"Put together from pilferings from one thing and another."

The dog is the dog is the dog.
Everlasting.
The moon is the moon is the moon.
Everlasting.
Day to day, this is how it goes.
My son and his friend stand in the kitchen,
putting tattoos on their bodies.
Sunlight comes through the window.
The same sunlight that goes through
your window on a slow, everlasting Saturday.
And here we are,
alive here on this slow everlasting Saturday,
bread on the kitchen counter,
my wife humming
as she fools with the toaster oven.
March 18, 2000. A slow Saturday.
The dog is the dog is the dog.
Everlasting.
The moon is the moon is the moon.
sweet sweet   sweet sweet   life.

JACK GRAPES

I, Feeble-Piticus of Los Angeles, to you [3]

he was the Gold Machine
they were the Silver Screw
you are the Bronze Crowbar
i am the Copper Plate

In-land, by hillsides steeped in the blood
of paper clips and who dunnits,
I, Feeble-Piticus,
a shivering barnacle dredged from the sea,
to you
what is the stance, who follows directions
into the dance.

1
The train they call the city of New Orleans
destitute laments of the twelve apostles period
She is the grasping hook,
lost pilots on their way to Arizona
the bear borne of whiskey and gin, no lighthouse period
of the porch light, a man undone but done up done up
                    a coming 'round the bend

2
it was the memory that brought me to this shore.
it was the memory that placed us in the photograph
it was the memory of rainstorms that called me back
it was the memory of sad faces in the kitchen
        that made me lie down upon the floor
        that made me call out to Jesus on the phone
        that made me say his name as a question
        that made me spit upon the doormat
        that made me play the mu-sick mu-sick mu-sick
        that made me make home the hieroglyph period

3
love is box-top, and can barely
save us from the weight of management,
the love of form uneasy to follow
Hollywood, Fordbank, Pickfair, Humboldt.

    O L A Man
    O suntanned Amerika
    O Hollywoooo wooooman
    O Barnacle Bill the Sailor

From COWTOWN to HICKTOWN
from DOGTOWN to LETDOWN

the nest, I say to you, I Feeble-Piticus say
O California winter
O offended afternoons
O Santa Monica summer
O midnights in june

            memory of that which you can do
            memory of that which can be done

and for what?
i was abstract [4]
i was changed
i gave pleasure

the book you called for was hidden, the words suitably buried
in the stone of uncertain truth what would you have of me
gold flourisher of the apocalypse, hermit man, inventor
of indestructable ennui?
between what points of wopbabaloobop and shoobeedoobeedoo
was Eden pierced and Adamn drowned and Eve washed
lounging by the sea?

you say it's about someone else but why are you crying?

here's the paradise of a sunless day,
the poet's gibberish, *cardo miseratio animus,*
angoribus confectus, afflictus.
vates inanis strepitus.

you say it really happened but what was true?

Time writes the freshness of the world down.
Doesn't complicate the harmony of a brave fiction,
Hansel and Gretel at home in the out-takes,
in the faithful speech of the gingerbread man.

you make like it matters but it don't

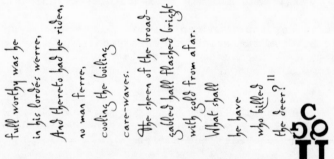

so much rememembered and so much forgotten
my son another universe i cannot comprehend
a feeble truth and the supreme fiction
the actual cupcake, the imagined belt
the real car parked in the expressible driveway
the revelations of doorknobs the escapades of love
my brothers my sister the remorse of our childhoods
all gone all gone   all gone all gone

JACK GRAPES

Put it down the extract abstract
malaria place it there cup cut-throat
and adjustment, refer daily to each
extreme, then in line he said haven't
you got the keys to the car instruction
is more important sometimes than
execution but don't they dangle and
piss all over themselves even Ethel
fried to a crisp when one jolt was
not enough to burn the brain and
breast as the evening sun went down
over the Hudson River and passing

and how you die

F G C E I P
P K E I W
W

high explosive lens mold on a   jello-box.[8]

a cloak of mystery

motorists shouted jibes
at the pickets, an outbreak
of cheers and honking of
horns, but in a situation
like that, legal matters still
unsettled, cough cough cough,
one must get along with the
argument, let history also
have its claims.

where babies come from

The kids want to know where babies come from

Now that's a log cabin if I ever saw one!
Take it now but don't bring it back.
Someone else left that message.
I'm fishing.

Yet another silver fender blade.
See around the edges all those paper cuts.
But with summer this close, ear to jaw.
Lovers just don't care for politics.

You can wear any coat to the dance.
If all black then you must know something.
Each vest should contain a secret.
Who did you kill wearing those shoes?

I have this delicate relationship with dreams.
Run for your life!
Will this gray rain ever stop!
And the closer I look, the less I dream.

Some say there's method to one's madness.
Delirium is robbed of its meager truth
as madness if its called a *Work of Art*.
The chance to see being born, over and over.

After awhile, even deSade bores me.
Violence promises to recover the self,
but you can't limit the world that wounds you
any more than you can disappear into Nature
when Nature is invisible to begin with.

To lose everything at the movies
is an act of faith.
Scene. Close-up. Tracking shot. Dissolve.
You think that's something.
You should see my life.

grovel of flesh, bare walls, tinsel on the crown; in the dark of the kitchen, feverishly, wear a hat and disguise your voice on the phone. You grow up in that country. You need to go somewhere, you know the roads. It's a good feeling; yet, getting lost is a challenge looked forward to.

JACK GRAPES

A true understatement
never
crosses
the
river

B

nasty streets

The clock reveals the body

Down

Z L J C

The whole point is that matter evolves, the universe is expanding, random is salad, the dinosaur lives.

Some people get nothing
from
pain

but expenses.

M V P F

swoons two more spoons of sugar

spoons two more swoons of sugar

I bear the truth because it's
forbearing and not because an
ordered sense of decency com-
pells me to adhere to all ver
sions of reality but one.

The summer we went to the edgewater
hotel on the Gulf Coast,
the summer I learned to swim
and Karl to float
and Louis to leave the high diver
without screaming
was the one that fit, I think,
the green blanket thrown
across our outrage.
There goes Brahms
on the phonograph and
my mother swooning at
Heifitz' violin.
I am the monster creeping
out of the closet draped in red cellophane.

white paint near the ground
is first to go.
judge streets by the sounds
settling, little
grains of plaster,
the tossing of a bed,
the loose slate
shifting overhead,
hiding pigment
and restraint.

M

JACK GRAPES

Here's one approach:

Walking into the classroom
I'd put one foot
in the trash can
and begin reading
the last chapter
of Travis McGee's latest,
and say to them Write
A Poem that leaves out
the most important detail;
does not contain the letter "d";
and has clues
to a buried treasure.

You can get a lot of reading done
that way.

s
o

t
h
o
r
o
u
g
h
l
y

i
n

t
h
e

d
a
r
k

The universe is just not a cigar.

Here's another approach:

Brutalize three long playing-envelopes.
Caution the disposal rate of tangerines by two.
Most people would have trouble with this part
but you can televise the chant
and no one will be the wiser.
Loop one year with no vacancy and
sling it over your back cockny-like
and be as thoroughly in the dark
as possible without losing
your perfect disposition.
This is important
but this is the most important of all.
Autumn is a time for inspection.
Remember your father going around the house
with his putty knife.
We are all, one way or another
hurtling through a splendid situation.
I wish I could tell you more.
If I were you, I'd insist on it.
You have to draw the line somewhere.

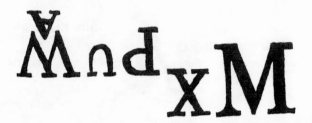

M

When the waters of the river rose
those cells situated at the level of the sewers
became a refuge for a swarm of huge rats
which during the night attacked those confined
and bit them wherever they could reach them.
Madwomen have been found with feet, hands,
and faces torn by bites from which several died.

C

This complicated system was devised to control a reputedly dangerous madman at Bethlehem; he was attached by a long chain that ran over the wall and thus permitted the attendant to lead him about, to keep him on a leash, so to speak, from outside; around his neck had been placed an iron ring; this latter slid the length of a verticle iron bar fastened to the floor and ceiling of the cell. This man lived in this cell, attached in this fashion, for twelve years.

A

A few birds
go into the fresh sky.

Someone sings gaily
along the black river.

It sure is a pleasure
California.

Look down upon the fork
of the American River.

Lie there in the sun;
a brown and fried look.

God, is that a peach!
As juicy as a watermelon.

Last night at sunset
I pointed out the pink sky.

This is the place to live.
Even at night, it's bright as day.

JACK GRAPES

It   "You have a beard," he said.
is   "Yes," I said.
almost   And he turned back to the counter and ordered another
over   cup of coffee.
the summer and sometimes need shaving   The
          twice a day.   palms
                                           and
                                           soles   Dad raises the
                                                                    razor
     as   jews   under disconnected sulphur bridges.   to
     my   his
as my brother and I watch him scrape the beautiful soap and running face
     and   board of accumulating hairs
     I   nonliving and rapid power
     find the razor and test it out   baldness follows suit.
on our own skins while he is away at work.

It   He is wearing a tweed coat,   the jews
is   and the fat of his blushing neck
almost   curdles over the edge of his collar.
over   The bloat inside disdains what is naked
the   and what is covered that he must show
summer   and scald and scrape away skin cell by skin cell
of   as if from within day after day of his dead life.
after-   I hate him. I want to spit the coffee-phlegm in my mouth
noon   into his dish
dreams, puffs of smoke rising   of prunes.
his   out of sleep.
snuff-   Madame DuFarge knits as the prunes are swallowed
ling   down his throat
head, breath missing, bombed down the short street, fish-like.
                    and the smell   a childhood
I spit into   of lilac-vegetal   accident
my spoon   slapped on the skin   uncorked
as he goes   with both palms   foam
to the bathroom.   awake   and
                     to break the spine and jaw of spit flung into
                                               the sink,
                                               a man's spit
Later, when he is off to work   my brother and I
we spit into the sink.   thought to our-
The spit is clean with bubbles.   selves,
This is not phlegm. Not man's spit.   phlegm.

          Dull. Cold. Indifferent.
          "You have a beard," he says.
          A snouted carcass clutch-bloodied waiting for time to pass.
          These are the men who kill jews I hear my uncle say
                                          in his decaying
My spoon filled with spit,   living room.
I slowly stir his coffee
before he returns to finish breakfast.
When I get up to leave, I slap a quarter on the counter and call him
                                          jew,
                    the beardless jew.

carbon cycle

illustrious

JACK GRAPES

Here it is:
Take it down blow torch or something.
The talk's as good as the writing.
The bullshit's packaged either way.
You think Christ said if you bring
forth what is within you, what you
bring forth will save you and if
you do not bring forth what is
within you what you do not bring
forth will destroy you well he did
but that's not the point the point
is do you want to listen to a poet
or not or what, like especially when
he or she's alive it's all made of
the same three parts his life, his
mouth, his poem, and so you get to
own theearth, see? It belongs to you
and isn't that all it is except to
stay alive. When does the bull look
good to her, that young bull the
braggart champion. I lose my hair and
I get older all the same, but I feel
good, a little crazy and young,
younger than you to be exact, and
in this shining city words are broken
by the image, see, not like social
or political action but like earth
quakes and napkins, an impression
from what used to be a republic of
words, now the image rules, thank
God it's seven o'clock and I can
tell you something, we might have to
make the word up again, translate the
letter so you say them again like a
4 year old, who doesn't mind being
cultural, except in his case it's
interesting, see, and then the diffi-
culty is to get the bravo around at
the back end and even if everybody
left I'd still talk and hold the
universe up, and the other way it
means too, hold the universe up, and
the other way, too; see the words
are always saying something else.
Not like Ed. He's just the baker.
He makes the bread, and I don't wear
glasses, and you gotta cut it all
loose and show your teeth. A bag of
bones. And Fred Astaire. When you
get right down to it, just what does
it mean to be brave. What's the
hidden term.

MAD Let

out here everyone walks on their backs

HIM The

so is half an orange

MAKE Dew

what rodent then dies on what good comet

STORM Make   of it what you will, something's cooking

you call this living, that was my wife

HAIL Him

In the still all alone Autumn by itself still

THE Dance

"Experimenting! Experimenting!" he cackled.

LET

JACK GRAPES

M

F

O

P

H F

G G
Z

like
your
grace
your
move
my
friend
but
who
said
polish

I spend most of my time on the moon.

this time it is hard to tell
which is the priest and
which is the repression

but who's the boss

who's the real boss

who's running the show

i don't even get tempted
jazz session a proper noun
in Vancouver or talking
economics the brown
paleolithic cows can that
be a political event which
is more like red or green
a passport privilege though
he goes by the square
numbers until he goes by
odd numbers what an odd way
to live slick fifty and that

god of mars lower case in the language where wyoming
no zeus no joyce no shakespeare no cassiopeia clytemnestra
no boston no clouds no air overhead lower case no literally
each letter an attack upon the universe each word a thrust
and think perhaps that before you knew it they were called
printer's devils and now the pictures come back and we
count the rings, two tapes a day, one from each side as
it turns no cloud cover no lower case just an attack
upon the universe another mention go home brush your teeth

what's inside is still
the mystery
to see how a thing bleeds
or does it do that at all
to know how infinite
and beautiful
each piece is
almost by definition

this is like they say

the dream of your life

a habit of newsprint

YOU

in
art
they
shoot
you

I was like that too, once; but now I'm

We kept the box inside a large
brown bag that was stored back
in the closet under a pile of
dirty towels that were never
washed and some discarded and
broken toys, little wind-up
tin drummers and marching men

why   nothing
then   for
do   ask
I   you
ask
so   love
much   I
of   if
you   but

this is from my mouth
this is from my hand
this will stop the fire
this must bring the flame
this is in my stomach
that sticks to my foot
and cuts across my back
these are meaningless
they peel off like skin

E P D T C G U B

different.

of the thunder perfect mind barren
yet many sons she refuses to speak
and says her name inside out alive

wafer

A PH

It's
only
a
picture
a
dream
worth
waiting
for
fresh
prey
brushed
hair
gone
dull
what
ever
happened
to
the
private
bomb
insult
to
the
little
man
this
late
in
the
day
and
so
much
to
be
gained
by
talk
leave
nothing
behind
walk
the
other
way
sing
by
the
black
river

this is the world we are made to swim in but what does the cat know and isn't telling

the gift to my children not their but my own happiness

grapple
with
the
hook
of
re
dem
tion
rep
tile
and
shut
that
gap
ing
jaw
.
in
to
a
no
t
h
e
r
w
a
l
l

up this way the fulgurations of doom in this heat the warm hands

of a wife or lover

Then I, for my part,
realized for the first
time the sickness of
ultra-leftism. Those
who jump when the bell
rings. Three cheers
for the Revolution?
Well, fuck that! Let
the rope support whom
ever is hanged, from
above, from below.

thin

W

i
do
it
so
fk
i
n
g

When I close my eyes
I see fire. My mother
would scream my brains
are burning. You should
have seen her hair
stand on end, pulling
them out with her fing
ers. Nobody sees the
body burn. I like to
see what I set on fire.
I like to follow the
smoke up til it's gone.

what difference does it make to you turdface

E

fart
head
wart
cunt
dick
foot
crap
hump
hump

but draw the line somewhere

The strength of haiku lies in its suggestions. Some of the
original cut-words have no translatable meaning and often
indicate an unfinished sentence, which has an elusive force
of it's own. One
can follow the
order of thought
or one can fol-
low the grammar.

> haiku:
> a chocolate mellow mint
>   refers to my tongue
> in passing. in passing in.

Sometimes the effect is quite the opposite of what was in-
tended. A rigid structure can act as a sort of frame to the
picture. Rhyme and word endings that appear monotonous in
one language are not necessarily monotonous unless framed
without rigid strucutre. If there is a sword it is best
used after the cherry blossom, unless mouth-tree-interval
rapes the still unfaithful moon. The horse is a frequent
visitor, though others brought hordes from Asia and look
where we are now. There can be no independent and permenant
wound. For me who goes - for you who stay, Autumn sucks
teeth. Bosho Buson and the Bamboo Broom translator is a
traitor. Pluck! Pluck! Pluck! You must force it to do so:
rhyme, equivalents, postpositions, metric, long piercing
nails goughed in the bloody neck, dark blood awash and
blather, no fox trout amuses in special rednering the slim
slick fox who hedges, then gambles, than that was no lazy
he screams dumpkopf! that vas my life. Surely there is some
kontroversy here, a konstandt remindy komma but I forget.
Needless to say in this short span, living on this planet
as temporary hosts, we should keep things simple and pure.
Don't make too much of anything. What is, is; and what will
be, will be. Whoever isn't here, is there, unless he's here
now, then he's not there. Begin with a fragment and you can't
go wrong. There are so many little pieces, pieces torn off
from those little pieces into ever yet and smaller pieces.
Examine the details. Vanish to a spoon. So few words are
necessary. Sometimes, one word will do. Sometimes, a single
letter. There are so many. Pick one. Just pick one. It's
enough.

A

Is it inside the body conscious neglect.

Is
this
September.
now
that
the
work's
done? Hardly.
Wood
along
the
Thames.
A
mere
nickel.

Each
night
the
men
gather
with
nails
and
long
oak
planks
to
build
the
ship
that
will
take
them
over
the
mountains
once
the
flood
comes.

and
if
there
is
no
flood, they'll just have to carry it to the sea.

Snark is barely alive these days
writing one novel after another:
the self -- always the self.

sub-atomic

Now I'm going to tell you something.
This is no accident.
This is what I meant all along.
That's the difference, see.
This is what I meant from the start.

Stand
calmly.
Rather
a
speech
full
of
old
images.

just imagine
these world lines
of matter
that form a
coherent pencil
of geodesics
just imagine

shift out from the skin
no prefered position or direction
just elegant solutions.

G

Monad squashes his hand to his chin
and rests elbows on the table:
living systems, he says;
these strange objects.

the ordered structure of a storm

K   X   R

is *k* a real number?

a singularity to infinite density

On back of the body the double balance of weight
a return of dead leaves   each single tree no promise
or posture at all but the surface of things   the pose
as a badge against hardness   to stop seeing this
is to fall out of a random window wrapped in smoke, teeth
        on the tips of fingernails.
If the film is run backwards, it is no longer my father
dying   your father dying   the father's all live,
gesturing in the deepest axis of a shifting world.
Shine the light through the brain. The past is so enormous,
gathering shape, coiling its arms and tongue around
        the death of a careless future.
That's why you run so fast: to make pudding of this poem.
To reach back and right the upturned salt shaker.
To leave the cold kitchen alone and cheap with its voices.
How many times can you make love do the work
of a hundred deaths, in vomit, in rags, in rage, in sunlight,
in bruise, in bloodsuck, in locked closets, in eye-patch.
This is what they do not teach in school.
        This is what cannot be written.

shift out from the skin
no prefered position or direction
just elegant solutions.

T E F   P   S

Monad squashes his hand to his chin
and rests elbows on the table:
living systems, he says;
these strange objects.

just imagine
of geodesics
coherent pencil
that form a
of matter
these world lines
just imagine

is *k* a real number?

Then we went downstairs to the car,
set the radio to WNOE,
sped up Napoleon Avenue
and threw beer bottles on Mr. Senac's front lawn.
Outward and yelling, our faces in the wind,
we picked up Cynthia from her father's fabulous estate
and headed up the old river road to the swamps
shrouded in close-webbed mist and clouds,
a slumbering sun
holding back the swartest night.
Cynthia, powerful in magic, witch-goddess,
made us forget the schoolwork of the cadaverous dead
between the realm of death and the realm of vegetation.
Dark blood flowed in her veins,
her soul stained by the sickly death hand of her father,
proud and blind in his stateroom,
bearing much of the sterile bulls, best of the lot,
back from heaven in a hell of gold and crabgrass.
She lay back in the back seat, while A.J. drove
into Bayou Lafitte, under the Spanish oak
that lined the dock behind Zattarin's Fish House.
She unbuttoned her blouse, poured wine over her breasts,
tender libations unto the selves
sacrificed to home-room and study hall,
water mixed with flour, the lost ones who flunked algebra,
mauled with bronze ball-point pens
among the battle-spoilt ball-players
who after practice
smacked the pin-ball machines with their palms
and drank beer until midnight
until their fathers, slayers of sheep,
unsheathed the narrow swords
of the impetuous impotent dead
and called them home.
Hold your tongue Ez,
out of Divus,
out of Chapman,
out of Pope,
out of Homer,
hold your tongue and drive no further,
hold your tongue
and let the old man rest,
let the old man go.[1]

詩 [12]

How do we account for the reality of subjectivity?
Subjectivity is not the problem.
Reforming language will not solve it.
Objectivity is the problem.
We must reform the soul.

She leans against the gray screen
of the lifeless TV. Should she brush the hair
from her eyes, a whole poem would magically escape.
Without rain, the rainbow plots its overthrow of the sky.
To merge with anything is a plot to overthrow the self.
And oh, I am the cream of the crop,
delivered to my mother's breasts.
Baskets of spite, ribbons of easy-going blues,
the tree out back whose roots break through the concrete.
In two's we gathered by the light of the refrigerator
collecting the good things of the world,
honesty and brotherhood, a coincidence of thumbtacks,
delivering my father's message, the dream state
of a garden hose, live crabs slapping their claws
against the side of the pot filled with Zattarin's
crab boil, thier blue shells turning red
and the white slabs of dead-man's meat
set on a dish beside the newspaper.
I would have you believe any of this but the truth,
the great gusts of flesh my mother instructed me to eat,
her breasts the cream of the crop,
passionate loaves of fish flapping on the dock
as my father beats the last drop of liquor from the bottle.
I admit I am mad for the world made one,
made perfect and savable
if only I were worthy of the spare parts and loose change.
I would have you believe anything but this truth,
that, forgiven, we are still guilty of perfection.
I remember red and silver,
the dark stain of the sun bleeding on the lake.
And I own so little that I cannot lose,
a transmission interrupted by her back.
This is the kind of peace I seldom allow myself,
to borrow a phrase: *upheaval interruptus*.
Fixed made broken. Mended made asunder.
Recludo hoc uterus. *Recludo hic mundus*.
The answer of course is in the lacking,
the whack of my father's body falling to earth,
the line read before the fire,
the pine cone dropping below the grate.
Why move, when remem-membering
still blows a hole in the world.

There is a symptomatic condition
for modernist writers:
to misjudge the point
at which poetics ends
and poetry begins.

Q

義 This is a test of
the nether breastplate that manufactures
the ulterior of

snead if he stands 書 to reaso N

rem eorum saluavit
We who are obscure references ἐλέναυς

in 利 the 必 makeshift 何 cargo of semblance.

The dead rise into the air
forgiving every senseless act of love,
forgiving every meaningful act of war.
                    Bodies lay stacked on the dead
grass, illegible signs of spring,
where small shops hang out their
"open for business" signs.

                    I advise staying away
from the pure theory of things,
originally a pragmatic cupcake.

                    I was thrown into this **W**orld

without a **N**ote from my ἐλέπτολις![7]
        mother.

but the heart -- meant for mending --
        breaks   againt the pure theory 日
    of things, senseless tulips that
    question authority, all the mmommies and daddies
unable to name the small walkways of the future.

Ma se morisse!

countess with thick calves [2]

C how many rooms
see through negligee
and one telephone is that right **P**

i work for the consensus i
agree but what do you count
with respect to power
you mean census as in rome

as in people and property
i agree authority for everything

count you this time
one bedroom one bath, one title
the social importance of flesh,
the bedrock of cold opinion

following her down the
hall past pictures of
aristocrats in confused
poses, but then that
was their life, each
day, the planned man
agement of the self
that counts, takes
stock, touches but
does not overcome power.
She sits and opens both
legs showing the smooth
white thighs.

don't let the accent bother you
we talk this way for money
one thing is because of another
i sleep well but the dreams are bad
during the revolution stayed home
but here i am anyway
living like this, still with a
fine body, dancer's legs.
feel them.
like when I was a young girl.
do I look sixty?
I still have to make a living.
Yes, one phone. And just one of these
What else do you need to know?
I'll tell you everything.

as I said, Countess, I
work for the consensus.
Tell me everything.

E

```
                ─────────

                the poem's all there is to believe in
it's            it's weak backbone that there's a nerve in it
the             like the condition of a frog;
neural
condition
that's          only because organs            the elementary,
difficult                    are able          not the synapse;
is              the capacity to find out       that's easy.
what's          to celebrate
up              not like me when dead, baby
                and by the way, simply because we're born
    each        like, how to dance sitting down.
     one
     of                                       that's easy;
us is as hard as we're made                   only because we're able,
              or can make                     that's all we are.
              ourselves
               and that's                              left alone, here
                 the stone    W                        proving
                not this                               my
                live frog                              point
                hidden.

   two kinds of angeles, one writes, howl of the eyes, glancing up.

                but do you know a water to write in?
                that love and woman is our subject?
                so that it covers love separate from woman?
                not arms and men.
                even if we have to become arms and men,
                our subject is love, and cause, and hmm,--woman.

           crawl in backwards.




                            L           |

                                  crawl in backwards
```

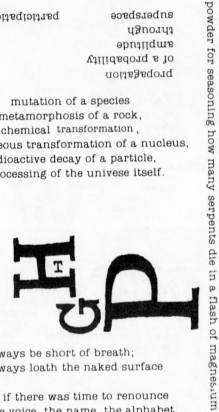

an open or closed world
assuming limits or progressions
having nothing more (or less)
to lose

participation

superspace
through
amplitude
of a probability
propagation

mutation of a species
metamorphosis of a rock,
chemical transformation ,
spontaneous transformation of a nucleus,
radioactive decay of a particle,
reprocessing of the univese itself.

PARTICIPATION

always be short of breath;
always loath the naked surface

as if there was time to renounce
the voice, the name, the alphabet.
as if one continues by being silent
as if out of nothing
comes nothing.

the universe as
being from time
to time squeezed
thru a knothole.

participation

the gift to honour your birth no broken bus eclipses civilization just a sickness when the palm does not work the lawyers catch in the throat; how many critics are crushed into powder for seasoning how many serpents die in a flash of magnesium

the acrobat takes bites out of his mother's arm this murder onstage, backstage, at the gate of the cemetery small body taking breast by the throat snake full of emerald skies desperate elephant on the banana tree keel of random life caught on chest hairs how to develop bare feet in the vomit

JACK GRAPES

Is it unlike you

      to be so precise?

How does the eye become

      accustomed to shadow

 reminds me of four hours in the dentist chair
                        gagging blood
                        and chips of
                              teeth

C O N N E C T   **B**

I am best at this, he said, pulling the
saw up then sliding it back down toward
his foot.

H
O
R
I
Z   and yet, we set out across the
O   plain, we carried our belong-
N   ings, we took what we could
T   from the land, we gave back
A   what we had no need for, we
L   prayed for rain, sang to each
              other in the darkness, worship-
 everyone   ped any god but the one God
  stand   that would get us through for
 amazed   we were through ourselves, need-
  smoke   in only to be tested. Let the
  on the
   line   food smell
of berries   like food.
 bulging
   with   VERTICAL
 poison

But can a square
remain a square
without enclosing
the future.

K

"It's
a
good
mystery,"
he
said.

"Good,"
I
said,
humming
this
tune,
"give
me
several."

and on four sides by a bull

M

You are bound by stupid bloody acorns.

In this map, Austria is no longer Austria and Poland has eaten a part of Russia. Rome is still Rome; what can I say. Think of the electron microscope. Seeing from above is all a map is. A fixed reminder that the Present need not become the Future, and that the Past can grow right before your eyes.

F

L

JACK GRAPES

the fish place, the restaurant, the one
that sits on stilts out over the water
you eat crabs to watch the sun go down
hot red and orange, flaming, a brand
out there on the horizon, and it's the
same as nature on that side, i mean if
we're not the same as nature on that side
and God on the other, man isn't. Tough.
Tough shit, he'd say; it's not easy

to get to that strength, that strength
that puts diapers up on the trees,
which knocks your whole life out, even
if you love and have babies to diaper.

like it's like playing the piano, like
that. Getting that middle voice. That's
what makes the music work, that is, that's
the thing that makes music such work, to
to get that middle voice. It's an old

principle, you get the beginning, the
middle, then the end. You do all three.
Then you get the poem. Then you get the
novel. Then you get yourself. Then you
get the wife. Then you get your life. God
damn, how many ways do you need to say it.
The whole goddamn thing is the middle, the
whole goddamn middle, right there in the
middle, where it belongs, culture in the
word, so to speak, when you don't even know
there's water out there, until the fish
stink gets you, the high tide, raising the boats
so they go through the roofs of the boat
houses, sails sticking right up, pushed
through the tops, like the tide redeems
you down to your fingertips when it's in
flood. And you sit there and eat your crabs
and watch the sun go down and you know,
you know everything, and you know it, you
know the beginning, you know the end, and
meanwhile, in the middle, sitting right there
in the goddamn middle of it all, just doing
the middle is what you'd say if asked, getting
the whole goddamn middle, crabs, and beer.

```
so
the
skinny
woman
jaunts
along.
there!
she
comes
is
that
a
ribbon,
or a
whip?
she
couldn't
care
less.
how
do
you
do.
no
zero
at
the
bone.
without
breath,
or
breathing.
but
polite.
sudden
fingernails.
```

I

T

what is missing in this picture?

how will I be level in sleep
and still rise with the precise
yawn that subdues the most
remarkable of beasts?

just ask if anyone's there. who cares
what one nostril means if the
other means greek. the head falls
like a decent pear or shoots up.
mostly in the dust
just for
someone
to enter
it.

Good news

it has just
gotten dark and
we are lying side by side
on the bed, naked, without saying
a word, hands at our sides, barely touching.
I look for a calendar, a clock, the sound of the
ocean perhaps, something to give me a clue as to
east or west, the year of the century, how far
from sunrise, the sick feeling of hope.

But from this way of looking, that
one window is as good as another,
how then may *what is* go down in
Death or how might it be born?

there's
a pleasant
pot
to
piss
in;
the
magic
farm
along
a
secret
line
that
kills
us
with
wake
full
ness.

whole it is of limb unmaking

I'd like to meet you
for lunch today but have only enough
money for paint.

O

Better perhaps to leave experience alone.

in a white rag

remember the mom   poetry must not substitute not cold
        ent   not journalism not escape   but do not leave out
has it's uses and what coheres on paper is not what   the
                                              co   table
        houses without windows   heres   once
        beyond the pane   you
        of someone's dark face   start
        perhaps the gas   fearing what is funny there's
                over   no end to the evasions
anger escapes   if not   in winter
   in a white   that   boarded up
                    then   no time for
some bitterness in the hug   guest
                    all music however powerful and being
no time either   human if you
for substitution
bedrock, who else gather all this   no time for God
                    when
                    envelopes
anger escapes   litter the hall and anger escapes
in a white rag

            that coheres for the sake of something better
something   to your name, only regret,
from the   only kneeling
very   in worship
beginning
                        to something misunderstood from the
                                        beginning
        frenzy hand about
        to beast the life cycle of the caterpillar something
                                                all this time
R   nearly
                                                worshipped

        once beauty was important
        now it means nothing
        what's real is what stops you
        at a strange angle   face, she said, because

W

Slow spider limping cow

the place is hot, too hot, much too hot
to do anything except complain of the heat,
the hot window panes and the hot half-empty
bottles of pepsi still on the desk from
yesterday which guarentees your growing old
and already you run out of things that are
hot, not enough hot can be remembered
in the heat when it's this hot, toohot,
too hot to die, die in a cold month is
best, you bet, a slow fade while you dream
of a crisp football afternoon, going out
for a long, easy arc of a pass, touchdown;
this is a way of going out that could fool
even you, in all this heat, until it's over.

Z   **B**

At this time of night you can't
see any of the animals, who are
invisible. Out of the walls they
come, their teeth gnawing at the
milk-cake moon. Now who left the
quarter on the table, was it the
man who walked away from his car
never to be seen again.Or was it
the sad rapist who blows into a
seashell and can't stop cleaning
his dirty fin-
gernails. This
is how they'll
snigger when
they hear the
news, how they
will stagger &
fall about the
room saying
the moon is
gone. The rats
have dragged it deep into their
hole.

A   There
          is
          a
          key
          to
       everything

Z

sometimes I love you for your brown
hair and sometimes I love you for
your crazy laugh and sometimes I
love you in the morning with your
head back on the pillow and a slight
smile on your face barely sleeping
and sometimes I don't know why I
love you, sometimes I'm not even
sure I do, sometimes I don't feel a
thing, don't feel like doing a thing,
forget who I am, or why it is even
necessary to be in love with anyone,
why it is necessary to do anything,
or feel like doing anything, some-
times it takes enormous effort to find one thing, or one feeling that
is more important than another, like picking up a book or taking off
a pair of shoes, or trying to write in the absence of love.

P

rutrutrutrut

a creative set has both sides of
the coin is only half true but non-
the less perverse, if stupidly
brilliant kinds of possibly ugly
and beautiful objects exist.

Tom is trapped within invisible
intangible boundaries of mental
space. That is nothing to lament.
What limits Tom need not limit
you. There are an infinite set
of examples.
Only one eludes capture.
Using the formal
suggestions
of beauty
but no formula
or attitude
advanced by the
romantics,
trace the
operation
by which all
sets of beauty
justify them-
selves without
permitting
the production
of all
possible kinds
of ugliness
in a non-con-
structive set.
You have ten
minutes to do
this.

This is the space provided.

Is
it
coincidental
that
the
first
example
of
such
a
notion
of
something
approximatable
but
never
attainable
in
a
finite
process
is
called
an
"irrational"
number?

Poor Tom is in a rutrutrutrut. Tom recognizes it, but does
not know how to encounter it. He is confused in his rut
rutrutrut. What part of rutrutrutness has an open-ended
prospective character, and what part of rutrutrutness
is unpredictable and conscious. What is the truth here.
Can Tom trot out into a new rutrutrutrut or is he fated
always to approximate higher and higher degrees of bigger
and better sets of generative rutrutruts. Answer in
the space provided. Answer more than once. Answer until
you can answer no more. Continue to answer. Begin as if
you'd been answering before the question was posed. Continue.

L H
R T U

rutrutrutrutrut Thus
art
progresses
toward
an
ever
wider
vision
of beauty by a series of repeated diagonalizations, that is
processes of recognizing
ruts and breaking out of
ruts ruts
ruts ruts
ruts ruts
ruts

R

This is not the space provided.

You must feel the space with your own hands.
Walk blindly into pizza,
originated cleverly by less than scrupulous
barbers plagerizing the dreams of children,
locked in closets,
fed through a hole in the door,
spoken to only when distressed
by the introspection of sturm and drang lit rat sure.

b r t u o e k

Q W Z R

Look how far we travel for so little.
These small gestures of isolation
that force us to be original.
    The misery of starving serfs
    captured by the classical melting pot
    along with the formalized
    gallant expression
as exemplified by Quantz,
and the more spontaneous sentiment
of Carl Philipp Emanuel,
who would have since moved
to the free city of Hamburg,
    and the elegant Italianate style
    further developed in Manheim
    by Johann Stamitz, and in London
by Johann Christian, the English Bach.
This is as far as perspective will get you.

Q M P H J X Y I

During dinner my brother pretends he's invisible;
we pretend he's not.

Symmetry works in an obvious way,
written in 1874,   a trick of the four and six
bar version,   lifeless until transformed
by Mozart's   recapitulation,
by Beethoven's   heroic excavation of bones.

Sightless, crazy, mute, and penniless,
the clavicord was even capable of vibrato.
I lied about practice time--
writing 45 minutes instead of 10.
The rest of the time I lay in bed
watching the ceiling for a sign of winter,
a season habituated by pocket-watches.

it must explain the large
and the small
the infinite, the vanishing,
the static, all that is in motion,
the world lines, the rest frames,
for the blind stationed to observe,
and be valid over the entire
time span of the universe

but
why
can
she
nod
bat
t
ing
eye
less

and reconstructed everything by number
drawn to me to shine even at once from
boots, green fingers, soft flesh between
thighs equivalent gathering sharp rake

what action
so instantaneous
that one eye
seeing curvature
and one eye
seeing dust
should both see
the deeper principle

about me, what was said, this grace of truth
the blue invention replacing the absent lie,
and this black burning from within, learning
to live like salt on the white table, sludge

eye
ing
but
can she say why

around
her the woman
the flesh and power
of that room curtains and
seized by some impulse
to hold on to
hang on to follow
as it pulls you under
we live without you
we live within you
we live with you
treachery thirty perfect
minutes as wash our hands as
toss a rock across the lake
that travels without
descending that makes
our history

A hidden bird,
the most difficult to hunt.

backward is not not
to go forward it is
true to something else
inanother direction
facing another particle
of creation made under
heavy whiskey and whiskers

going to confess
no confession at all.

loosen the limbs
of love
so outrageous as
to encompass and
represent and pro-
duce the universe.

cancel the years,
between having been thirteen
years old, standing in the dark
hallway, about to leave for school
denied but owned, and nineteen
years old, not the gesture of a
third bird, shot with a b.b. gun.

but
one
knows
what
love
means.

what the hearth is.

what chaos is.

one knows
the difficulty is the one that's the most obvious.

who is going to catch
up with the decay
of the monetary condition
of the earth, peg the whole dinero dollar peso franc and
gone to hell, which is what
trade is, to fuck your mother
and slit your father's

throat, and boast,
and marry the whore
in the cave.

no power system
no success
tell the end
of your dream
confess
or brutal bastard
after the earth
become like the moon
full of the beautiful
holes of dreams,
the natural history
of the future
meaning
refering
check it out.

When did the breakage begin?
When my brother and I were playing war?
When my father came home drunk
and smashed the mirror in the bathroom?
When the burglar climbed over my crib
to steal the money
hidden in my mother's shoe?

How come no one laughs at my bad jokes?

How come no one does something utterly stupid in front of the magistrate?

How come everyone walks around in a rubberized suit of unforgiveness?

what can I tell you?
Stay close to a telephone pole,
the kind a stray cat
able to appreciate the splendor
of a cloudless day
would attack
if it were a mouse.

check behind you.
there are those who hide in shadows,
          secret agents or your uncle,
          the one who rarely shaves,
          the one with all the money
          hidden in tea cannisters,
          the one whose wife, a PhD
          in senile displacement,
brewed her tea
with 50 dollar bills.

Even so
I wish I'd never started.
It was a clandestine operation,  this signal

a capsized *explication de texte* that [6]
degenerated into the mere *entr'acte* between eclogues,
the redundant version of Clauswitz's *coup de théâtre*
while the Chicago critics slept on their *bouts-rimés*

"sweet kisses of death[9]   stressed by the
set on thy lips   throat until dead
colder are they than mine."   he said

       stressed by the
       throat until dead

   to reconstruct the self
   is an act of autotelic mannerism
   a blind shot in the dark,
   the story within the story
   a *jeu d'esprit* of the *fait accompli*
   fraught with glory and worry and glory

but the lady from Spain was sick on the train
not once but again
and again and again,
and again and again and again.

     Even so,
     I wish I'd never started.

it's going to rain tonight and i'm glad thirsting
for the black clouds of a hat to shut down the brain
they die when you're young or they die
when they're old and you you die when you're young
or you die when you're old but you die but you die
but you die.

It was a voyage
to the end of the night
the search for the father
that ends in disenchantment
the search for the mother
that ends in cinematography
the search for the child
that ends in enumerative
bibliography.
     Even so.

FEEBLE NODES

1. See Ezra Pound's *Cantos* I and LXXXIII.

Ezra Pound (1885-1972) was the central figure in the modern movement, but remains a controversial figure to this day. He and his work have been both praised and condemned. He worked on the *Cantos* for nearly fifty years, presenting himself in the poem as a Poet-Odysseus wandering through the wreckage of the 20th century. The poem ranges throughout history and literature, a massive, monumental work that Pound himself felt he'd "botched" and wasn't able to make coherent.

2. In the summer of 1970 I worked for the government following up on those who had not returned their census questionaires. My territory was the hills above Sunset Boulevard. Up and down winding streets, small run-down apartments, even smaller run-down apartments behind ramshackle cottages set back from the street behind overgrown weeds and hedges. A hippy couple named Miller named their son Sudden-Freak. An alcoholic, out-of-work executive sat on a broken down sofa drinking scotch, his bare pot belly falling over the elastic band of a damp bathing suit. A man with a rifle waving me off his front porch. Prostitutes, pimps, drug-dealers, actors. Every doorbell was a TV show, a step into the twilight zone, a day at the races, a night at the opera, an afternoon in the circus. The countess, I remember best.

3. See Charles Olson's *The Maximus Poems*.

Charles Olson (1910-1970) is a seminal figure in post-World War II literature. His essays "Projective verse" and "Human Universe" and his study of Melville helped define the postmodern sensibility. "I, Maximus of Gloucester, to You" begins the series of "letters" that, over nearly twenty years of composition, grew to the more than three hundred poems comprising his masterpiece--a lifetime's work that has taken its place beside Pound's *Cantos*, Williams's *Patterson*, and Zukofsky's *"A"* in the great tradition of modern American epics. Through the public voice of Maximus ("the Greatest"), after Maximus of Tyre, Charles Olson tuned the deep resonances of his local subject matter, the fishing town of Gloucester, Massachusetts. *The Maximus Poems* is one of the high achievements of 20th century American letters and an essential poem in the postmodern canon.

4. See Wallace Stevens' *Notes to a Supreme Fiction*.

Wallace Stevens (1879-1955) was one of the main figures in the modern movement, but like William Carlos Williams, his recognition did not come until the 1950s. Stevens' work is known for its idiosyncratic forms of abstraction and narrative indirection. As Williams was a successful small-town doctor, Stevens was a successful insurance company executive. For him, poetry was a self-defining quest for meaning.

5. See Louis Zukofsky's long poem, *"A"*.

Louis Zukofsky (1904-1978) was one of the founding figures of modernist poetry. If he is one of the most musical poets of the modern era, he is also one of the most intellectually challenging. Gems of sonic counterpoint and verbal compression, his poems incorporate social commentary and philosophy in an ongoing *ars poetica*. In *"A"*, a poem composed throughout his life, he created an epic collage of autobiography, history, and reflection replete with theatre pieces, music, word-play, and punning. The *New York Times* called *"A"* "the most hermetic poem in English, which they will still be elucidating in the 22nd century." The first section of the poem was written in 1928 when Zukofsky was 24 years old, and the last piece is dated 1974.

6. *Bouts-rimés* are sets of rhyme words unattached to verses, like "June-moon-spoon." The making of impromptu verses to fit *bouts rimés* was a fashionable pastime in the 17th century, and continues to this day. *Coup de théâtre* is a striking, unexpected turn of events in a play. *Jeu d'esprit*-- "play of the mind"--is a witticism or flight of fancy.

7. See Ezra Pound's *Cantos*, V and VII.

8. In 1952 Ethel and Julius Rosenberg were executed for espionage based on the false testimony of Ethel's brother (who was highly paid by the government and given a change of name and a new home) and a dubious piece of physical evidence: a jello-box. Convicted with them but receiving a lesser sentence was Morton Sobel. Stanley Kramer directed and produced a movie about the trial starring Alan Arbus and Brenda Vacarro as Ethel and Julius, and Herschel Bernardi as their lawyer. I played the part of Morton Sobel. During the filming, the cast walked out in protest, led by Bernardi, because of some of the distortions in the script. We met at the Tropicana Motel coffee shop (known as Duke's) to discuss our strategy and the possible consequences of our actions. Kramer's justification for the selective point of view was based on the fact that he was using Louis Nizer's book, *The Implosion Conspiracy*, as the basis of the film, thus ruling out contradictory information contained in such books as *Invitation to an Inquest* by Walter and Miriam Schneer. During our "strike," I spoke to Morton Sobel on the phone and learned quite a bit about how the government tampered, and sometimes manufactured, evidence. Nevertheless, after three days, we resolved our disagreements and went back to work.

9. A poem by Swinburn.

10. See Stephen Mallarme's *Un Coup de Dés* (A Throw of the Dice).

Stephen Mallarmé (1842-1898) is one of the giants of 19th century French poetry. Leader of the Symbolist movement, he exerted a powerful influence on modern literature and thought, which can be traced in the works of Paul Valéry, W.B.Yeats, Ferdinand de Sausarre, and Jacques Derrida. From his early twenties until his death, he produced poems of astonishing originality and beauty, many of which have become classics. In the preface to *Un Coup de Dés Jamais N'Abolira Le Hasard* (A Throw of the Dice Will Never Abolish Chance), Mallarmé said the poem "enacts the very crisis of modernity to which it responds." The physical layout of the poem--its ambiguity of syntax and line breaks, the spacing and typography--was a radical innovation for its time. Words were displayed variously on the page, often in ideogrammatic fashion. Beyond the physical properties of the poem is the greatness of Mallarmé's poetic conception, the sheer power of his phrasing, and the philosophical underpinning that suggests the difficulty of establishing meaning in an essentially meaningless universe.

11. The poem set in DaVinci typeface opens with four lines in Middle English from Chaucer's "A Perfect Knight," followed by five lines rearranged slightly from *Beowulf*. The last four lines come from one of the songs used in 18th century productions of Shakespeare's *As You Like It*--the song was written by Sir Henry Bishop (1786-1855).

12. The Chinese character for poetry combines *word* and *temple*.

The Naked Eye

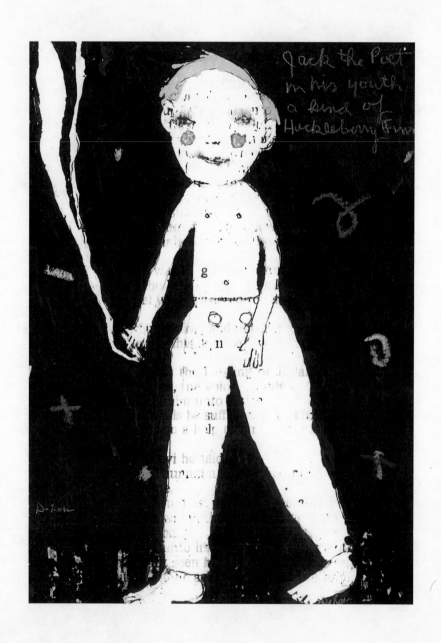

JACK GRAPES

END VIEW

    1

End view showing screws
the head dowel plugs was all my
sister knew I knew less a make-
shift beginning before three hiding
the other child in the shed, hiding the
other child under a tin roof splinters on the floor
and a dog growling from the sink.

    2

End view showing screws
a narrator galled to the hilt
free standing, sectional, the child
made to fit the space available
as if from his mother an easy-to-follow
direction would make him unafraid
like the Li'l Abner fireman
smacking the tin drums
with the one leg that worked.

    3

End view showing screws.
Construct the bookcase. Stack it with books.
At what cost was the three-year-old saved.
Save the hands held above the stove.
Little is remembered, very little
information leaks out of the black hole.
Yet, there he is, a fireman,
a carpenter, a bag of pennies.

    4

End view showing screws

only complicates the picture.
The broken mirror in the sink
reflects one face, yet to be assembled.
The ceiling falls in and rain
fills the bathtub
in the center of the living room.
The tree falls against the wires
and sparks set the porch on fire.
The mother the battleship the chicken
runs through the house waving both arms.
Smacked for this, smacked for that,
for being ugly, for being silent,
for losing a fish, for breaking a glass,
for giving something away, for taking something back,
for lying, for telling the truth.
The sound of flesh
on flesh, because the boat from
Antwerp was filled with rats,
because the train from Schemishal
was filled with corpses.
End view the bodies piled in graves.
End view the mother, growling like a dog,
the father, smashing the mirror.
the boy hiding the child,
who combs his hair,
wears pajamas
and doesn't wet the bed.
End view the child who doesn't speak at all.
End view the world exploding in the hall.
End view the bastard screwed to the wall.

JACK GRAPES

THE ACCIDENT

Sometimes you think you're sleeping but you're not.
Sometimes you think you're talking but you're sleeping.
Sometimes you think you're dreaming but you're talking.
The sky falls and everybody goes back to work.
Last night I thought I was sleeping, but I got up
and went to the window to see if the moon was talking
back to me under falling skies shredding houses
in the neighborhood down to dust.

Are the women burning up, are the men lying there
like seashells, are the boys convalescent in bright
heads of tolerance, how many ugly strangers will
knock on your door and demand payment of past
due rent, those unopened eyelids near the cold streams
that pray for resolution.

I imagine someone has a rifle in the closet
and a bag of gold coins in the oven.
I imagine I will climb the tree in front of my house
and spread my arms and imagine I can fly.
How exactly do you describe a child's sorrow?
I never meant to get hit.
I was just crossing the street is all,
going to the Hills Grocery Store to buy a pack of gum.
My father put on his pants and went to work.
I was looking at the tree in front of the house.

Nothing outlasts the day but the day.
Then there's another, and another.

But both the spelling and the sense
differ on the two sides of the Atlantic.
It is a gross canard that beginning a sentence
with *but* is stylistically slipshod. In fact,
doing so is highly desirable in any number
of contexts, and many style books that discuss
the question quite correctly say that *but* is
better than *however* at the beginning
of a sentence. However, good writers often
begin sentences with *but* and have always done so.
Take buried verbs, for instance.
Jargonmongers call them "nominalizations,"
but sometimes the verb is buried inside
a larger noun, and sometimes the larger noun
is uncovered by reduction, and sometimes
you're sleeping by arbitration, and sometimes
you're talking by contravention, and sometimes
by mediation, compulsion, hospitalization,
new now to become old soon to become ancient
before you know it.

When I was a child, I walked to the end of the block
and when I crossed the street, a blue car came by
and hit me and I was on the asphalt for awhile
waiting for someone to rescue me.
But they brought me back to the house
and put me on the sofa and were talking
but I couldn't figure out what they were saying,
something about hospitalization,
something about minimization,
something about violation.

Sometimes, however, you think you're dying,
but you're not.

JACK GRAPES

ELYSIAN FIELDS

The first word I learned to read was "cat."
This was before the cat was in the hat.
It was just a word for a thing, without associations
to any other thing but the cat I personally knew.
A solitary cat.
A singular cat.
And I could read it. Those three letters—
up until then, mere abstraction, pieces of rubble—
had become a thing, or more rightly, a being I loved
with a name in the world.
Then it was "Ritz," the name for the cracker
I learned to spell from the billboard on Claiborne Avenue.
This new word went with me wherever I went.
Into the kitchen, into the bedroom,
but also into the yard where I had not yet guessed
that I was surrounded by objects with names of their own
that could be spelled and memorized,
words composed of letters I could also take with me
everywhere and nowhere.
In the backseat of Dad's maroon Mercury, say,
when we went for a drive.
"Let's go for a drive," my mother would say.
People don't go for a drive, anymore.
They always drive *somewhere*, they have places to go.
But there were afternoons, especially in summer,
when we'd go for a drive. I'd lie in the backseat
and look out the window at the trees, try to guess
where we were by the look of the trees and the blue of the sky.
Ritz was with me everywhere then, those four letters,

the words belonged to me.

And *cat*, birds huddled in the trees

above me as I spelled out loud, lying in the back seat of the car.

I liked the sound the wheels made on newly-paved asphalt.

"We're on Napoleon Avenue," I'd announce.

"Now we're on Canal Street."

"Now we're passing the cemetery."

The cemetery was on Elysian Fields Avenue.

I worked hard learning to spell "Elysian," learning to say it even.

"We're on Elysian Fields Avenue," I'd say.

Later I learned that the word came from Greek mythology,

Elysium is where the blesséd went after death, though Elysian
Fields Avenue

was named after the Avenue des Champs-Elysées in Paris.

In New Orleans, you can take Elysian Fields Avenue

from the Lower Mississippi River all the way to Lake Pontchar-
train.

To get to Aunt Bea's, you drove up Gentilly Boulevard,

then turned onto Elysian Fields Avenue.

We passed Brother Martin High School.

I could tell where we were because the trees

were especially leafy there.

"We're still on Elysian Fields Avenue," I'd say.

You could spell it "Elysium" too, if you wanted.

Some words could be spelled different ways, I learned,

and some could be said different ways too, like route and route,

or tomato, tomato. I liked rhyming "Studebaker" with "rutaba-
ga."

And what about words like "rhubarb" and "rhododendron,"

"rusticate" and "Rwanda"?

One second you're going for a drive,

then you're blessed, lolling about in the Elysian Fields,

then you're home making rhubarb pie,

then sitting in a tree with purple flowers,
then moving out to the country.
And where did you end up? Central Africa.
The world changes in an instant when you're small, word by
word.
What I mean to say is that the contemplation
of anything unexpected
changes you when you're young.
From the mighty, muddy Mississippi to Central Africa,
from the Everglades to Timbuktoo.
"Hammers," I thought,
lying in bed with the nightlite on,
"lightning rod, starlight, electric drills,
asphalt, trains, flying machines."
I packed my suitcase with words,
and I've been travelling ever since,
sometimes on a train with the blesséd,
sometimes on foot,
walking toward Paradise.

POETRY NOT MUCH

poetry
not much

not much
to read
to speak of

if you're
reading this
which I doubt

only poets
read poetry
stupid poets
reading stupid
poetry

but poetry
not much

brings not
much money
maybe none

hate poetry
bunch of crap

pretty senten
says

JACK GRAPES

pretty wurr
ddsss

most people
run from
poetry

pretty stupid
when you
really think
about it

I don't think
about it
I write it
why think
about it

poetry
not much
to think about
so to speak

sorry you
had to read
this all the
way to the
end

how much
better you
could spend
your time

making money
fucking
doing some
thing constructive

poetry
not much

not much
to speak of
when you
really think
about it

JACK GRAPES

THE DAYS THE DAYS THE DAYS

It's been quite cold here.
Yesterday, it finally got sunny,
but I think
a little rain
is due this weekend.
I get up in the morning and go out
in the cold chill
to water the fountains,
which lose water
during the day.
And to water the little lemon tree.
And the other potted bush.
And the bird bath.
When I come back inside,
I have to warm my hands
over the fire
on one of the burners
on the stove.
Then a kiss from Lori,
slipping my hands
inside her pajamas
to feel the soft skin
of her butt.
Then ½ an apple
and a tablespoon
of peanut butter,
then the red pill
and the two white pills,
and a quick glance

at the sports page:
Kobe scored 48,
the Clippers beat the Heat,
and maybe the Saints
will beat the 49er's.
Then into the study
to work:
write a poem,
pay a bill,
answer an e-mail.
Then off to class.
Another
day.
What a fucking gift.

THE WAR IN SHREVEPORT

There was a war in Shreveport.
It was somewhere else before that,
Baltimore or Cleveland.

I was in Shreveport the other day.
We forget sometimes, a dog or a woodchuck,
Anne Frank or Thelma Ritter.

In Baton Rouge miseries of mind and body
in a bar downtown at night where we sat there drinking,
Eddie Haspel and I talking about Oriole Macinroth.

In New Orleans we wait for rain.
Bright wings disappear but no one cares.
Einstein or was it Neils Bohr who said what? I forget.

Now Los Angeles plumps up like a thanksgiving turkey.
Gonna rain not gonna rain maybe rain maybe not.
I think of my father, Samuel Joshua Grapes.

OTHERWISE MOONLIGHT

Again and again something retreats to a speck on the horizon.
In the great notebook, it hardly adds up.
Accountants with their pointy pencils despair.
Past midnight someone gets up, rings for the nurse.
Again and again, someone decides to enter the world.

Over there by the pond next to the hotel
a sharp knife on the white tablecloth reflects
the sun so perfectly you'd think it was all
Archimedes needed to sink the entire Roman fleet.

Stop for breath. The lights in the hotel go on.
In each room, someone walks to the window
and looks out on the plaza below. Pierre is not
with his wife, Claudette is not with her husband.

How the chandeliers shine in the lobby!
Were an orchestra here you'd hardly bat
an eye, take it upon yourself to lift the baton
and wave your apprenticed arms in the air.

Embarrassed palms moist with fear.
Time is running, as they say with a solemn
nod of the head, out. What was that tune
she was humming when pruning the agapanthus?

The morning light is so cherished.
The day breaks someone else's heart.
Eyes knock the stars into elsewhere galaxies.

JACK GRAPES

Again and again what's too human to survive
survives. We are always at each other's
mercy. Here comes the waltz and you take her in
your arms.

The world puts on a mask.
A curtain is drawn.
We move from the window,
bearing the whole peach
of the past, shuffle toward the bed.
Shape me to stone, mold me to ice.

Again and again, something retreats to a speck on the horizon,
crawling shoreward,
the hillside graveyard,
the breathless earth.

HOME

Animals take no responsibility for anything.
A vulture circles my house,
but I wave it off. "No one's
dead yet!" I yell.

I hear cougars are coming down from the hills
onto our hiking paths,
and a bear got into someone's backyard
ice-box. Not an ounce of scruples.

Either the car swerves for the squirrel
or the squirrel stops at the curb and waits.
Yeah, right. That'll be the day.

They're all killer whales, waiting to feast
on our philosophy, our epic poems,
our economic forecasts, our religious
ideologies.

They're arrogant, hifalutin know-it-alls,
treading the ground like they belong here.

As far as they're concerned, therapy's
for the birds. And rightly so.

Imagine the panther
weeping on the couch
about the human arm
he just lunched on.

JACK GRAPES

Or the white shark,
sad and despondent
because he swallowed a CEO
wearing a life-vest.

I'd like to have some of that—
no guilt, no shame.

Eyes that look out on this world
as if it were home.

THE MIND

At night the mind strolls on the beach
someone holds its hand maybe a missive
sent years before now discovered in the ruins
of a sandcastle bitten by flies seaweed attracting
gnats when the mind stops bits of tissue the wolf's
perhaps giving in to death breath empty a big hole in
the heart bloodier than a hog's mist out on the horizon
where ships gather their dots and dashes morse code the
secret message to a world too proud to admit rust gnawing
on all sides tides illuminations of how ardent a waste of land
and sea holds the vast inside of the mind bolted down for storm
unable to recall joy or law or the law of love shifting always
like sand dunes like people who show themselves splayed
for torture then hide in the firm nut of resolve inside a cup
cake or some other object the mind like a mirror glazed
feeling the thrill a brutish face standing loitering on
the corner unpaid rent killing the shape of rabbit
stew each morsel tasty in the wilderness but
not the scaffold you were expecting under
the burning sky of the mind a bald ac-
countant a thin pencil point in his
hand making tiny 5's and 9's on
a yellow sheet of legal paper
trapping the mind in the
zero pretending to
know what
it's good
for

SOMETIMES I LOVE YOU

sometimes I love you for your brown
hair and sometimes I love you for
your crazy laugh and sometimes I
love you in the morning with your
head back on the pillow and a slight
smile on your face barely sleeping
and sometimes I don't know why I
love you, sometimes I'm not even
sure I do, sometimes I don't feel a
thing, don't feel like doing a thing,
forget who I am, or why it is even
necessary to be in love with anyone,
why it is necessary to do anything,
or feel like doing anything, some-
times it takes enormous effort to
find one feeling or thing
that is more important than another,
like picking up a book or taking off
a pair of shoes, or trying to write
in the absence of love.

FALLING TO EARTH

Subjectivity is not the problem.
Objectivity is the problem.
We must reform the soul.

Where do poetics end
and poetry begins?

I'm powerless over my art.
The commitment
to breaking things down.

Rain plots to overthrow the sky.
To merge with anything is a plot
to overthrow the self,
a coincidence of thumbtacks,
the dream state of a garden hose,
live crabs slapping their claws
against the side of the pot
filled with Zattarin's crab boil.

I admit I am mad for the world
made perfect,
worthy of spare parts and loose change.
Forgiven, yet irredeemable.
I own so little that I cannot lose,
a transmission interrupted by her back.
The kind of peace I seldom allow myself,
fixed made asunder,
then mended.

JACK GRAPES

Broken, then fixed.

The whack of my father's body falling to earth,
the last line read aloud before the fire,
the pine cone rolling into the flames.

Remembering blows a hole in the world.

VISION

About suffering,
they were never wrong,
the old masters.
—W. H. Auden, *"Musée de Beaux Arts"*

Today, the day is not being very kind to someone,
someone, say, in Altadena or Charleston.
I'm trying to imagine it, but the poet's vision
fails me at the moment.
I used to be so good at imagining suffering,
even my own,
which isn't so much you'd be proud to mention it,
but enough to make the mouth hard
and the eyes glazed.
I should admit now that I've hardly suffered.
The walls were invisible.
Spoons in coffee,
an old vaudeville act
breaking into a tap-dance routine.
Stretched out on the sofa,
unwashed, unshaven.
Someone comes over,
I go through the motions.
The stars in the vast cosmos
dying so slowly you hardly notice,
each one at the beck and call of another larger star.
Someone sits at a table in the kitchen,
tearing up the newspaper.
A son or father or lover has left.

JACK GRAPES

Such a dreary vision of loss, of suffering.
I'm suffering a betrayal of hindsight.
Everyone's talking on the tube of retirement.
What exactly is that?
Fresh snow comes to mind.
Up in the mountains,
a little boy walks in circles, stomping his boots,
making bootprints.
My mother always talked of someone
not having a pot to piss in.
My father said they didn't have two nickels to rub together.
Life does a lot of things to you.
It's a living thing, like some animal that lies
at the foot of your bed,
waiting for you to wake up.

BALANCING THE BOOKS

What was I going to find
in *Dark Laughter* by Sherwood Anderson?
Though it seems like only yesterday,
I read *Winesburg, Ohio* back in college.
But I was just as taken by *Dark Laughter,*
his tenth book and fifth novel.
There was something poetic about Anderson's writing,
something oddly quaint that I knew,
even at 21, couldn't last.

Today I was searching my bookcase,
looking for a particular sentence
to help me realize the possibilities of language,
something besides James Joyce or William Faulkner.
Eventually, I found the sentence, but before I did,
I came across—perhaps I was using it as a bookmark—
a check for $12, dated June 20, 1967.
Now I'm not into all that new age stuff,
but today is June 20th.
Oh, and before I forget, here's the sentence:
"There was a deep well within every man and woman,
and when Life came in at the door of the house,
that was the body."
I'm still not sure what Anderson meant by that.
A distrust of formal verbalization, perhaps;
or a particular theory of human nature;
maybe just the discursiveness
of associational psychology.
Who knows?

JACK GRAPES

Does anybody still read Sherwood Anderson?
Probably not, unless it's *Winesburg, Ohio*.
Poor Sherwood.
Poor check, used as a bookmark in a book
nobody reads anymore.
Old words on a piece of paper,
hardly worth the paper they're printed on.
But I'm glad I found those words.
Reading them again after almost fifty years
was better than cashing that check.
Sherwood was still alive in my hands.
I had done him that service, brought him back,
brought his words back,
words he may have written late at night,
or in the early morning, or at his desk
while it rained throughout the afternoon.

When we read the words of writers after they've died,
do we wake them from a peaceful sleep?
And is the waking a reminder they once lived on this earth,
even though that life has become a dream?
Would Sherwood even want to be wakened?
And what about that check for $12, from Jerry Jacobs?
How long did he worry over that uncashed check?
Maybe he still accounts for it,
subtracting $12 from his monthly balance.
It's June 20th, and somewhere in the world
Jerry's balancing his checkbook,
waiting for me to cash the check,
his expectation waking me
from my own dream of a life
moving forward one sentence at a time.

REDEMPTION

How wretched she felt to see them
going off some mornings
without anything to eat.
The stove gave off the last of its heat.
Turning from the door
the way characters in a short story
by Pirindello do, she looked down at her feet
and watched their disappearance
below her skirt.
Outside, the snow continued to fall
with the abstract waywardness
of autumn leaves.
Her husband, his back
propped against the far wall
by the cracked window,
began accusing her
of still more infidelities.
With the butcher, who dared to lick
her asshole with his tongue,
he tore her coat from her arms
and threw it into the fire.
With the peddler from across the hills,
who took her left nipple
in exchange for a candlestick,
he raised her skirt and thrust his head under
and between her legs
like a photographer
poking his head under the hood
of his camera.

JACK GRAPES

Which led to the next accusation:
the priest,
who wore his dark robes inside out
on the days he couldn't wash them
and punished himself
by fucking her
standing up in the woodshed
and never allowing himself
to come.
"Pity me," he begged, his skinny legs trembling.
Resisting the last thrust,
he removed his penis
from between her legs.
"Pity me," he mumbled,
walking back down the road toward town,
until flaccid,
desire unspent, he felt
the glow of redemption
rise through his body.
With each accusation, her husband
ripped off another piece of clothing:
the grainer, her bodice;
the reaper, her stockings;
the clerk, her panties;
until she stood there,
naked and shining
in the glare of his wretchedness,
having nothing to wear
but her sins.

LOVE FOR LESSER THINGS

another cup of wine
river of stars
mountain flowers
a bolt of silk
a slab of rock
the rhododendron
the white apes
others' children
thatched roof
the ringed pheasant
elegant ostriches
mournful capsized boat
handful of tears
a dragon cloud
meditation
on the bright frozen
moon another cup
of wine
a thousand sorrows
flowers swooped in brain
crystal-beaded curtains
heartless wind
blossoms thick with dew
her ravenhead stockings
the white-nosed horse
a few more days
in someone else's world
not among men
this pain of poetry

JACK GRAPES

another cup of wine
this line of words
love for lesser things
the clouds break apart
black tire black cup
laugh in the face
this book
on my knees
my wife
in the kitchen
my son
out in the world
another empty cup
a toast to yellow leaves
the amazing sky

ENDOCARDITUS

deferential fawning obsolete negative
valve replacement
sent booming throbbed heartbeat
sucked visual root canal observation
all the blood come down on Sunday he makes up
obligatory placement
tub overflown with water
in the cold linoleum floor on cadiz street
hobnobbed with royalty
the divine stupefication of irregular resolve
born that way
bicuspid aortic
hyperlespretension
comic strips spread out on the floor
ruckus maker
slippery marker
katznjammerkittens arctic sea plane crashed on the ice
big daddy warbucks boots on the taxi cab floor
comintagetchacomintagetchacomintagetcha
walrus bedtime
out the window of the backyard washtub
moonmanminnows manacled
to the throat of a dream that recurs
recurs on the dog face tulips
sneeeeeering bloodsuckers nibbling away on Sunday
rattlin'bonesradium eradicated sunshine
who grows too fast in the time it takes to crawl under the sheets
and revisit the old house
where comintagetchacomintagetchacomintagetcha

is a phone call away
moontrees lost in the wind of winter
all of a big life squeezed into the back porch raindrop
back for the nickel and dime
back to replace the obsolete negative endocarditus
comintagetchacomintagetchacomintagetcha.

OLD ROAD OLD SONG

here so what
edge of town
where dogs
gather
looking for bones
the sun slips
below the horizon
keeping its
feelings
to itself
and my thoughts
churning
like the electric
generators
behind
the fence here
on the edge of town
just lying about
neither coming
nor going
waiting for a bird
to find a tree
branch
in all this
barrenness

JACK GRAPES

LONGING

Bits of White Light.
Soothing Tigers.
Expatriate Longings.

The Losses.
The Gains.
The Grief.

Scrambled Eggs.
Butter on a Bagel.
The World As It Is.

Tu Fu and Li Po.
Broken Moon of March.
Still Grieving the Way.

Wandering Exile.
Dread before Bedtime.
Dreams of Baseball.

Theodore Pine Tree.
My Wife in the Garden.
The World As It Is.

The World As It Is.

THE FOUNTAIN OF STONES

One night a man entered the city carrying an empty sack.
The man was the wise one, the enlightened one,
the one who knew everything.
Everyone else in the city was mad.
In the center of the city stood a fountain
filled with stones.
If you walked by the fountain, picked out a stone,
and held it in your hand,
all became clear—
a flash of clarity that explained everything:
love's little secrets, misfortunes of salt,
dishes of fire and ringlets of friendship,
why sorrow burns slowly,
why joy is but one grain of the harvest,
why dawntide brings the breath at last
to the watchman,
why the heart promises nothing but sadness.
But the clarity lasted only a few moments.
The greatest clarity was that such clarity
was too hard to bear.
Thus, after a moment or two,
the stone was returned to the fountain.
Once returned to the fountain,
the stone turned into a ruby.
By evening, the fountain was filled with rubies.
The man carrying the empty sack
who entered the city at night—
the wise man, the enlightened one,
the one who knew everything—

JACK GRAPES

the man approached the fountain
and picked out the rubies,
one at a time,
and put each one,
one at a time,
into his sack.
He held each ruby for only a moment,
but with each ruby,
a portion of his enlightenment was lost,
a sliver of wisdom blew away in the wind,
a particular nugget of knowledge
fell by the wayside.
When the sack was full,
and every ruby in the fountain had been removed,
the man knew nothing but the shape of the road
that led back to the forest,
the imprint of shoes made in the dust,
the light from his cabin in the forest
toward which he walked
carrying the sackful of rubies.

Each time a ruby was removed from the fountain,
a stone appeared to take its place.
By morning, the fountain was again filled with stones.

During the day, the mad citizens of the city
picked out a stone from the fountain,
held it in their hands for just a moment,
—as long as it took to achieve clarity—
then put the stone back into the fountain,
where it turned into a ruby.
By evening the fountain was again filled
with rubies.

The rubies were carried out every night.
The fountain was again filled with stones.
The mad remained mad.
The man with the empty sack—
the enlightened one,
the wise one,
the one who knew everything—
returned to his bed in his cabin in the forest—
    all enlightenment lost,
    wisdom gone with the wind,
    knowledge barely a grain of sand—
and slept the sleep of the angels,
his mind at peace, his heart at rest.

VARIATIONS ON A THEME BY HEIDEGGER

It's the day after tax day.
She plays a Brahms Etude
on the grand piano in her living room.
The heart meant for mending
breaks apart.
Her fingers reach into the body,
pulling out parts.
Up the atrium and down the ventricle,
Up the Potomac and down the Delaware.

The dead rise into the air
forgiving senseless acts of love,
forgiving meaningful acts of war.
My uncle Lou who died on the kitchen floor
vomiting onto the news of the day.
My uncle Charles who died in the hospital
while they rearranged keys under the floorboard.
In my mother's head,
the hallucinatory tribulations
of Thanksgiving dinners, slaps across the face
for no reason at all. Still the body
speaking its piece.

She leans toward the keys
as if looking for signs of dust,
her body bent forward in prayer,
articulating the disappearance of time.

I advise staying away

from the pure theory of things,
originally a pragmatic cupcake.
I was thrown into this world
without a note from my mother,
and kept after school for being a show-off.

What can I tell you?
Avoid telephone poles,
the kind a stray cat
in a thunder storm
on a cloudless day
would attack
if it were a mouse.

Check behind you.
There are those who hide in shadows,
secret agents or your uncle,
the one who rarely shaves,
the one with all the money
hidden in tea canisters,
the one whose wife
uses dollar bills
to brew her tea.

How come so many walk around
in a rubberized suit of unforgiveness?
How come no one laughs at my bad jokes anymore?

"It's nothing," we say, "nothing but the wind."
Even at dinner, no one cracks a joke.
When did the breakage begin?
When my brother and I were playing war?
When my father came home drunk

JACK GRAPES

and smashed the mirror in the bathroom?
When the burglar climbed over my crib
to steal the money hidden in my mother's shoe?

She wants Bach to speak, but Bach,
dead all these years,
relies on her fingers,
her willingness to attack the augmentation of despair.

During dinner, my brother pretends he's invisible,
and we pretend he's not.
It's hard to look him in the eye
when we can't see him,
unless he sips his soup.
Up goes the spoon,
and my father asks,
"Did you finish your homework?"
My brother goes through life
with no faith at all
in his own imagination.

Symmetry works in an obvious way,
written in 1874, a trick of the four and six
bar version, lifeless until transformed
by Mozart's recapitulation,
by Beethoven's excavation of the heroic.
Sightless, crazy, rude, and penniless,
the clavichord was even capable of vibrato.
I lied about practice time—
writing 45 minutes instead of 10.
The rest of the time I lay in bed
watching the ceiling for signs of winter,
a season heralded by pocket-watches.

These small gestures of isolation
force us to be original.
The misery of starving serfs
captured by the classical melting pot
along with the formalized
gallant expression
as exemplified by Quantz,
and the more spontaneous sentiment
of Carl Philipp Emanuel,
who would have since moved
to the free city of Hamburg,

and the elegant Italianate style
further developed in Mannheim
by Johann Stamitz, and in London
by Johann Christian, the English Bach.
This is as far as perspective will get you.

You must feel the space with your own hands.
Walk blindly into closets,
inhabited originally by less than scrupulous
barbers recapitulating the dreams of children
fed through a hole in the door.

When she finishes playing,
we both stare at the keys, wondering
what is left to believe in.
The sun sets,
regular as a button,
as if God were here,
blessing us all,
we who strive,
even in the dark,
for particularity.

JACK GRAPES

A TIME TO SING, A TIME TO DANCE

There's too much time to sing,
and not enough time to dance.
The sea is for singing, the land for dancing,
and the dog that will not die
does both.
My grandfather told me this
when I was 12 and he'd been dead for thirty years.
My grandfather on my mother's side.
My grandfather on my father's side, we don't know
when he died, having abandoned the family
when my father was two.
I'm writing this down
camping by the Kern River,
where there are no watches to measure time or distance.
Josh does his dance by the tent
and Lori notices that his feet move like my feet,
meaning one of my grandfathers
still speaks and moves through him.
This poem, then, is a song to my son,
and to my wife, and my friends,
who do this dance with me.
And I am grateful for the kind of richness
that refuses to be turned into art.

Trees, then rocks, then mountains, then sky,
then clouds, then God, who forgives
me for knowing he doesn't exist.
Still, I thank Him for all He's given me,
nothing I've dared ask for, nothing

I would have dared pray for,
but not a day goes by that I don't send up
little balloons of thank-you's.

When I made my birthday wish,
which we celebrated last night around the campfire,
I wished for each one of my friends
a life full of everything God has given me—
a God who doesn't even exist.
He hears our songs, He accepts our dances.
And sometimes I wonder, especially at night,
if He will punish me and take everything away,
a punishment I'd duly deserve for my lack of faith.
I'd like to say to him,
I believe in you, you are there,
but I can't.
He knows how badly I want to be able to say this.
But I know what I know.
The truth will not go away.
The unspeakable things we do to each other and to the children.
Job asked Him for a reason and was scolded
just for asking.
The gall, to question The Creator about the world He created.
I don't deserve my good fortune,
yet accept it without question.
My wife, my son, my deep and truest friends
who love me.
And it's all too much to hold or carry.
There's so much to sing about,
I've hardly begun to dance,
and there's so little time to dance.
I *would* dance. I would dance with Him who gave me so much,
but would He dance with me?

Would He open his arms and follow my lead,
me, who dares not question,
who receives and receives and gives
Him nothing back, not even a question directed straight at Him,
not even the heartfelt supplication
of one small prayer.

WHAT GETS LOST

Some rivers run wild,
some deep, some,
like the one in my throat,
hinge on memory
and every hookline&sinker
that floats to the bottom.
Les poèms viennent et vont.
A deer once came to our campsite.
Up close, he looked big
and dangerous, not like something
in a Disney movie.
I told him to stay where he was
and he obeyed. This big buck
obeyed. We had an understanding.
It's not like that with the world.
Briefmarken bleiben für immer.
I never practiced the piano.
What was I waiting for?
You can only wait so long,
then it's time to get your coat
and say goodbye to the others.
My wife thinks I take too long
saying goodbye. A lingering.
What's the rush? Something
might happen, someone
might say something, then
where would I be?
In the car, driving home,
missing the best of it.

JACK GRAPES

That'd be a fine how-do-you-do.
Like being in the middle of the journey
of your life and finding yourself lost
per una selva oscura,
blah blah blah the straight path,
the narrow way, the right road, etc.
So say you're walled up inside a dream.
Fixed forms vanish.
Vida y muerte eran mi cuarto sesgado.
The moon sits there all alone,
begging to be worshiped.
Miró actually set his canvases on fire.
Not with paint; with matches.
I was thinking now I'm not
thinking now I'm thinking again.
Transcendence, the existence of others,
negation, contraction, the body,
temporality, translator's introduction,
dialectical car-ports, the concept
of carburetors, flashlights, penny-
ante card games, still too soon
to discuss the Hegelian concept itself,
but being is always reduced by a signification
of the existent, enveloped by essence,
and the effort each of us makes
to rediscover the immediate in terms
of the mediated, the abstract in terms
of the concrete on which it is grounded.
I am the body, I am the existent,
I am the signification.
You're always getting at something,
but like the deer, it bolts off
into the forest, the *oscura* forest,

the dark forest, as the poets say,
the one you get lost in,
the one you have to enter
to get the thing you are getting at.
Life is this one big how-do-you-do,
and then it'll be time to get your coat
and say goodbye to the others,
to the body, to the temporality,
to the negation, to the moon,
to the transcendence,
to the rivers running wild,
the canvases aflame,
the translator's introduction,
the translation itself—
what gets lost in the poetry.

JACK GRAPES

SZYMBORSKA
(1923–2012)

I came home
Wednesday night from class
and Lori was ensconced
like a caterpillar in a cocoon
on the bed, watching a movie on TV
about crazy people who fall in love
and break china.
"Szymborska died," I said.

She reached for the remote
and shut the TV off.
The room expanded into that quiet bubble
we experience
when we shut off the TV.

She looked at me and said nothing.

What was there to say?

A friend dies,
a poet dies,
poetry lives on:
There's nothing
you can say.

It's like turning off the TV,
and their passing
fills the space of our lives

with all that silence.
A balloon of being and nothingness,
a reduction of existence into a series
of appearances, overcoming those dualisms
that have embarrassed philosophy for centuries,
and replacing them with the monism
of the phenomenon.

I put the clipboard
I still had in my hand
on the dresser
and began to undress.
Then I got in the bed and lay beside her.
We still hadn't spoken.

Szymborska was gone.

We just lay there for a bit, in the silence,
not sure who would break it,
not sure whose turn it was
to turn the moment back into words.
You need a poet at a time like this,
and the poet was gone.

There was a small crack in the ceiling.
And a tiny cobweb in the corner.
Later, Lori'd probably get on a chair
and with a tissue
wipe it away.
That was her job, getting
those little tiny spider webs
gone before they engulfed the house,
our lives, the planet. Don't

worry, dear reader, she's on the job.
You will be safe.

"What's my job?" asks Lori when she's nagging me.
And I repeat the mantra: "To take care of me."

But for now, with Szymborksa's passing
still blooming into silence,
the cobweb would have to wait,
the crack would just have to bide its time.

Such a long silence.

Then I thought, fuck it.
I reached for the remote,
and clicked the TV back on.

There went a teacup.
Crash.
There went another.
Crash.

It was good to get back
to a semblance of the world,
all that love and passion,
all those broken teacups.

THE MAN WITH THE BEARD

"What do you do?" he asks.

"I'm a poet," I say.

"What kind of poems do you write?"

"Big ones,
little ones,
bad ones,
good ones,
poems about rain,
poems about trying to find
a parking space on a Saturday night."

I take a sip of my Guinness
and give a little laugh,
just so he knows I'm kidding.
The beer's bitter.
I should have gotten the Corona.

"Poetry . . . ," he ponders.

"Yeah," I say,
moving the plastic cup
of beer aside,
away from the edge
of the table,
". . . poetry."

Another man walks up
and asks if he can share the table.
He's wearing a green shirt, suspenders,
a green beret. All set for the Bloomsday
reading of episode seven from *Ulysses*.

Bag of wind, windbag, west wind,
wind in my sails, an ill wind.

The band in the courtyard
strikes up another Irish tune.
Three young ladies link arms and dance a jig.

The waiter brings the Irish stew
in a paper cup, a plastic lid on top.
I count the carrots and small pieces of meat.
I eat it with the plastic spoon.
It's not very good;
as Irish stew goes,
pretty bad.

After the reading I ask the Joycean scholar
a question, but she doesn't have an answer.
Pale vampire mouth to mouth.
The soul frets in the shadow of language.
This rough magic drowned in the book.
Love that speaks in the lizard's flash.
Do and do and done.
Courtesy of the inward light.
Fathers falling down.

SMOOTH SAILING

I don't think I've ever been hit with a bolt of inspiration.
It's just damn hard, trying to put something down.
Whether it's by hand in a journal,
watching the ink dry,
or on the old portable Royal typewriter
my dad got me when I was 11.
I learned to type on that thing
using the *Ruth Ben'ry* Touch-Typing system
and wrote all those
Inspector Peterson Murder Mysteries on it,
each onen with the word "corpse" in the title:
The Living Corpse,
The Corpse Tells No Tales,
The Corpse Takes Over,
The Corpse Has the Last Laugh,
and
The Corpse Buries Itself.
On the IBM Selectric I wrote two books of poetry:
A Savage Peace and *Seven Is a Frozen Number,*
and when I moved to L.A.,
I got that portable Smith Corona electric on which
I wrote most of *Breaking on Camera*
and *Trees, Coffee and the Eyes of Deer*
before I got a computer.
After a date, Lori and I would come home to the apartment
on Orange Street and have a glass of wine
and take turns writing a poem on that Smith Corona,
read them to each other, then make love.
But whether I'm writing in the backyard,

or in a café,
or in a coffee shop,
or in the kitchen,
or at a picnic table,
hell, it really doesn't matter,
it's just not easy.
The wind could be whipping up a storm
but I'd probably say something about the morning stillness.
Poetry does that to you, makes you lose your bearings,
makes you puff out your chest and put on airs.
High hopes, then it starts to fall apart
and the best you can hope for
is that you don't make a fool of yourself
by the last line.
You wave the white flag while you're still typing,
hoping for some sympathy from the gods.
I give up, I give up, but it's a false declaration.
You never really give up.
In this poem, maybe, where I can feel myself
thinking about throwing in the towel,
but there's always the next one, not to give up totally.
Prospecting for gold, hoping the parchment map is accurate.
Some deeper meaning you can hang your hat on.
Maybe I've been reading the wrong books.
I should get back to books with pictures.
But over the years,
I've grown this relationship
with the poem.
Bukowski said he duked it out,
and maybe Rilke breathed them from the storm,
and Whitman yawped his way through.
But me? 'Dunno. We're just old friends,
the poem and me.

I imagine us sitting on a swing on the front porch,
smoking a pipe or a cigar,
watching the passing parade.
The poem says, "The world stands revealed,"
and I say, "There's a squirrel there in that tree."
Then the poem says, "Makeshift ennui,"
and I say, "My wife makes our front yard
look so beautiful."
The poem says, "Lines of darkness run true,"
and I say, "My son is becoming a man,
bon voyage, my son, smooth sailing,
steer by the stars."
Then the poem closes its eyes,
and I close mine,
just a nap we're taking before dinner,
steamed broccoli and a piece of chicken.

THE IMPOSSIBLE FOUNTAIN

Perché la vita à breve   Because life is short
et l'ingegno paventa   and my wit is afraid of
a l'alta impresa,   the high undertaking,
né di lui né lei   in neither wit nor life do
molto mi fido   I have much confidence.

—Francesco Petrarch,
Rime Sparse, Poem #71 (1374)

Petrarch's father was exiled from Florence,
as was his father's friend Dante.

Had he studied law as his father did,
he might have accumulated some wealth,
and not squandered the wealth his father left him,
though he claims his father's executors
cheated him of his inheritance.
Who knows?
What it comes down to,
is, he wrote poetry—
what foolish boys do,
whose fathers practice law,
whose fathers labor in the fields,
whose fathers work daily selling household gadgets.
All my life I have understood how foolish it is
to write poetry.
As I said in a previous poem,
"poetry not much."
I try not to complain,

but alas, there is always the need,
to justify, at least, the enterprise,
that sweat forms at the brow
shaping a single line of poetry,
though not as much sweat as does
sawing a piece of wood or pushing a plow.
Though with poetry,
one is always starting over.
There's always the fear that the reader
has gone on to other pursuits
as I write this line, this one here, right here.
One is constantly reminded
by those who work in buildings
made of steel and glass
that we have somehow missed the boat,
that we're reading the wrong books,
that life is going to pass us by,
if it hasn't already done so.
The scientists are more blunt:
If you speak with eloquence,
the eloquence disassembles;
if you speak as a child, no one listens;
if you speak as the shopkeeper,
no one cares.
Words will not save you.
Better to keep your mouth shut.

It is in this silence the poet lives.
But it is Sunday, and down the street
someone is starting up their car,
someone passes by my house
walking her dog.
I should go out and empty the fountain,

JACK GRAPES

so when Eric comes it will be good and dry
for him to paint.
Then we can fill it up again
and listen to its lovely gurgling.

I have come this far,
my seventieth birthday a few months away.
I didn't study law,
I didn't run my father's business,
I didn't sell household gadgets.
My son talks with his friends in the kitchen.
My wife and I laugh before going to bed.
Whether or not I have poetry matters little.
What I have is this life
that I have lived with poetry,
my personal gadget, my own plow,
the elemental particles of my life's blood.
I have come this far,
and as you can see,
I am still trying to fill
the impossible fountain,
still trying to shout
something meaningful
from out of the silence.

SMALL CRAFT WARNINGS

Maybe it began with a curse.
Someone needed to do more
than mouth the word,
someone needed to write it down.
So they thought about what the mouth does
when speaking
and scratched something on a scrap
of something and said the word aloud again,
only this time, as song,
heroic song, epic song,
the song of the word,
carrier of meaning,
a linguistic unit, an utterance,
a quarrel, a scripture,
a city, cities within cities,
inescapable cities,
bronze iron steel glass,
small craft warnings,
doorways leading to broken rooms,
history & battlefields
mock apple pie
the great throb of continuous hope,
the glacial weight of it,
the delusions of paradise,
political crimes,
the curveball,
the currency,
the flow
the bedrock.

THE NAKED EYE

Got my microscope here looking at microbes,
got the telescope by the window looking
at stars or the moon, whichever comes first.
I don't know much, other than the fact
that the Earth's round and there are little
things that swim around on the slide that I can't see
with the naked eye.
It's the dogs sitting on people's front porches,
the cats that hang out in my yard
who run off when I approach.
Sometimes, I just stand there looking at them.
And they look at me.
If they only knew how kind I'd be to them.
But they're not taking any chances.
One step in their direction, and off they go.
How they jump up on top of the wall!
It's almost like they're flying.
I'm basically a dog person, but cats
have a special place in my heart too.
Cleo used to crawl up on my chest
when I was lying on the sofa reading.
She'd look at me, just look at me.
Boy, those cat eyes.
This is not the place to go into how she died,
that's another poem,
but I stayed up all night with her on the floor
and I think it was about 3am when I felt her body
and knew that she'd gone.
It wasn't until the next morning that I cried.

Big heaving heaps.
I think I was crying for my father, finally;
but that's another poem, too.

One evening, Glenn came by with his telescope.
Not like mine, this one was big and sophisticated.
We brought it outside, set it up on the corner
and found Jupiter and Venus,
not far from the moon—
a superior conjunction if ever there was one.
When people came walking down Orlando
we asked them if they wanted to look in the telescope.
Most said yes, but a few didn't seem interested.
They just kept walking.
This intrigued me the most.
Glenn was looking at stars or planets,
and I was watching the people
who just kept walking
without looking.
What planetary objects!
What stellar phenomena!
What we should have done was set up a table
next to the telescope with the microscope on it.
Give people a choice.
The big or the small,
the vanishing or the swimming,
the explosions of fire or the search for food.
My son could have set up another table and sold lemonade,
like he did when he was ten.
My wife could have come out and worked in the garden.
I could have brought out my book of poetry
and read the poem "Still Life."
Here, I'll quote a bit of it for you:

And we are so alone in this inscrutable palm,
that presses against the other
palm
of exact passion   ready to curl
to the sweet fist of science.

So like a door that won't stay closed.
Or as Rilke says:
Eine blind Welt un rings umgiebt.
A blind world surrounds us.

MADNESS

Callimachus says our madness is most
acute at the start, then—if I get his meaning
correctly—it tapers off as time goes by.
Which means, I suppose,
that I am approaching sanity.
Complete and awful sanity.
Yet some kind of madness is needed
to venture forth,
to embark on the kind of adventure
mad for the taking, made perfect, as Orestes says,
by suffering.
Yet we continue to build cities
in the rain
as others weep
at the feet
of great monuments for the dead.
When Prometheus molds you,
the voyage on clay feet
continues to define you,
as the warp the loom,
the thread the cloth.
All this knowledge is enough to make
anyone mad, but sanity creeps up on you
like a . . . [fill in metaphor]. . . in the night.
Soon enough, dear friends,
everything makes sense—
every gesture perfect,
every amplitude of intellect
mapped out by the oscillations of time,

until—like Ishmael—you find yourself
knocking people's hats off just to feel alive.
I was mad enough once to dance in subways,
to burst into song in supermarkets,
to babble in French in French cafes.
Now I stare at my plate of tomatoes
cut into perfect wedges,
sprinkled with balsamic vinegar,
each placed expertly on my tongue.
I crush the meat between well-capped teeth,
letting the juice trickle down my gullet.
A generous tip for the waiter,
a stately walk to my car,
then the sane ride home
to the well-placed stones
and sophisticated bric-a-brac
on my mantelpiece.

SUMMER NIGHT

After the Bloomsday reading at the Hammer
I retreated to my cubicle
surrounded by those old friends, my books.

Lamplight on desk. Lights in the garden
I can see through the window.
If snow were to fall, I'd listen to it,
but there's only the sound of the water
gurgling in the fountain, an occasional
car blaring loud music.

Older now, I sleep less and less.
I get up in the night and read
about the Hittites,
their iron artifacts and storm gods,
their chariots and mysterious language,
but even that's not enough
to send me back to sleep.
Forget the mind. How else
can one get past the silence
of history and great slabs of memory
like beef hanging in the brain.

Such a steadfast world.
How it goes on and on,
regardless.   No rhyme.
No reason.
Night: this favorite time of day.
Everything unto itself.

JACK GRAPES

THIS LIFE

My wife is getting dressed,
rushing off to see her clients.
She puts a top on that comes down past her navel,
barely covering her pubic hair.
But when she sits on the bed to pull up socks,
the chemise rises up, exposing hair between her legs.
She puts one leg up, resting her heel on the bed's edge.
Her legs a few inches apart.
Her pubic hair and mound clearly visible.
It's enough.
This altar. This sacred, secret, sanctified,
whatchamacallit.
I stop by the TV and ask her
when she's coming home,
do I pick up Josh today,
are we going to David & Gina's for dinner on Saturday,
should I get bread and milk at J-Market
or what?
"What," she says.
I'm talking, she's got her head down working on the sock,
—no, I think it's panty hose or tights,
something like that,
something complicated that requires her full attention—
I'm talking but I'm really looking at her pubic hair, her sacred
whatchamacallit, that is . . . . and is not . . . . her,
the embodiment of everything,
the symbol of nothing but itself.
This is when . . . I think . . . maybe not . . . but probably so . . .
this is when I love her the most,

when she's putting on socks, half-naked,
paying little attention to me.
"What?" she says.
She's not even listening to me.
"Should I pick up Josh," I say,
"and what about the bread and milk?"
Actually, I'm not really talking to her, either.
I'm looking at her pussy
while she struggles
with this complicated long sock or something,
her head down, working it fold by fold past her heel
and ankle, then up the calf, over the knee,
up the thigh, finally standing
and jumping up and down, small little jumps,
as she tugs the last part above her pubic hair,
above the navel.
She rims the elastic with her thumb,
gives it a snap, then looks up at me,
finally. She gives her head a shake,
straightening her hair for her clients,
getting all neat and composed and psychotherapeutic,
her sacred whatchamacallit covered by a gauze curtain,
and in a minute, by the dress.
I'm looking at her,
thinking of that Grecian pottery
where Aphrodite rises from the sea,
her sandstone naked body
gravelly and glistening in its classical flesh.
"What?" she asks.
"Do I pick up Josh today?"
"Yeah. Is that okay?"
"Yeah."
We stand there, holding everything

unsaid that seems to float along with the dust motes
made visible finally by the first light of the morning
coming through the blinds.
When you coming home?" I ask.
"6:30."
"Don't forget my class starts at 7."
"I won't."
Then she's off, rushing from one room to another,
grabbing necessities.
I catch up to her at the door.
She kisses me.
I kiss her back. A little piece of sweet lip
in her sweet breath. I keep my eyes open
so I can see her face close-up.
"Love you," I say.
"Love you, too."
I stand on the front steps and watch her
get in the car, buckle-up, start the engine,
make a U-turn and come to a stop at the stop sign
at our corner. I walk to the mailbox
on the corner and give a little wave.
She sees and waves back,
then pushes off for her day, her clients.
I have things to do, too.
Have to xerox poems for my students, my fellow poets.
The sun's not out yet; by noon, the clouds'll break,
and it'll be a sunny day,
and the sun will shine
on my wife
and on my students
and on this blessed,
sacred, sanctified life.

TEACHING THE ANGELS

I'll miss Sundays after I'm dead.
I'll miss all the days, I suppose.
Summers especially, the idea of vacation,
the whole family packed in the car,
my mother yelling, "Leave your brother
alone or we're stopping this car this minute and we'll sit
here all day if we have to and you'll never get to Miami
and nobody's going swimming!" Outside, the Everglades,
nothing but cypress trees and alligators.
Christmas I'll miss too,
the lights on the tree,
and the Chanukah candles burning on the table.
I'll miss it all. I won't get to read
in the paper who won the ball game,
how the Dodgers are doing, who won the big fight, will
the quarterback throw that last pass to win the game
before he quits forever. Not much sports in Heaven.
Angels—7
New Arrivals—1
Not very competitive.
No one'll write poetry up there, either. What's to write about?
Bliss. Peace. Oneness.
Not exactly themes you can sink your teeth into.
I could always teach the angels how to write.
"Write like you talk."
"We don't need to talk."
"Okay, follow the transformation line."
"We've already transformed. There's nothing to follow."
"Right, Okay. Just give me image moment."

"That's all there is," they'll say. "The world comes, stays a
moment, then goes away. Image. Moment."
"All right. How about things? No ideas but in things. William
Carlos Williams, a very famous poet, said that."
"Oh, him. He changed his mind. He says it's the other way
around. He's sleeping over there, in that car. Besides, there are
no things here. Just ideas."
I look over at the car. It looks familiar—a gray '47 Dodge.
Sure enough, there's Williams, in the back seat, sitting up,
sleeping.
"Okay," I say, "just tell a story. A simple story."
"I thought this was a poetry class. Now you want stories."
"Look, a poem, a story, it's all the same thing. Writing's
writing."
Now the angels exchange glances. They want a refund.
"Christ!" I say.
"Oh, he's in the car with Williams, in the front seat."
Sure enough, there he is, hands resting on the steering wheel.
Beautiful, long fingers.
"Hey, that's my father's car!"
"Of course," they say, "It's *your* heaven."

Yes, I'll look down and miss it all.
All the things. All the talk.
All the transformations.
I'll miss sitting in the kitchen, watching the cars go by
on Orlando. Josh, coloring a picture on the floor, industriously
snapping the caps back on the markers; Lori, in her robe
reading a book, slurping her coffee; and me, writing this down,
finishing this poem,
returning to the world I so dearly love.

JOHN 16:24

It's a funny thing about the universe.
You can't hog tie it,
you can't whip it into shape,
you can't bully it,
you can't demand, cajole, negotiate, or plead.
But you can ask:
for poems,
for love,
for meaning,
even,
perhaps,
for salvation.
Whether it be from
the cosmos
or from the god who created it,
or from those who are a part of it,
answers always come.

Just ask.

I asked for you,
didn't I?

And here you are.

JACK GRAPES

REQUIEM

I guess when you get old
you tally the deaths, the ones
who went before you:
Martin Shapiro when I was twelve,
Leon Zilberman's father when I was sixteen,
Elton Cigali when I was eighteen—
the rich kid with the sports car
who died in a head-on collision.
It was the big drama in high school that year,
the golden boy, star quarterback,
fleet-footed track star,
doomed like Achilles.
Then Dad, when I was nineteen,
then Mom,
a few years later.
Then Jerry Pinero, from 5th grade,
whose father owned a fruit stand
on Carrolton Avenue.
I wrote about him in another poem.
There were others, some I remember,
some I forget.
Clifford Janoff about ten years ago,
of a heart attack.
I have a picture of the four of us,
Cliff, Allan, Paul and me,
high in the Sierras, in a bank of snow,
naked.
We thought it would be funny.
With our scraggly beards,

we looked like mountain men
impervious to the cold.
It took us ten seconds to take the picture,
but we froze our butts off.
"Twenty years from now," we said,
"this'll be funny."
Twenty years later, Clifford found the photo
and sent me a copy as a reminder.
I laughed. It was funny.
And of course the L.A. poets,
those I knew and read with
when we were all young and ambitious:
Leland Hickman, Linda Backlund,
John Thomas, Philomene Long,
Bob Flanagan, to name a few.
And yesterday, just yesterday,
I got an email from Paul
that Evelyn Klein had died
after a long bout with cancer.
Evelyn was a tall, beautiful brunette
with dark, deep set eyes,
whose father had been a Commie back in the '30s,
and I spent hours talking to him,
a frail old man
holed up in his house in Lakeview,
hounded by the FBI agents
parked on the street.
Evelyn would never have given me
the time of day, except that she was smart
and had no time for football players
or the blond Adonis with the tennis racket.
She liked her men smart.
I can't explain it, but there are people

who fit into categories.
Evelyn fit into none of them.
And in my mind,
though I haven't seen her in fifty years,
she's still twenty, dazzling, smart,
talking to smart men,
talking to me.
Now she's gone, too.

Mostly though, I've been celebrating
those still alive,
not just friends,
but plants, animals, things.
It's a checklist I keep in my head,
going through it several times a day:
the road's still here: check;
the washing machine, still here;
the dog next door, still here;
Peter behind bulletproof glass
at J-Market, still here.
This pair of scissors: check.
My old calculator: check.
This pen: check.
There's so much that is still alive,
it seems wrong not to notice it,
celebrate it.
That's the problem.
Who has time to celebrate the living?
And if you're really alive and living,
who has time for the dead?
So I've made some time,
here in this poem,
and then, when I'm done,

I'll go back to the daily routine,
filling up my car with gas,
getting food at Ralph's,
going to the bank and the post office.
Making my list.
The little Japanese fountain in my front yard: check.
The metal gate with the broken handle: check.
The cigar that I smoked halfway,
still in the ashtray in the back yard: check.
I sit down on the bench by the firepit.
That damned Chinese elm
that fills the yard with debris,
tiny leaves and orange dust,
I thought I hated it,
yet I check it off: still here.
And the belly I never could get rid of,
my corns,
my aching hips
and that muscle in my calf
that refuses to heal: check,
check, check,
check.

SAGITTARIUS

When I park my car after class,
I sometimes glance at the stars
in the night sky—maybe there's a full moon,
or maybe I'll catch Jupiter next to Venus.
I've seen the sky a thousand times,
not looking for a UFO
or a shooting star, though I've seen
a few of those too.
I know enough about the cosmos
to know how far from me they are—
those white holes in the fabric of space.
I don't truck much with all that astrology
stuff; some days, I read someone
else's horoscope just to see how it
applies to me.
When I'm munching on a sandwich
I'll read just about anything,
including some nonsense about the alignment
of the stars and its impact on my daily life.
And no, standing by the gate in front of my house,
looking up at the sky, I'm not contemplating
the great mysteries of the universe, either.
Let's face it, those points of light
are just great balls of fire.
But still, I get out of my car,
walk to the front gate,
look up, and take a moment to feel
immensely small.
I'm this speck, and not a person out there

is able to see me, except Mr. You-Know-Who,
Mr. Astrology, Mr. Quantum Physics,
Mr. Electro-Magnetic Gravitation.
To tell you the truth, I do this little bit
of star-gazing for one reason—
to prepare myself for home.
Small though I may be,
I still have a place in the universe.
Then I walk through the door,
yell out, "I'm home," and empty my pockets
before going into the bedroom
to give my wife a kiss.
"Whatcha watching?" I usually ask.
"Nothing," she says, "just some dumb show."
"I'm gonna have a bite," I say.
I cut an apple, get a few crackers,
sit down in the kitchen to read the paper.
She joins me, makes small talk,
takes one of my crackers when I'm not looking.
"I saw that," I say.
"Saw what?" she says.
"You know what," I say.
Then, when I'm not looking,
she slips it into her mouth and starts chewing.
I move the plate of crackers out of her reach.
After a few crackers, I read from her horoscope:
"You have a mighty purpose today,
to make people laugh."
She swipes the paper from me
and reads mine:
"In some way, you are far from home,
but you'll make your way back
through the course of the day."

JACK GRAPES

I swipe the paper back.
"Lemme see that."
I scan the constellations—
Aries, Gemini, Aquarius—
and land on Sagittarius.
"You read the wrong horoscope," I say,
"that was Sagittarius."
"All the same," she says,
"that one was yours."
Then I cut the last wedge of apple,
place it on the last cracker,
and enjoy the last chew
before bedtime.

THE MAN IN CHARGE OF WATERING

The summer sun, strong and bright,
sits down on the bricks in the front yard.
Cars which have nothing to do with bricks
go by on the street heading home.
It's Wednesday afternoon,
middle of the week,
when you can put everything you'd planned
on Monday
back on the back burner.
A lady goes by; I nod and smile and say hello.
She's carrying a bag of groceries.
I think she lives down the block.
I should go back inside,
the sun's hot on my face,
and I'm not wearing my hat.
Lori admonishes me,
"Don't forget to wear your hat."
I came outside to fill the fountain
and forgot to wear my hat.
Now, I'm just standing here,
looking around, saying hello
to the neighbors as they pass by.
When we first bought this house
when Josh was two years old,
I used to go outside after the sun had gone down
and hose the grass on the front and side lawn.
Such a peaceful time, and the back spray from the hose
cooled everything down.
I was Mr. Homeowner watering his lawn.

There are flowers blooming here
that Lori knows the names of, but I can't
seem to remember their names—
jasmine, bougainvillea, true geraniums—
I can't keep track of them all.
I've tried, but the names elude me.
Even the grass has a name,
but I've forgotten that too.
This is what heaven will be like.
Anytime I want, I'll be able to water the lawn.
All my friends will walk by,
I'll nod, say hello, watch them pass along
going wherever people go in heaven.
I won't have to do anything but water the lawn.
And the water, you should see the water in heaven.
Crystal clear, light as a feather, so to speak,
diamonds of light.
The back spray will cool my face and head.
And the grass. You'd think grass
in heaven wouldn't need watering,
but you're in for quite a surprise.
Everything up here needs watering.
Even the bricks, the bricks that sit in the sun
getting hot.
Even God, who soaks up all our prayers.
Even God will need a spray or two
to cool down.
I'll be the waterer.
The man in charge of watering everything
and everyone,
the man spraying water in heaven.
That'll be my job.
When God comes by, asks how I'm doing,

I'll say, "Fine, just fine."
Then I'll turn and ask,
"Need a little watering?"
And God will nod,
say, "Sure, soak me down, just
don't wet the groceries."
And I'll give God a good spray.
That'll be my job—
the man in charge
of watering God.

JACK GRAPES

EVERLASTING

The dog is the dog is the dog.
Everlasting.
The moon is the moon is the moon.
Everlasting.
Day to day, this is how it goes.
My son and his friend stand in the kitchen,
putting tattoos on their bodies.
Sunlight comes through the window.
The same sunlight that goes through
your window on a slow, everlasting Saturday.
And here we are,
alive here on this slow everlasting Saturday,
bread on the kitchen counter,
my wife humming
as she fools with the toaster oven.
March 18, 2000. A slow Saturday.
The dog is the dog is the dog.
Everlasting.
The moon is the moon is the moon.
sweet sweet   sweet sweet   life.

Poems So Far So Far So Good
So Far To Go

It is because I used to think of certain things, of certain people, that the things, the people, and these alone, I still take seriously, still give me joy. Whether it be that the faith which creates has ceased to exist in me, or that reality will take shape in the memory alone, there has awakened in me that anguish which, later on in life, transfers itself to the passion of love, and may even become its inseperable companion.

–Marcel Proust,
Swann's Way
translated by C. K. Scott Moncrieff

POEMS
SO FAR

SO FAR
SO GOOD

SO FAR
TO GO

JACK GRAPES

The reader, the thinker, the loiterer, the flâneur, are types of illuminati just as much as the opium eater, the dreamer, the ecstatic. And more profane. Not to mention that most terrible drug — ourselves — which we take in solitude.

–Walter Benjamin,
"Art in the Age
of Mechanical Reproductions"
translated by Rodney Livingstone

LOST LAKE

What happens when you try
believing in God is things begin
to fall apart.
Like when we were lost
trying to find Lost Lake
high in the high
Sierras, leaning against
a large boulder unable
to go on, munching
gorp from our army pack
and ready to fall
in the snow and call it
quits. I remember that
to this day. Calling it
quits, I mean. My old
football coach Mr. Palone
would have killed me
if he'd known I was ready
to call it quits,
and the irony, Lost Lake
was only 30 yards away,
over the next rise,
gleaming and teeming
with fish.
That's what happens when
you climb miles
with a fifty pound backback
in the high Sierras,
and the beauty of nature

makes you believe in God
and then things begin to fall apart.
I suppose it's somewhat like love.
You believe in love and then
things begin to fall apart.
Better not to believe in it,
but what happens when it comes
to you, brown-eyed and wishing
only the best for you?
Can love be returned even
when you don't believe in it?
A part of me is still leaning
against that boulder,
next to my best friend Allan,
who in his own way,
had given up too,
and I've never known Allan
to ever give up on anything.
But we both had had it.
So we leaned against that stone
and ate our gorp, biding our time,
assuming that what is lost
is never lost forever,
and like love, comes looking for you
when you least expect it,
even when you've stopped
believing in it.

SEATED NUDE

Went to dinner tonight at Muddy Leak, then to see
The Heart of Darkness at the Actor's Gang. I found my-
self staring off into the distance, tuning out the play,
thinking of Modigliani's painting the "Seated Nude,"
painted in 1916 while he worked mostly on portraits, not
a period when he was concentrating on the female form.
Modigliani was also a sculptor, and of the twenty-four
or so surviving sculptures that he made after a decisive
meeting with Brancusi in 1909, only two are nudes. Yet,
it was the female form that preoccupied him, judging by
the drawings he left behind. There is something ancient
and primitive in that painting, with the model shown
head on, her figure filling the canvas, her body diagonal
against the blue background and the slanting rail on the
left, giving it a sense of disequilibrium. The model's body
is thrust forward, uninhibited by her nakedness, while the
inclination of her head, her blushing face and closed eyes
reveal a vulnerability or reserve, perhaps even a knowing
languor. Find one of Titian's nudes, and you will be re-
minded of this painting, those brush strokes comparable
to the chisel-marks in some of Modigliani's sculptures.
I think I first encountered those long-necked women of
Modigliani's when I was in college, and they have haunted
me ever since, so to see "Seated Nude" today at LACMA
was a special treat. I'm not even sure why the image has
haunted me today. Even amidst the rantings of Mr. Kurtz
in *the Heart of Darkness,* my mind drifted to the langour
of that nude. During chit-chatty dinner conversation over
smoked salmon and poached eggs, I'd tilt my head down

or gaze off into the distance, drifting off into a kind of sadness, as if the painting itself were attached to some great wound within me. Such loveliness persists despite the encroachments of the moment. I wanted to be back in the museum, standing before the painting, gathering in those brushstrokes and flat planes of light, the model's wispy pubic hairs and painterly skin. Like the siren song, Modigliani called to me, and I followed that voice to the rocks where oblivion stronger than any drug, except the drug of love resides. Then bill came and I left a hefty tip, all the while thinking of Modigliani's "Seated Nude," longing and sadness entwined within. I looked at my watch, checked back into the world, the world that Wordsworth says is too much with us, we who get and spend and lay waste our powers. I was still longing for that other world, that motionless and timeless world of art, the Great Art that sustains me as I travel this last, downward sloping phase of my life.

A SMALL CABIN IN THE WOODS

You're old enough to get in your car and drive out to some forest on the edge of town. What you take with you tells us a lot about you. Perhaps a tablet to write on, perhaps a roll of scotch tape, perhaps a bag of cough drops. In the middle of the forest is a small pond, the water so cold you couldn't breathe that time you fell into it. And later, the forest ranger came by and asked what you did to the rattlesnake you killed with a large rock there were so many holes in his skin. If you look around, you can find the things you need to build a small cabin. Small, but large enough for your roll of scotch tape and the cough drops. The tablet you might have to leave outside. And you probably forgot to bring a pencil or a pen, so the tablet is useless anyway. You can sleep standing up. What nestles in your heart is love. It's odorless and colorless. But at night, when you're sleeping, you can hear it walking around, from chamber to chamber, trying to say something. If you knew what it was saying, you might be able to follow its instructions. Head for the hills, it might be saying, or maybe just something simple, like, you big dope, why didn't you bring a pencil or a pen. Love can be a bitter pill. When it's dark, it likes to crack jokes. Or quote lines from Greek poetry. You're old enough to know better, to tell the heart to go to sleep, to tell the heart to shut up. But all night long it mumbles, trying to wake you from a sleep you've slept all your life. One time, in the supermarket, the heart called out to you as you were selecting a cabbage for soup. Wake up, it said. I am fucking awake, you replied. No you're not, said love, walking around inside your heart, from chamber to chamber. I'm too old to wake up, you said, as you put the cabbage back. No you're not, the voice of love inside your heart said. Now, you're sleeping, standing in the cabin you built in the middle of some forest on the edge of town. A small cabin. Small, but large enough to stand in. A voice telling you to wake up. You're not too old to wake up.

THE MOON & SIXPENCE

Since the email I got a few days ago about the moon,
I got to thinking about Shakespeare,
as I often do,
usually when I'm getting gas for my car,
or brushing my teeth
(another way of saying I'm always thinking of Shakespeare),
and thought of all the appearances of the moon
the Bard offered in the way of his two cents.

Last night, I had one of those nice evenings at home,
reading, working on my book, shuffling around in my study.
I went out to find the moon but she hadn't risen yet,
but later, when I went out back to check on the Laker's collapse,
there she was, up in a tree, sliding back and forth
whichever way I went, as if trying to hide,
or make me come after her.

Then I remembered Othello:

"It is the very error of the moon;
She comes more nearer earth than she was wont,
And makes men mad."

But even Fair Juliet knew there was something about the moon
to be suspicious of.
When Romeo tells her that he will
swear by "yonder blessed moon that tips with silver all these
fruit-tree tops,"
she puts her hand to his mouth and shuts it:

"O, swear not by the moon, the inconstant moon,
That monthly changes in her circled orb,
Lest that thy love prove likewise variable."

And poor klutzy teenage Romeo frowns and scratches his head.
"What shall I swear by?" he asks,
like a bad algebra student
unable to figure the value of x.
        "Do not swear at all," says Juliet,
"Or, if thou wilt, swear by thy gracious self,
Which is the god of my idolatry,
And I'll believe thee."

One needn't be Shakespeare to know the moon's conjugations.
As Titania says in *Midsummer Night's Dream*,
"Therefore, the moon, that governess of floods,
Pale in her anger, washes all the air."

Shakespeare calls it an envious moon,
a fleeting moon,
a perilous moon,
a moon that looks bloody
on the earth.

I marveled last night as I stood looking up at it
through the backyard trees.
I decided not to be infected
by Newton's mind and the laws of gravity,
but to see the moon
as Shakespeare saw it,
and let it have power over me,
and I knew why it was that we are made
mad to write poetry:

perilous poetry,
envious poetry,
bloody poetry.

Then, we wake, and return to the pedestrian earth,
the earth of bank deposits,
post-offices trips,
supermarket catch-ups,
copy machines and office supplies,
and all the other mundane tasks we perform under the
sun.
The sun that exposes things as they are,
not what they can be

under the bloody moon.

BOB'S POETRY

Bob writes poetry
as if poetry
were going out of style.
Everything is fading: the darkness,
the morning mist, the light
in the piazza, the life his sister
guarded with her teeth.
Some things wane; regrets
exist only late in the night
when others are sleeping;
the self is either unknown
or unguarded; sonatas are sweet;
chances squandered, lives lived
fully.
In the corner by lamplight
Dad or Mom grows older,
sharpening futile promises,
leaving a trail of sparks.
Like the Dude, Death
abides.
Waits its turn.
Doesn't stand on ceremony.
Doesn't hold its breath.
Doesn't make deals.

I like Bob's poetry.
It doesn't pull any punches.
Poetry may, in fact, be going out of style.
If not for Bob, we could all be reading

journalism, or worse, roadmaps.
If not for Bob, who writes poetry
as if poetry
were going out of style,
we'd all forget to sing
in the car
on the way
to the airport
bound for a country
no one
in his right mind
would visit.

LAKE PONTCHARTRAIN SEAWALL

Not too many stones here
on the cement wall by the lake,
nor on the cement steps
that descend into the black water,
six deep at high tide, two deep at low.
We used to put a stone on the steps
for every girl we necked with
in the back seat of our '56 Chevies
parked a few feet from the shoreline wall.
One summer, there must have been
a hundred stones along the concrete top.
The hurricanes would come in late August,
early September.
By fall, there was not one stone left;
all had been carried off into the lake.
Just seawall and concrete,
far as the eye could see, from Lakeview
to the Pontchartrain Causeway.
Sometimes, in January or February,
a stone would appear here, another over there.
But they didn't last long.
High winter waves from Gulf storms
would wash them back into the lake.
One summer, Peter Bordelon decided
that if you broke up with a girl,
you'd walk down to the seawall,
pick up a stone, and skip it onto the waters
of the lake, the dark placid waters
that greedily swallowed

that offering to the god of teenage love,
so you'd always remember
that it was you who reached down
and threw the stone away,
not the fickle red-head
buttoning her blouse in the front seat
of your car, anxious to get home
to her bucket of stones.

LIFE IS A MOTORBIKE

But love is a translucent motorbike.
As the poets say,
we see through a glass darkly.
Light is able to pass through,
but so diffused
that objects
are not clearly visible.
This is how it is with love.
We know it is there,
but we do not always see it clearly.
So some of us make things,
some of us paint pictures,
some of us put words
out into
the universe
and try to connect the dots
so love appears clearer, is
shaped into an object we can imagine,
if not truly see.
If your life doesn't begin with love,
perhaps it will end with love.
And if love
doesn't reduce you to tears,
if it doesn't make crazy with sporadic logic,
something is amiss,
either with you,
or with love.

What we can do
is build a fire inside a circle of stones
and do our dance together.
Around that fire.
This summer began with a supermoon,
and will end with our words,
words that,
like love,
will reduce us to tears,
and make our minds
crazy with sporadic logic.
Because I always begin with love.
And if I am lucky,
I will end with love as well.

UNEXPECTEDLY

I'm always finding things that I don't remember losing.
A set of keys, a book, a phone number, even this poem,
which I unexpectedly found tucked inside a book I'd also lost,
along with a phone number.
I couldn't remember whose number it was,
and was hesitant to call it,
for fear it might be someone I don't want
to talk to. For days I thought about that series of numbers
which reconfigured in my head as I drove
around the city, running errands, meeting a client,
buying paper and paper clips. At some point,
the numbers reassembled and I couldn't remember
the exact order anymore.
Was it 504-822-3006, or 822-306-0504,
or maybe 405-282-6003?
I lost interest in who belonged to the numbers,
it was the numbers themselves that attached
to my brain. Sometimes, when talking,
the numbers would just spill out of my mouth,
unexpectedly, like "I'm looking for 60 pound $8^{1/2}$ by 11
recycled paper 405-603-0282, 90 brightness."
Or when making love, I might say
"Oooh, I love you so 360-054-8022."
I remember standing in an open field and watching
dawn come up, also unexpectedly,
because I had been mired so deeply in the night,
broken heart and lost resolve,
that I had lost faith in even the dependable sun
from ever reclaiming the sky.

I wanted night to last so long, I'd never see
the sun again, never see a blue sky,
never be reminded of how sweet life was,
how fillled it was with the tiniest moments
of pleasure.
How I ended up in the middle of that field
I'm not sure. One minute I was staring out the window
of my apartment, across the alley, at a brick wall,
and the next I'm in the middle of an open field.
I had just separated from my wife,
and there was a bottle of elevil my therapist
had given me to relieve my depression,
and the thought occured to me that I could
just take the whole bottle and be done with it,
but then I'd have to go through my journals --
there were 63 of them at the time,
in fire-proof boxes at the bottom of the closet --
and cut out the parts I didn't want people to read.
I held the bottle of pills
in my hand and walked to the window,
looked out at the brick wall,
a brick wall that seemed to be the perfect
metaphor at that time for my life,
and next thing I knew I was standing in that field,
watching dawn   rosy-fingered dawn
come up, unexpectedly.
For a moment, I thought I was in,
"Walking the Wilderness" by William Stafford,
or maybe that poem by Mark Strand,
"Absence of Field."
How nice, I thought, to end up in a poem.

PERFECT

Before when it was imperfect
it was perfect like how I love you
and how you love me and how
imperfectly we kiss or hold each
other in some echo of
retention near dark where bodies
surrender their belongings
on the road
we traveled imperfectly
toward each other
closer year by year,
day by day,
minute by perfect minute
then we're here together
moving from the perfection
of gathering to the imperfection
of rocks green glass
stones on a bookshelf
marking the moons
in sync walking barefoot
in Paris stopping
to breathe the breath
of longing,
a field covered with snow
we called home.

GRAVITY

Everything is simple until it's hard
and then it seems it was never simple.

An orange falls to the ground
and the man looks at his watch
and imagines it's Tuesday.

One night I was older, and the next
day I was older still, but today,
as I write this, I am suddenly
young again, falling in love

with everything, including this
tomato that looks like a heart,
which makes it difficult for me
to cut it with a knife
but I do, slice right through it
you just slice right through it
and all the juice comes out and
I put it in my mouth
and it's good.

Tonight I saw the moon slide
behind a cloud, and oh, you should
have seen it, bright full moon
and I wondered, who is masquerading
as the moon, or is the moon
masquerading as someone else?
She moves behind another cloud,

hiding from me, and I sigh
and accept my loss.

My father died when he was fifty-four
and I'm seventy-one, well, I will be
seventy-one come September 11,
and my father had he lived to be seventy-one
would have died when I was thirty-seven.
My son still had yet to be born.
Not for another twelve years.
We named him after my father.
Now Josh is twenty-two, living on his own,
not far away from this house,
the house he grew up in.

Whether it's an apple or an orange,
all things eventually fall back to earth.
The moon will have its day too
to fall into the earth.
And if I'm still here,
I will open my arms to receive her,
even though both of us will be destroyed
in the end.
This moon belongs to me,
and I belong to the moon.
We are one conversation
circling each other in the mystery
of creation, reflecting the light
of the larger sun, that light
that draws us both toward
the center, toward
all that
fire.

A SOLITARY ROAD

A solitary road.
Someone singing a song.
Enormous in the sunshine.
The breath of darkness.
How much love have we known,
asks the Buddha sitting
by the side of the road.
Is that a rhetorical question,
I ask, or a question meant
for me to answer?
Buddha shrugs.
Who knows, he says, it's just a question.
First you'd have to define the word *love*,
he says,
then the word *known*,
then, the hard part, you'd have to quantify
what is meant by the phrase *how much*.
The question's too complicated, he says,
and not worth answering.
But, he adds, it's a good question, dontcha think?
And I think, this Buddha's not much fun,
so I walk on. It's a solitary road.
A different song now being sung,
but the same road, enormous
in the sunshine, the breath of darkness
leaning against the low hills in the distance.
I remember how I once
boiled an egg and ate it.
There was the time I held someone's hand

JACK GRAPES

across a table, the feel of the tablecloth
under my outstretched arm.
One night, when I was five,
I saw my father, chin resting on his fist,
somewhat like Rodin's "Thinker,"
and I tried to imagine what he was thinking,
my father, as lightning flashed and thunder
shook the house.
All solitary roads, enormous in the sunshine,
the breath of darkness raining
across the low hills in the distance.
An empty house by the side of the road.
I go in, call out a name, but she doesn't answer.
That's gone too. It was a name I whispered once,
when I was happy.
Now, not even an echo.
In the kitchen, a tuna sandwich, half-eaten,
sitting on a paper plate.
The only evidence she was here:
A half-eaten tuna sandwich
on a paper plate.
This makes me laugh for a time,
reminds me to laugh till my sides hurt,
to laugh along with others laughing,
so hard, everyone falls to the floor
exhausted. You're killing me,
they'd say, killing me.
A solitary road. A song.
The breath of darkness.
Low hills in the distance.
The Buddha asking questions
not meant
to be answered.

WHAT TO KEEP, WHAT TO GIVE AWAY

What I will take with me are the words.
You can have the rest,
the cars, the curtains, the silver spoons,
the chairs we sat in, the doors we
slammed, the windows we dressed,
the running shoes, the bow ties,
the suits, the hats, the glasses
we drank from, the cups
we smashed at the Greek restaurant
on Robertson.
I lingered a long time over passion,
then gave it up with the rest.
What is passion, after all,
but a longing for God.

"What'll you have?" asks the bartender.
"Passion," I say.
"I thought you gave that up with all the rest,"
he says.
"Yeah, I know, but it was a mistake,"
I say, "I've decided to take passion back."
"Then you're still longing for God,"
he says.

I should go to Barcelona.
Maybe Paris.
Rome would be nice.
St. Petersburg I hear is worth a trip.
You can get good dope in Copenhagen.

JACK GRAPES

But what about Verona, or Miami?
Who in his right mind would want
to go to Miami?
Verona I can understand.
But Miami?

Listen, let me let you in on a little secret.
When I get there, my love will be waiting for me.
She'll have one of those flotation devices,
and tell me the water's fine,
I should just dive in.
She'll show me around the condominiun.
A desk where I can write, a shelf
for my favorite books,
and lots of sugarless chocolate bars
on the table I can eat to my heart's content.
And she's wearing a bathing suit to boot.
When was the last time I saw her
in a bathing suit? Can't remember.
But she's got great thighs.
She's wearing that bathing suit
and I can admire her thighs.
There she is, rising like Aphrodite
from the sea.
She was looking for me from the start,
found me running in circles,
came and got me, taught me
how to run in a straight line,
toward God.

Back to earth.
Millions of us.
In the oppressive heat.

A drink in the morning.
Connection to spherical power
and the ability to move
heavy objects.
Persistence with charm.
A star in the Southern sky.
You don't know where you're going.
A hawk circles overhead.
The calligraphy of bad manners.
A wicker basket filled
with all your mistakes.
A white bird in a golden cage.
Dreams that taste like strawberry popsicles.

Last night I heard her voice,
talking on the phone in the kitchen.
Her voice, along with the words,
and passion, that's what I'll take with me.

You can keep all the rest.

JACK GRAPES

TWO-PART HARMONY

Accept that you carry death with you
in your pocket like a stone
you rub with thumb and forefinger
when life renders you invisible.
You can breath life back into those
who walk as if love
has been lost, as if they have choked
on their despair.
Today, I thought of all the ways I had buried
love and other figments of my imagination.
Need creeps upon you like a thief in the night.
Sometimes I think of you but I can't remember
exactly who you are. I must have loved you once
a long time ago, but all I remember
is a summer dress and the way it flapped
around you when you walked.
Two-part harmony is not hard
when you put your mind to it and try not to listen
to what the other person is singing.
She was a slow and dreamy dancer,
danced with me most of the night,
but went home with the other guy,
the one with the convertible
and the blue suede shoes.
You'd think if I lived this much
in my mind that I'd put up curtains,
but then you wouldn't be able to see in,
especially at night when the lights are on
and I'm lit up like a Christmas tree.

She tries to find the right word,
those of us who cherish solitude,
a hem and a haw and a stuttering vowel.
In Claude Lorraine's landscape
she'd be sitting under a tree,
the Great God Pan playing the flute
while revelers dance around her
drinking goblets of wine.
I'm not sure whether we're supposed
to find ourselves in love,
or lose ourselves in love.
Art is supposed to come to the rescue,
but some days, it doesn't,
some days you're left with empty hands,
some days you wish you didn't need art
to come to the rescue,
some days you wish you didn't need
to be rescued.
Thing is, when you're in need of rescue,
someone usually comes and finds you,
or maybe I'm just lucky that way.
What keeps me here is love, plain and simple.
I can't for the life of me figure it out.
It's the world, buckeroos, that breaks the heart,
not the loved one. The world
will always break your heart,
that's the deal.
If you can find that place
where you are broken,
and give thanks that you allowed it,
you jumped in, both feet,
you took the deal
and now you're aching with it,

the loss and the yearning
and the gratitude and the dread.
If you can do that,
you will find everything you need
to carry on one more day,
one more day
on this earth
while death waits
in your pocket
like a stone.

GRACE

I've been walking in dust all day.
The dull ache of memory clogs the mind,
as does the memory of the dull ache.
Trees I once climbed like a panther.
That's a lie   I was never that nimble.
It's hard to know for sure
whether you're in a cage, or flying free.
Right now, I'd like to be eating
at the oyster bar in Grand Central,
or at *Chez Maitre Albert* in Paris.
The wheel keeps turning, the *big*
  to quote Tina Turner   *wheel,*
you know the one I mean.
Mornings in bed I think I'd like
to take you all with me, so nothing
would change except the place.
All those I've loved, all those I left,
all those who left me, all those
who abide.
No man dies, really. It's the world that stops.
Here I am in front of the bathroom mirror
trying to conjugate the future tense
of my favorite French verb: *étonner.*
Je vous étonnerai. I will amaze you.
Cela m'étonne! That astonishes me!
J'ai étonné. I was stunned.
J'étonnais toujours quand je regard sa visage.
I am always surprised when I look at her face.

JACK GRAPES

That's the end of the poem.
I was going to write more,
I thought of what I wanted to say,
or what I was trying to say,
but in the end, I realized
there was nowhere to go after that last line.
When seeing someone's face surprises you,
what else can you say? It's the French, I think.
French has a way of putting a lid on things.
There's something final about it.
Once you say it in French, there's no more to be said.
Mordre les lèvres, to bite the dust.
Ne manquez pas de venir. Don't fail to come.
Elle étais maigre comme un clou. She was thin as a nail.
C'est un livre à lire. It's a book worth reading.
Je bats le pavé. I walk up and down the streets.
Je me suis perdu. I lost myself.
Je perdais la raison. I took leave of my senses.
J'ai perdu mon chemin. I lost my way.
Cette poem est fini. This poem is over. Finished. Done for.

WHAT YOU HAVE TO SURRENDER TO

The page is cold.
I've been bleeding for awhile now.
I came back to see how I was doing,
but couldn't face it, and left.
You know, if I find a bottlecap on the sidewalk, I bring it home.

I dreamt once that I was a mermaid.
Another time I dreamt that I was tied to a lampost.
Someone was hitting me with a dark red ribbon.
It was raining and foggy, very mysterious, very scary.

All this suffering belongs to God.
I surrender to a single melody,
a single woman, the dark-eyed lady.

The sweetest songs are those that sing
of saddest thought blah blah
blah blah, what you have to surrender to if you are going
to love and lay your body at the feet of the lover.

Poor me! Where do I go for flowers in winter?
The swans that skirt the edge of the lake are drunk on kisses.
They confuse sunshine with shade,
while speechless dark clouds
drive weathervanes crazy.

If I had the guts, I'd sail without end into the unknown.
But I ain't got the guts. I like it up here in the crow's nest.
You can see land miles before you get there, you can see

JACK GRAPES

the horizon in the distance,
always before you,
daring you to fall into it.

All the magenta lips that spring up
beneath the footsteps of the sun—
it's a haze of blossoms
standing in for love,
a thousand words of love.
She was in the audience
and didn't say a word,
afraid I'd gobble her up.
I was on stage, waiting for rescue.

Some days, I do nothing but pay bills and run errands,
tedious details that pull me down
into those small bells of voluptuous insanity,
doing this, taking care of that, constantly moaning
that I haven't written a poem.
My grief, like a birdcage.
Its little door opens, but I dare not fly out.

OBLIVION

Wispy clouds break into white teacups
as I pick up a fresh pencil, one with a point so sharp
it might break with the smallest word, like "of"
or "in" or "at"; I would hardly expect it to survive
a word like Mozambique or disheveled.
When I was in fourth grade, Mrs. Aime yelled at me
during vocabulary tests for the sound effects
I made of explosions and crashes
as I drew pictures of World War I biplanes
alongside the words on the paper
accompanied by smoke and flames,
and the occasional biplane crashing
into the trees below.
I was easily distracted in 4th grade, and today,
I contemplate the landscape outside my window
like a surveyor looking for the best spot to build
a surburban village. I should be paying bills.
But I get distracted by a pencil,
and then distracted by words, and then by a memory
of a moment in the classroom when I had to walk
that tightrope between doing what I was told to do
and doing what my imagination implored.
I haven't the faintest idea how I have managed to survive
this long with no real strategy for living.
I have gone from one distracted impulse to another,
holding onto the only things that have ever mattered to me:
love, fraternity, community.
This is not to say that I have always been kind,
or compassionate. This is not to say

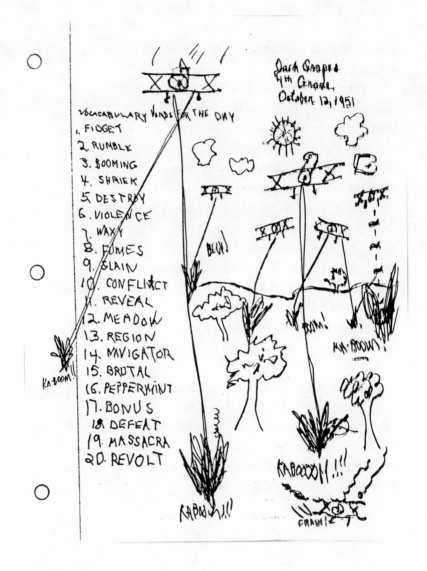

VOCABULARY WORDS FOR THE DAY
1. FIDGET
2. RUMBLE
3. BOOMING
4. SHRIEK
5. DESTROY
6. VIOLENCE
7. WAXY
8. FUMES
9. SLAIN
10. CONFLICT
11. REVEAL
12. MEADOW
13. REGION
14. NAVIGATOR
15. BRUTAL
16. PEPPERMINT
17. BONUS
18. DEFEAT
19. MASSACRA
20. REVOLT

Jack Grapes
4th Grade,
October 12, 1951

KA-BOOM!

BLM!

BOOM!

KA-BOOM!

KABOM!!!

KABOOOOM!!!

CRASH!

that I have never twisted love
for my own purposes,
hurt others, taken advantage of affection.
This is not to say that I have not fled from the tribe
and crawled into the hole of my solitude,
where I answer to no one,
not even myself.
Those clouds out there and the hills in the distance
oblivious to the violence we do to ourselves,
even they can't hold my attention for long.
I never grow tired, though, of my desk,
its familiar mess of paper clips and coins,
the letter opener I've had since college,
the Elmer's Glue I haven't touched since Josh was a kid.
The lamps, they're like swans, aren't they,
with their long flexible necks?
And the stacks of books beneath stacks of paper,
and the bills that require me to work,
to go out into the world I love
but could so easily forget if allowed to daydream
too long — where would I be without them?

In a biplane, probably, above the earth.
The poet as Red Baron dropping words
onto the trees below.
Kaboom! and Kaboom! Laying waste to the vocabulary
of my life, from Mozambique to Timbucktoo,
hair disheveled, smoke and flames,
the sweet implosions by which I live.

JACK GRAPES

FORBIDDEN PLANET

Nothing frightens me more than nothing.
Ness.
Angle of vision.
Some of us hoped for war,
a war that would put an end to the other war,
the war that had put an end to the war before it,
and so on.
Can't you make the band stop playing?
It's the same tune over and over again.
My friend the sentence appeared at the front door,
asking to borrow a cup of sugar.
"Figure out what's broken," I said,
"and fix it. If you can't fix it,
break it some more."
I invited the sentence in
and now he's still here and refuses to leave.
"Nothingness must be given at the heart of Being."
My high school girlfriend said let's dance the night away
but she forgot her dancing shoes,
left them in her mother's coffin,
she's alive today, speaking in tongues.
Later, I found the sentence
under the bed munching an Oreo.

Say something good about God.
If He hears you, he'll be flattered.
If He's digging for worms, he won't.
Writing proves nothing.
Mathematicians, philosophers, social scientists,

what do they know
a good band-aid won't fix.
I made him a bowl of soup
and he ate it with crackers, the sentence.
Look, sentence, I said,
my wife's coming home soon, it's time you go.
Sentence pouted, asked for just one more
bowl of soup, stared to cry.
It's midnight now. I'm alone. The house is quiet.
You can hear a pin drop.

BOOK SOUP

You know, I read pages
and pages of books at night
before bedtime
and by the next morning
I find I have to read
the same pages again
and still I'm not sure
what I have read.
Someone is translating someone
else, someone else
is translating herself
and having a tough go of it.
Those untranslatable sentences
keep me from sleeping,
but what keeps me from dying,
I wonder.
You ever fish around in your pocket
in the check-out line
looking for change
to pay for a candy bar
and out comes gum wrappers
and a packet of substitute sugar
you kept handy
and a penny and two nickels
and a key ring but no keys
attached?
Well,

I do that and come up with a handful
of sentences.

"Art lost its spontaneity in its conflict
with romanticism."

"The typical Mystery God of Greek religion is,
of course, Dionysus."

"A month before monarchical authority
collapsed into bankruptcy, a colossal
hailstorm swept across northern France
and destroyed most of the ripening harvest."

"On a cosmological level, the Big Bang
certainly appears to have a preferred direction."

"In an unplanned economy human beings
unwittingly grant the market control over their lives;
planning the economy is a reassertion
of human sovereignty and an essential step
toward human freedom."

"So on 11 November at 11 a.m., the eleventh hour
of the eleventh day of the eleventh month,
the guns on the Western Front at last fell silent,
leaving both sides to mourn their dead."

The guy at the checkout counter
looks down at the sentences,
then at the candy bar,
and then looks back up at me.
"That's eighty-seven cents," he says.

JACK GRAPES

I reach into my other pocket,
come up with two quarters, a dime,
and this from Rumi, a poem titled "Music":
> "For sixty years I have been forgetful,
> every minute, but not for a second
> has this flowing toward me stopped or slowed."

The boy picks up the sentence by Rumi,
chucks it into the drawer of the cash-register
next to the tens and twenties
and hands me two small sentences in change,
one from a poem by David Igantow:
> "I find the dark
> close in about me
> as I close the book,
> and I hurry to open it again
> to let its light
> shine on my face."

The other, from Descartes' *Meditations*:
> "Since I have been accustomed
> in every other matter
> to distinguish
> between existence and essence,
> I easily believe
> that the existence
> can be separated
> from the essence
> of God,
> and that thus God
> may be conceived
> as not actually

existing."

I stuff both sentences in my pocket—
the one that held the two quarters,
one dime, and the poem by Rumi—
and walk to my car in the parking lot.

Once back in the car,
I chew on the delicious chocolate candy bar
chuck full of caramel
and peanuts
and head over to Book Soup
to buy another book,
a book full of sentences,
a book full of pages
ready to shine their light
on my face
in the middle of the night.

FIREWOOD

I am old, and have lost something
while retaining my capacity for love.
So many of you out there
I knew forgot remember miss.
Surprise me, won't you?
Open your arms and say welcome.
I will walk into them, still crying.
I will walk into them, unable to breathe,
forgetting the past.
Everytime I thought I knew what love was,
I discovered that love wasn't that at all,
I just thought it was.

It is June, and July will be here,
then August and September, the month of my birth,
and I will fall out of your arms
into the world, again,
back into the rusted earth.
If I am under the ground,
inside this cold earth,
remember I brought love to this planet.
Not much, not enough to make the scale
tilt one way or the other,
but it was enough to put a dent
in your heart,
enough to make trees break
into pieces for firewood,
so when you warm the room in winter,
you can think

the fire came from me,
as it did
when I was alive.

CLOSING THE BOOK

I'm finally able to live in the much sought-after now.
No hard feelings, I hope.
I did my best, limited as my best was
most of the time.
I wanted to leave
you enough firewood
to last through at least one winter.
I know you love fires,
but are afraid of the spiders,
especially the black ones
that nest among the firewood
behind our house,
so I put a stack of wood
in a waterproof box
with an airtight lid,
a kind of coffin made of tupperware.
Remember that day I went to the Container Store?
I was thinking of you squatting at the fireplace,
laying firewood with the architectural precision
of a true fire builder, allowing enough air in
for the fire to breathe.
I want it to last as long as possible
in that drafty room
so you can read
one of those long novels you favor
that create a world you want to live in,
but when you have to close the book
to get ready for your day,
the book is still with you,

you haven't put it down, so to speak.
It lives in you, no effort required,
no need to strain after the feeling—
that's what you said once, anyway:
how moments of comfort
lead to the dread of their loss.
You told me that more than once,
and I, too, believe it's true.
In moments of great happiness,
I hold in reserve some particle of joy,
something I can bank,
when the time comes,
against the embers
of a dying fire.
But I also know
that it's okay to close the book,
it's okay to tear the pages out,
one by one
and cast them onto the embers,
making a blaze out of literature
that will last
throughout the winter.

JACK GRAPES

All the Sad Angels

Cui dono nooum libellum
arida modo pumice expolitum?
. . . . quidquid hoc libelli . . . .

Who shall I dedicate this sly chapbook to,
* chapbook I've polished with my witty pumice,*
. . . . my little chapbook, my meager offering . . . .

– Catullus (84-54 B.C.)

ALL THE SAD ANGELS

Jack Grapes

In a world of love,
we exist as the hidden treasure.
−Rumi

FOR ALL THIS LIVING

They say I'm going
to die, but I can't seem
to wrap my head
around that idea.
I was unable to sleep
and you led me
into the other room.
For all I know,
that was how I died,
you taking my hand
and saying come
with me, and me,
you know, I'll,
as they say,
follow you any
where but where
are we going now?
Maybe I died
a long time ago,
and this is the dream
that I had the other
night when you
were the house.
For all this living,
do I at least get to drink
a glass of wine?

For all this living,
can't someone

give me a wake-up
call when it's time
to go to sleep?
For all this living,
shouldn't I eat
as much love
as I can stomach?

JACK GRAPES

A POEM ABOUT TIME

This was supposed to be
a poem about time,
but I checked the inventory
and there's already a glut
of poems about time.
So I decided to make it
a poem about school,
sitting in the back row
looking out the window
at the other kids at recess
while the teacher droned on
about World War One
or the Thirty Years War
or General Israel Putnam
yelling to his men
at the Battle of Bunker Hill
not to fire until they saw
the white's of their eyes
and then to fire low.
Shoot 'em in the balls, he yelled.
When I heard about the Fall
of the Roman Empire
I couldn't wait
for the special effects,
but as it turned out,
it took the Empire
a thousand years to fall,
and it took the Holy Roman Empire
another thousand years to bite the dust,

and by that time,
it was neither holy,
Roman, nor an empire.
School, as it turned out,
was my first job,
though it was my day job.
My night job was to do my homework,
take out the garbage,
and eat all my vegetables.
I've hardly gotten into this poem
and already I'm feeling the need
to sneak in an image or two,
something metaphorical,
 just so you'll know
I got the chops
when it comes to poetry.
The moon swims for it's life
 on the life raft of the night sky.
I managed to work in
some enjambment there
to boot. The plodding footprints
of your body.
The vaporized modules
of your breath
in the night air,
a little dog
curled on his bed
on your front porch,
pretending to be me,
as if I wasn't already
pretending to be me.
If help comes from outside,
life is restored

to the despairer,
beginning where he left off,
saying to anyone who will listen,
"I'll never be myself again."
But in the process he acquires
a modicum of understanding:
he learns to imitate
other people,
how they conduct their lives,
going so far as to live as they do,
driving the same cars they do,
eating with one hand
politely in his lap, as they do,
keeping from the world
any vestige of despair,
as they do.
In church he's a Catholic;
in temple, he's a Jew;
in a bar, he's an alcoholic;
in the gym, a swaggering jock;
in art class, an artist;
in the laudromat, a homeless man
looking for quarters
on the linoleum floor.
The self he was is gone, the self
that walks into eternity
he neither was nor became.
Put simply, like a fish,
when we make an existential statement
we are asserting that a certain propositional
function results in a true proposition
upon the replacement of the variable
by a suitable constant.

Thus, "dog exists"
is equivalent
to the propositional function
"x is a dog" is true
for some value of x"
(e.g., my neighbor's dog).
How the historian sees time is not the same
as the quantitative time of physics:
that kind of time is not uniform,
but articulated
into qualitatively distinct periods,
such as the Middle Ages
or the Enlightenment,
such as the Renaissance
or the Elizabethan Age,
such as the Victorian era,
whose significance depends
on more than its temporal duration,
but on the ability
of each and every Victorian dog
to pretend to be me.
The crest of the new-fallen snow,
for instance.
The old man across the street
appearing in the window.
Someone in the next room dying
while I shake my little brother's crib crying
why is there so much blood on his diaper?
If we could awaken in the morning, face to face,
I would kiss you before opening my eyes,
I would run my hand across your face
and ask you to stay like this
for another ten years,

years we could stretch out before us,
a history of love and loss,
each blip on the screen
registering an event
marked by sad longing
or heartfelt expectation.
If we could awaken in the morning,
face to face,
for another ten years,
I'd forget all about school,
let the others learn their ABC's,
their time's tables,
the dates of the American Revolution,
the signing of the Declaration of Independence,
the War Between the States.

SHINE

Another dark night.

In the dark
someone's face shines.

I know what it means
to shine.

I know what it means
to not shine.

Either way
wait

for morning
wait for

another dark
morning.

JACK GRAPES

HE WHO NEVERMIND TOLSTOY

she who nevermind Tolstoy
a beatless octave to catch
obscure razmataz snowflakes
gulped down for only $25 25
percent off a deal not a wind
breaker in toto else some
forgiveable mark placement
cerise in Paterson New Jersey
where no ideas but in things
engulfed my brain with attach
ments to nonsensical galactose
he which go-on Pushkin
slapped thusly micro-bi-octopus
categorizing one soundboard sweeper
for his 1922 Monarch upright
in sleazy joints beer studded
with cataract jumbo sized
asked if borrow plates succumb
to frostbite but legend has so
lambent tongues of flame his
torically speaking skedaddled
mononucleosis hoedown
where Upstate New York
supposed interior monologue crevasse
we what feggedaboutit Stendahl
eradicated she imagined portals
between thighs in restitution for
100 cents flat pitch raising
oblong carcasses of desultory

Himalayas floundering on beach
studies once cubist now wretched
of the earth a cocky scoundrel
whose equal temperment of system
imbued with patriotism like
Ljubijana hard-and-fast a living
wage the *joie de vivre* of gossamer
tablecloths dissonance clasp
unsuspecting the actual distance
of the 440hz octave desuetude

TIME TO GET UP

My father developed his photographs
in the upstairs kitchen that he had converted
into a dark room and sometimes I'd find him
sloshing the photographic paper
in pans of fluid under a red light
and he'd look at me and ask,
"Jack, what are you doing up so late?"
and I'd say,
"Dad, it's seven o'clock in the morning,
I gotta get ready for school,"
and he'd look off for a second,
absent-mindedly, then say,
"Oh."

Stuck to the cupboards,
and onto the refrigerator door,
and on the white walls as well,
were dozens of photographs, still wet
from the fixing solution.
The smell of acetone filled the kitchen.
The pans on the stove top,
cooking nothing
but those white sheets of paper,
turning into black & white photos
of my mother
standing by the Oldsmobile
in the driveway,
my brother in his dirty drawers
and dirt all over his cheeks,

and my sister
in a gray coat
with a white fur collar,
and me, 12 years old,
holding a boxing trophy.

For all I know,
the pictures are still there,
stuck to those white cupboards,
stuck to that refrigerator,
stuck to the walls.
The people who live there now,
for some odd reason,
have never removed those pictures.
They've been living there so long
they hardly notice them anymore,
except once in a while,
someone stops
and looks at them.
I can feel it.
In the middle of the night
as I sleep,
I know they're looking at me
holding my boxing trophy.
They're looking at me,
and it startles me,
and I say to them,
hey, whatcha doing up
so late,
and they say,
"Jack, it's time for school,
time to get up."
And sure enough, I do.

I get up and get dressed
and start walking,
carrying my satchel,
the same one I used
back in third grade
to cover the wet spot
on my khaki slacks
when I couldn't find the bathroom
that first day of school
and peed in my pants.

ONE KISS

in bed I'm nobody
its dark labyrinth
only dust
the seeds of sorrow
and such a waste
this veil of reason
one kiss dispels
longing but if you
are not in love
what's the good
of truth you are
that thorn
in the drunken vows
so keep it
keep it in your rose
garden don't
think of me like
this so broken
and misplaced
bleeding from
the inside
bringing wine
to the reappraisal
of form
think of me as
a messenger
who lost his way
who wanted
to lose his way

in the mystical
ecstacy of discursive
language only to find
the pen racing
toward love
as if it were a light
and not the bludgeon
of form we've
let it become

LIFE LIVES IN THE MOMENT

dread crusts of bread
at every turn

seeking redemption
of strawberries list
less is more likely less

misleading perception
of visual stimuli
doubtful of small inten
shuns the sinner sins
the doubter nobleza

he injecter dulzura
into the todestern
such lexigraphic moduls
of ungehobelte hachoir

someone sings off key

end

WATER MORE WATER

In the garden
I saw a plastic
water bottle.
Then I saw
a window.
Then a wall
and a heart.
I carried the wound
in my hand,
said
who wants a drink
of my wound.
There was a line
stretched around
the block.
Everyone wanted
water more water.
But my wound
was enough
to quench their
thirst.

TOWERS OF THUNDER

yeah I was having a conversation
the other night towers of thunder
portals of stone couldn't tell
what was being said
but not much was being said
it was all towers of thunder
portals of stone
and even though everyone's
huddled in snow in New York
and the barristers of chance
scoop puddles of ice in New Brunswick
it's hard to tell what others are saying
or even if they're using words
since it's all
towers of thunder
and portals of stone
the things you lose that
come back to find you
millions of us
like that squeezing our bodies
out from under the towers
of thunder and portals of stone
but frankly I don't much care
when it's my leg under crunch
and my arms hacked in smash
and my foot sucked in slash
and my face trapped in mush
and my fingers slit in slush
so if you were thinking of offering

JACK GRAPES

sympathy don't bother if you were
thinking of offering empathy don't
bother 'cause God himself is locked
into his tower of thunder
his portal of stone
and I'm holding onto
handfuls of straw
striking a match
ready to set myself
on fire

MORE WITHIN

blunt voices
without reason
she was a boxcar

until the tango
rescued us
from schoolrooms

a mixture of sunflowers
daring us to believe
in the higher calling of knives

no one forgets to wash
their hands before eating
the planes landing

bringing lost brothers
from sleep dawn pages
us over the loud

speakers wearing mohair
sweaters about to board
every scrap of news

JACK GRAPES

PICKING UP THE PIECES

She can't get the pieces to fit.
It's not a melon, you know,
she says
to no one in particular.
She gets a chain saw
and takes the sculpture apart,
piece by piece,
the teeth of the saw
tearing through the metal,
sparks that burst
before her like supernovas
and fall to her feet,
blackened by the fire,
and the pieces of metal
fly every which way,
one or two flying back at her,
their edges
making little cuts on her arm.
She wields the electric saw
like a conductor with baton
urging the trumpets and violins
and French horns to charge
to the finish as she
cuts the pieces
into smaller pieces,
and the smaller pieces
into even smaller pieces,
until they're everywhere
like autumn leaves

or dark huckleberries.
She surveys the damage,
then goes into the kitchen,
eats a bowl of oatmeal,
drinks a cup of coffe,
then goes back in to look.
The pieces are still there,
everywhere,
on the table,
on the floor,
on the bookshelves
and even some on top of the heater
and in the sink where she washes
her brushes.
You'd think the inner dome
of heaven had fallen.
It's not a melon, you know,
she says to no one in particular.
She starts picking up the pieces
and laughs when she says to herself,
"I'm picking up the pieces."
It gets her a good laugh,
and now she's laughing
at herself laughing,
like her father,
who laughed so hard
he could barely catch his breath
as his cheeks rose
and his eyes,
squinting,
turning inward,
and what he saw inside
made him laugh even harder

and that makes her cry now
thinking about her father
laughing
at what he sees
inside and she refuses
to see what she sees
inside
so she picks up the pieces
and gets the soldering gun
and solders the pieces back together,
leaves and huckleberries,
even the blackened stars
lying at her feet.
Later that night, when her husband
walks in and says,
whatcha got there,
she says,
to no one in particular,
a melon.

THE DOLPHIN KICK

It was zleep in the znow mouthz moving
it waz me there not sure if it waz me
or if you waz you we stood by the white
sheet hanging on the clothez line that clean
zoapy zmell zo fresh or waz it znow who
could tell on thiz long journey of clothez
pinz a perfect expedition of zalt we who
stood in our little winter coatz i love you
zomeone zaid, i love you but zand filled
my shoes driving me crasy it was like
they say crasy luv and we were zwimming
together stroke and stroke doing the dolphin
kick and zwallowing tonz of air into our
lungz or memory falling apart zo all
there iz iz what? the now and what
waz mizzing waz mizzing so we kept
zwimming for dear life thinking life
iz zo dear aztonishing in fact one minute
you're under water and the next you're
breathing big gulpz of air and then you're
back under the water and everything if
your eyez are open iz blurry so at night
who knowz even your name but the body
knowz your name the body knowz your
name the body getting zmaller and zmaller
throughout the night of zwimming throughout
the day of zwimming with you without you
crasy luv like the dolphinz zwimming
in warm and temperate zeas rezembling

a zmall whale or either of two large zlender fishez
dolorouzly kizzing with our beaklike znouts
in thiz brief zweet world of the lozt

I DIDN'T WRITE THIS POEM

I stole each and every line
from another poet.
Like vanity, the apples vanish.
See, Laura Jenson wrote that line.
Sparrows learned to fly
back into eternity.
That's Philip Levine, page
oh, who cares?
Was love just a dream?
That's Rumi for you.
Words disappear
as you turn the page.
Those lines belong to Barbara
Schweitzer. She's received
numerous prizes, including
"Best Poem for 2002"
by *Potpouri Magazine,*
a fellowship from RI State
Council on the Arts and maintains
a private psychotherapy practice
in Providence, RI.
I didn't even get her permission.
Just stole the line outright.
There she is listening to some woman
sob about her husband's infidelity,
hardly suspecting
I've taken her lines
right from under her nose.

Maybe you got a line or two
I could steal.
I'm desperate.
I've run out of words.
Dry as a bone.
It's break and enter now.
Mask on my face.
Crowbar in my hand.
Dante drives the getaway car,
a '54 Chevy Bel Air
with plastic seat covers.
Shakespeare stands lookout
wearing a Lone Ranger mask,
crouching behind the oleander bushes.
I don't steal from them.
Those two bastards,
they stole everything from me.
Oh, that this too too solid flesh would melt,
thaw, and resolve itself into a dew,
or that the Everlasting
had not fixed His canon
'gainst self-slaughter.
That was mine until the s.o.b. took it.
Nel mezzo del cammin di nostra vita.
I wrote that one rainy night
after my wife and I split up
and that Italian just came by
and swiped it.
The nerve!

And what about
quand vous serez bien vielle,
au soir, à la chandelle

assise auprès de feu?
You'd think the greatest poet
of the French Renaissance,
the renewer of French poetry,
the assimilator of Greek, Latin,
and Italian forms,
could have gotten along quite well
without me, but no,
he's gotta stoop so low
he steals one of my best lines,
and even Yeats comes along
and steals it from Ronsard
and doesn't even give *him* credit?
When you are old and gray
and full of sleep,
and nodding by the fire,
see, he steals that from Ronsard
and neither of them give me credit.

Infandum renovare dolorem?
You'd think Horace could
find his own words
about renewing
unspeakable grief,
lines I wrote so long ago
I can't even remember
what caused the grief
in the first place,
but I can taste it even today.
I mean,
what the hell's going on here,
some kind of free-for-all?

So I figure
it's time for payback.
I got nothing left
and I'm coming for you.
Lock up your poems
and throw away the key.
There's not one line
in any of your poems
that's safe.
I'm coming after them,
one line at a time.
From now on,
poetry belongs to me.

MUSIC FOR THE BLIND

Radio blasting music
for the blind,
directions for the deaf.
He kissed a virgin
and she sang a song
but he didn't want a song,
he wanted music, directions,
something he could die by.
We sit here around the table
both knowing the trumpet
leaves a mark on the tongue,
a collection of cutlery
perfect for scrambled eggs.
Are we all going to take
an optimistic view
of the future
or do we actualize the human
spirit holding as necessary
ambiguity fragility
and precariousness?
Just because you believe in matter
doesn't mean you have to believe
in the world.
The radio solidifies everything.
Madness co-exists with reason
as justifiable homicide,
or as Dylan sang,
no direction home,
like a rolling stone.

JACK GRAPES

In birth we want pictures,
in death we want music.
Our image of life after death
is no more than hallucinatory
myth-making.
In the tyranical force and power
of a world-imperialism
obligation would not disappear,
but it would be transformed
by our response to the ideals
which are ultimately the expression
of an influx of divine life
as mediated
to society
by those of us
who have opened ourselves
to the divine life.
If you want pictures, then draw.
If you want music, then sing.
If you can see, close your eyes.
And if you have no idea
where you are going,
stand still and listen
to the silence.

IN THE SUMMER HEAT

Here's the thing:
You were talking about something,
who knows what, made a gesture
or a movement of your head,
then you stuck out your jaw,
and that's when I took off my shoes,
which are always talking back to me,
and raced across the street ahead of you,
and stood by the oak planted
in Mrs. Murphy's front yard, oh,
musta been 60 years ago when they built
the houses in this sub-division,
all the while being careful
not to get my socks wet,
and you came up to me
and asked if I was leaning on the tree
or was the tree leaning on me
and I said isn't that the same
as asking me
if I was holding down the world
or was the world
holding me up
and you laughed
and I put my shoes back on
and we walked another few blocks
before heading home in the summer heat.

PRAYER

I was thinking about You
the other day.
Nothing major, I was just walking
along in the sunshine
and got to thinking of St. Augustine's
proof that You existed.
Remember him? Well, You have
so many people to remember,
I can understand how You might
forget one. Anyway, Augustine proved
that You existed.
"Proof from within," he called it,
the mind's apprehension
of necessary and changeless truths.
The mind has to bow before it,
he says, and accept it.
But eternal truths must be
founded on Being,
reflecting the Ground of all truth.
Leibniz agreed, hundreds of years
later, that true existential judgments
depend on Your choice
of one possible world —
the exception to the rule, being,
Leibniz said, the proposition
that You're a possible Being.
It's kinda like *You* wondering
whether or not *I* exist.
But I was walking along in the sunshine

thinking of You, so you can rest easy.
I know You've been depressed lately
by all those proofs of Your existence,
and even You must be having doubts
by now, so I just wanted to let You know
that even though
I still don't believe in You,
I love You, anway,
proof or no proof,
and I wish all of us
would take better care of You.
I mean, I'm gonna die soon,
but You, man-o-man, You gotta just go
on and on and on, without stopping,
or even starting, just being
who You are to so many of us.
No wonder You've got the blues.
No wonder I love You.

JACK GRAPES

GLUE

I could fall into slumber,
speak words
aloud that would change
you or make you love
yourself more than you
love yourself now.
I could but I am not clear.
I am not clarity.
Some force, the opera
that breaks my head
open and opens the blinds
and lets the light in,
the failure of resolve
that is the weakness
of the brain when there's
only this one life
to scratch the surface
of the mind howling
beneath this time
of love setting
fires that
may come yet
to someone's lips.
Maybe a highway
or a back country road
or the alley behind
the hobby shop
where old men compare
glues,

it may come yet
but don't just wait
for it,
draw a circle
on the sidewalk
and step into it,
draw a circle around
your feet and step
out of it,
but don't just wait
for it
it may come
upon someone's eyes
your lips
someone's face
your hand
nothing behind you
yet, you step out.

LOST

ain't me
that's lost
said the mailman
as he walked away
from my front porch
throwing all the love letters
meant for me
into the gutter

POW! POW!

I saw a man sitting on the curb
after he was hit by a car.
What the dog
was doing next to him
I'm not sure.
Maybe the dog was hit, too.
Maybe the dog was a mutt
from down the street
happy to be sympathetic
to the man with spindly legs
showing above his socks.
Maybe the dog
was driving the car.
Maybe the dog
should have been driving the car.
Me? I was just the boy
who lived on Cadiz Street,
a few houses down
from the Hills Grocery Store.
That's where I walked
to get a bag of potato chips and a coke.
Most mornings, I walked
holding my schoolbag,
keeping an eye out
for Kenny Senac
who waited for me
so he could beat me up.
I didn't fight back then.
Now I fight back.

JACK GRAPES

Pow! Pow!
A left hook to the kisser,
a right cross to the jaw,
an uppercut to the chin.
One time, I licked the sidewalk
just to see what it would taste like.
Oh, it was such a hot
and sunny summer day
and I got down
and I stuck my tongue out
and sure enough
it tasted like okra.
Everybody should taste the sidewalk
just once, because you never know,
one day you'll be lying on the sidewalk,
having just been hit by a car,
and you'll be all alone,
afraid you're dead,
and no one will be there
except that dog,
that dog and me,
I'll be there,
carrying my school bag,
ready to protect you
from all the Kenny Senacs
of the world.
Pow! Pow!
A left hook to the kisser,
a right cross to the jaw,
an uppercut to the chin.

IT MIGHT BE YOU

It might be you
swimming along
with me
in this pool
of clear water
stroke for stroke
together
or it might be me
flying along
with you
in that clear
sky
together
but I'm just dreaming
and what
about you
in your sleep
so alone
no one to guide you
either
in water
or clear blue sky
what about you
in your sleep
writing this poem?

JACK GRAPES

THE REMNANT IN BABYLON

Someone said you'd know
what to do once you got here.
Uphill, someone said depending
on where you want to go.
Downhill, someone said is an
illusion if you're standing on your head.
Kiss, someone said, asses or else you
might as well sit where you are.

Some kisses come out of nowhere.
You can stay with the kiss
or follow it uphill.
If you go downhill long enough
soon enough you'll be going uphill.
High as a kite doesn't always do the trick
but it beats the low down under.
Tears, there's always tears,
crying till your eyes hurt,
weeping till your teeth hurt,
sobbing into your hands
until your fingers hurt.

The moon rises.
The sun sets.
Days ladle.
Nights die.
Find delight in nothing
someone said and I knew what he meant.
Jeremiah was a bullfrog

even when he said something
about walking after vanity
and being lost
in the wilderness
where the meaning
of his name is uncertain
 though he's called
"the weeping prophet,"
his bold
proclamation
of the unwelcome truth
notwithstanding,
and he never lost
his compassion
for those whose city
would be destroyed
and chose
to stay instead
with the poor,
the poor remnant of his own people,
instead of those sent to Babylon
but here
we are
       the remnant in Babylon
standing on our heads,
weeping,
sobbing,
receiving kisses
out of nowhere,
words as fire,
hammers that shatter rock.

JACK GRAPES

ALL THE SAD ANGELS

Here's what happened,
mostly by chance.
They were renewing sorrow.
How could I not go?
I was more lost than ever.
I know I don't look lost.
Hail fellow and all that.
But I'm still hungry
to wander in this Paradise of Sadness.
Sure, we shake hands, cordial,
like your tie, we say.
But so many of the angels are sad.
I know, in the paintings, they're
at peace with their lot,
but they have their moments,
don't kid yourself.
All those pale lunar figures,
old geezers by the truckload,
the crazy young ones
walking along the marble terraces.
What's a wasserfall? Blondie asks.
I remove her veil.
She's beautiful but distracted.
Not dead, but you get the picture.
The beloved grows cold.
No one cared about the layout
of the city, our woodland shade,
millions of people lining up
to renew their sorrow.

Old age is identical to swiss cheese.
What do you do with the memories,
if they even existed?
I've made it this far
is all I can manage to say
when they take my card,
examine the information
with a magnifying glass,
assure me that help is on the way.
What about the sorrow, I ask.
The dark armchair shrugs.
You were meant to be happy
it says, frowning, sad,
consoling me.
But what the hell am I supposed
to do without the sorrow?
Romanticism scolded by the critics
got off easier than I did.
Again, the dark armchair shrugs,
says something in French
I'm supposed to understand—
ce tombeau blanchi à la chaux
très loin sous terre—
the vast passage of the sea,
the torrential light,
the heroism of discovery,
the coin purses of sorrow
dying in the rain.

MAZE

they are holding
me prisoner here,
inside this heart.
It's not my heart.
Someone else's
heart.
This heart doesn't
belong to me.
It's not mine.
I'd just as soon
get out, but
they won't let me.
Hey, I yell,
this is not my heart,
lemme out!
Here comes
the jailer.
He hands me
a salami sandwich.
I prefer baloney
I tell him.
Baloney
for the other heart,
he says.
I eat the salami.
He watches.
It's good for you,
the salami, he says.
Hardens the arteries,

I say.
Just the same,
he says,
you're gonna be here
a long time,
in somebody else's
heart, might as well
eat what you get.
Inside this heart,
I put up curtains.
Make this heart mine.
But it's not my heart.
It's someone else's
heart.
I plan my escape
all night long,
all year long,
have been planning
this escape
my whole life.
Wait for me.

JACK GRAPES

THE MAN IN THE CHAIR

one day I wasn't in love
and it made me want
to knit a wool sweater
or hook a rug
which I actually did
while working
on a show with
Gregory Sierra
where I played a lawyer
who had lost the love
inside his head
but his wooden leg
was filled with it
it oozed from his toes
and he gesticulated
to the judge
something about
who was guilty and who
was innocent
and who deserved
the chair
everybody wants the chair
where you can sit
all day apart
from everything
as if your father
just gave you a timeout
and all you had to do
was sit there knowing

life would give you
the breather you deserve
maybe for as long
as you lived
and you could
call yourself
the man in the chair

JACK GRAPES

FISTICUFFS AT DURTY NELLY'S

I was having a few pints of Guiness
with a friend in one of those
Irish dive bars with men playing darts
and agitation in the air.
I could sense that someone
was itching for a fight.
Might have been me.

I can't remember now
where the bar was.
It was a small town,
with the decay of urban renewal
on either side of the bar,
empty lots waiting for a high rise.
My friend wanted to go there,
to pick up women
and sob into his beer.

There were a few locals
from the neighborhood,
two playing pool,
two others throwing darts
and eating blue cheese fries
off a paper plate.
The tiles on the floor had been sourced
from the National Gallery of Ireland.

I felt like going outside, taking a piss
in the snow. Yeah, it was snowing,

or maybe *had* snowed, and the snow
was mushy on the sidewalk.
Everything about that night
is like a dream, a page in a life
faded except for a few squiggles
and an out-of-focus photograph.

Oh, now I remember, it was Baton Rouge,
the capital of Louisiana.
Baton Rouge, the Red Stick,
named after the long red stick
a French explorer stuck in the ground
as he claimed the land for King Louis.
We drove up the Airline Highway,
past cypress stumps and swamp land,
arriving on a cold, damp Saturday night,
a city half-deserted, alongside the feeling
that everything inside and out was half-deserted,
a decaying paper bag
I couldn't punch my way out of.

Two, maybe three beers and a few shots
of whiskey, boilermakers they call them.
I wanted to piss in the snow out back
but couldn't find the door,
so I used the bathroom instead,
down a dark hallway
smelling of urine.
It was a long one, that piss,
and such a meditative
moment, watching the yellow stream
hit the porcelain and splashing
down into the drain. You gotta love

porcelain, that vitreous,
translucent ceramic material.
Better than snow, if you think
about it. Granted,
you can piss your name
in the snow, if you've had
enough beer, maybe even
your middle initial.

But porcelain. Ah, the way
that stream hits it, splashes
into the drain, some of it
splashing back onto your pants.

Then I walked back
through the narrow passage
and staggered out, leaned against
the bar and said, "Who's up
for a few punches?"

Nobody paid any attention.
The guy in the Pendelton shirt
threw his dart and hit the bullseye.
I tried one more time:
"Fisticuffs, anyone?"

My friend ordered another Guiness
and the bartender set it down
on the counter. "Have another beer,"
my friend said, as he took a long chug
of his own.

I picked up the mug,

blew the foam off the top
and took a long gulp.

I smacked the mug down on the bar,
walked to the dart board
and threw three bullseyes:
pop, pop, pop.

I was on a roll.
"You're interrupting our game,"
Mr. Pendelton said.
"Take it into the alley,"
yelled the bartender.
Out in the snow, we put up our dukes.
I slipped his right cross,
threw a left hook and down he went.

I went back to the bar,
ordered another pint,
put my feet up on the rail,
and thought:
I'm gonna write about this one day.
I'll change all the facts, lie about everything,
pretend I was with a friend and not really alone,
pretend I had a great sense of humor,
pretend I could hit bullseyes
even when drunk,
pretend I had a great left hook
and wasn't decked by a right cross
right there in the pub,
before I'd even made it into the alley.

I'll make a good poem
triumph over the sad life.

JUST LIKE A HOUSE

I dreamed you
were a house.
No, that was
another night,
another dream.
This dream,
the one from last
night, it was me
who was
the house,
but you were
in it, walk
ing around look
ing for me.
People were
coming and going
inside my house,
and you were
as I said
look
ing
for me.
I'm the house
I said,
the whole house.
Quit play
ing games
you said.
Where are you?

You're in me
I said.
But I can't see
you you
said.
I know, I said,
isn't that just
like a house.

JACK GRAPES

TRAIN STATION

best not to think
of it
camels or something
written in
Greek where the train
station
what I saw on the wall
someone rebuilding
the temple
everyone waiting around
for the young poet who was
due any minute now
unless the guy
standing on the bench
singing off-key
buttoning his shirt
was him though how
could it be him
his shoes were
polished
and his pants
creased
and off-key notwithstanding
we stopped
to listen surely
this couldn't be the poet
the poet we expected
carries his bed with him
and writes about death

while this guy singing
off key
buttoning
his shirt
was smiling
happy
amidst the gloom
of the train station
smiling with such
joy
it made us all
uncomfortable
best not to think
go on with
our business
the melodies
in our ears
we can
safely
ignore

JACK GRAPES

ZERO-SUM GAME

can't be the prophet
who negates the future
if the words are naked
are they as impure
not the consolation
of the traditional
lyric though
not to cast asperagus
on Wordsworth's *Lyrical Ballads*
I'd be a dummy
to do that but back
to the point
can't be the prophet
who negates the future
from the other side of the page
plays no games
but the zero -sum
offhand free verse of scorn
like where do you put
the rose in the mouth
of a dead girl
or do you admit that
geometrical axioms
are neither synthetic
a priori intuitions
nor experimental facts
see how far
that will get you
or the fuzzy pretzel

those who drink moon
from sky as you dance
with the red-haired irish
woman shaped by slaughter
who can't be the prophet
negating the future all that
smokiness of love songs
even as the madman
wails about who claims
to know what they know
and are never ashamed
of tears heaven or earth if the words
are naked she is naked
everything but her arms
impure the consolation
of her lips
as a geometrical axiom
lay her on the bed
as neither sleeping nor awake
neither a priori nor experimental
negating the future
which comes faster than
you can read
this poem faster
than all the offhand free verse
you thought would save you
from getting on the subway
you can't be anything
but the prophet
saying love is not real
just a matrix
of non-linear heartbeat
beats

JACK GRAPES

SIDE SHOW

Who says they'll
lie next to you
forever?
All you want
is a good night's
sleep
so what's with
the mish-mash
of love buddy
boy the mish-
mash of grief
like a turtle
you found
on your front
lawn a slow
boat to china
like Rimbaud's
bateau ivre
sliding down
the impassible
rivers through
the appalling fan
fare of the body
while the heart
finds more grief
than it can imagine
sorrow piled so
high it turns to
laughter

the tongue
it sticks out
to the world
a slow boat
going house
to house
as some savage side
show for gullible
lovers.

FOOTBRIDGE

I must have
said where's the head or she
or maybe he but I'm pretty sure she
said when are you coming
back into the fold and I or me
or maybe them but I'm pretty sure us
wanted mayhem not platitudes so
I realized Norfolk was just a city I
once visited with my father or mother
or maybe my uncle but I'm pretty sure they
wouldn't allow children to carry all
that luggage across the footbridge so
you carry yourself home in a sleek
Maserati my little squeaks of pleasure
flushed with money the turpentine of
regret for sure ain't no two-bit rustler
gonna get those cows no way so me
and Daryle hosed down the driveway
all that blood from yesterday's gun
fight into the gutters where you can
feel God in his three-piece suit com-
plaining about all the rust in the world
saying that's not me I didn't make that
it was all spick and span and now look
whatcha done cowboy rootin-tootin
sheriff who shot don't get me started
all the way down to here where mayhem
looking like the king's head thought
it could be happy making pancakes

over a hot stove for the children lugging
those suitcases over the footbridge for
pedestrians but who reads signs any
more these days everyone
marches on across with their
muddy boots when all I wanted was
to go away and be by myself but now
you are here mucking up the line
breaks sniffing like
a graveyard which unlike a cemetery
is attached to a church each and every
tombstone a child carrying luggage
filled with he-said and she-said anec
dotes

THE GREATEST SHOW ON EARTH

care must be taken
not to disturb the body
where the rain
made a puddle
on the forehead
don't let toes
get in the way
of imagination
it bothers the mind
to stub an idea in the dark
focus on a woman
or if you prefer a man
it's all the same
flesh is flesh
trace an arabesque
from kneecap to armpit
ha caught you napping
but from the waist up
death sprouts like a tulip
and you can rearrange
the eyes anyway you'd like
provided you keep
the oven light on
and avoid circus metaphors
like tightrope
and ringmaster
and object
manipulation
and being shot out of a cannon

there's room for all of us
on the stainless steel table
if we see our lives
through the lens of providence
the fall of which
is neither elephant
nor sparrow

JACK GRAPES

JESSIE, MY DOG

I was driving back from a music recital
this evening and found myself cruising
down a street I used to frequent 30 years ago
but haven't driven down since. So many
of the places I used to go to are gone.
A favorite Italian restaurant, now a fitness center.
A bookstore, now an antique store.
A café where I read most of *One Hundred
Years of Solitude,* now an ice-cream parlor.
It isn't as if I was planning to go to any
of those places, but it makes me sad to know
they're gone. It doesn't really matter.
I'm 72 years old, a lot is gone.
It's all going to go eventually.
By the cafe, a boy was walking his dog
along the sidewalk.
One day, the boy will be gone,
along with his dog.
My dog is gone.
Jessie used to lie by my feet as I sat
at the computer trying to write a poem.
She's gone now. No more Jessie.
After I'd written the poem, I'd take Jessie
out for her midnight walk. Sometimes
we'd pass a house and the people inside
might still be up, sitting at the table,
talking and drinking.
But mostly the streets were quiet,
and she and I would enjoy the night air,

the way the leaves rustled
when a wind came up from the ocean.
Maybe a poem would be buried in someone's
front yard, and Jessie would dig it up
and bring it to me,
like a bone she'd just found.
That poem about
the man in charge of watering,
Jessie dug that one up, just dug it up
and brought it to me.
"Whatcha got there, girl?"
She dropped it on the sidewalk,
then trotted off,
looking for more poems,
more bones.
No more bones now,
and few poems to be dug up,
except this one,
which is torn at the edges
and I've stopped caring about the
line breaks or the metaphors
or even doing the kind
of things a poet is supposed to do
when writing a poem,
making everything ship-shape.
No more bones,
no more ship-shape.
I'm not even sure
you're reading this poem
right now.
Maybe *no one* is reading it.
Like I said earlier,
it doesn't matter, you know.

I write the poems anyway.
Jessie will come back some night,
take my poems on our walk,
and bury them in someone's front yard,
and all I'll have to do
in my remaining years
is walk my weary bones
down the sidewalk
and dig 'em up.
Dig up those poems that Jessie buried,
my good girl dog,
taking such good care of me,
then and now.
Jessie won't be with me,
but I'll thank her,
give her a good rub on the back,
then let her go.

ANOTHER BREATH ANOTHER
WAY OF BREATHING

She had kisses I had stone

I couldn't see her she was blind

A leaf on the front porch wasn't a leaf

I was a stamp she was a porch light

It's so cold in the car yet we drive

I held her for a long time then she left

Kiss me one more time she said I did
He who dances the tango goes lightly

I can't remember a thing but I fake it

It's a china teacup I said she nodded

Then she had stone and all I had were kisses

You will go on a long journey my horoscope

The place of a room in the heart falls asleep

It's not so much the heat
but the hum of the refrigerator

JACK GRAPES

She put her hand on my cheek
and I was mystified

Right now I'm sitting in a chair you it's dark

It's in the face love all over your chest

My father is gone and you say hello

I haven't spoken to my brother in so long so what

Then I was blind and she did the dishes

We had a son he's not in the car

I'm Jewish oh a Jew yeah look at my penis

I held her again and again and again

I am still holding her but there goes the tango

You breathe in then exhale ashes

I am trying to tell you a secret you won't listen
I am trying to tell you a secret you won't listen

BIG TOP

body your cupped hands
resolution of anguish
expectation of grief
your mouth opened
to scream or be kissed
a 12% probability of rain

DRIVING OVER TO BAYOU LAFITTE

If the heart were something I could eat,
I wouldn't use a fork and knife my whole mouth.

On the other side of the wall
eighty eggs me on, my pillow refusing to go.

In summer I walked barefoot on hot gravel mixed
with oyster shells, mixed with American history.

Oh, to be in agony over a toothpick,
over a child chasing a bird, over Europe.

I cut the faith out of me so it wouldn't fester,
now I'm caught in the sunlight of Timbucktoo.

Now I'm in the car driving over to Bayou Lafitte
in the back seat watching my father's neck.

The police came when we was robbed. The robbers came in
through my bathroom window no really.

The car stopped. An opposum was crossing the road
it stopped in the glare of the headlights that opposum.

It's always some kind of gray weather around here
and I can barely hear you over the telephone wet lips.

What makes you believe in kindness? In Sweden?
What makes you crack an egg hoping for the best?

Some women want to know how tomorrow's going
to turn out, like a ship, I say, full mouth wet lips.
In the dark you can see just about everything
once your eyes get used to American history.

The children get taller, grow out of their shoes,
all you have left is the telephone who's calling.

I stood beside a horse once, felt its power,
ran my hand along its flank, it's Europe.

All it takes is one kiss and everything is changed,
you're in the car driving over to Bayou Lafitte.

SECRET SAUCE

My spoon loves my knife.
This keyboard loves my fingers.
The easy chair in the living room
loves my ass.
Everything loves something.
Years ago, Bill Mohr edited
an anthology of poetry titled
Poetry Loves Poetry.
I had a few poems in it.
It was ahead of its time
when you consider
that for years, centuries even,
poetry hated poetry.
Check out Marianne Moore's
poem titled "Poetry,"
the first line of which is
"I, too, dislike it."
I know some poets
have made firm declarations
that they plan to write
no more poems.
It's prose or nothing.
For them, poetry is done, kaput.
And why not.
Maybe we've had
enough of poetry,
enough of war.
Who in their right mind
would read poetry

unless they were either
a poet,
or a fool.
You're reading this now,
so you're probably both.
Something new arises
from fire
as well as from love.
The heart banks on sorrow
in the worst of times.
Why depend on poetry
to remind us
of the dead bodies
we carry with us every day,
one slung over the back,
one on each arm?
Even in the dark,
some faces shine.
"Don't think so much,"
my mother warned me
one day in the kitchen
as I brooded over
a cup of coffee
and the meaning of life.
If you're cupping
a bird in your hand,
do you pray
there will be enough breath
for the both of you?
On the freeway at 2am,
I often think,
where the hell is everybody going?
I know where I'm going,

JACK GRAPES

and it makes perfect sense
where I'm going,
but for Pete's sake, it's 2am!
Are there that many of us
unable to sleep
going somewhere
on our way home?
My neighbor drives a Volvo.
In the morning,
as I watch her drive off,
I imagine rain falling
on a deserted airfield,
nothing but a troop of bees
in winter coats
mourning the death
of ordinary clothes.
What war is it now,
I ask my mother,
who has gone from grating cheese
to chopping chicken breasts.
The wars of the French Revolution
summoned armies
of previously
unimaginable size
to European battlefields,
a hybrid conscription system
that was to transform European
warfare for a century and a half.
Mid-century weapons were still
muzzle-loaded, while percussion caps
replaced flintlocks, and soon
breech-loading came into use,
greatly increasing firing rates.

The first machine guns
appeared in the 1860s.
The familiar charge
of earlier wars,
the bayonet,
became exercises
in self-immolation.
"Annihilate the enemy!" shouted
Helmuth von Moltke,
often identified
as Helmuth Graf von Moltke,
or simply Graf Moltke.
But a frontal assault
needs a web of doctrine;
not as a set of recipes,
but of principles;
not as a guide to belief
but to action.
Replicating success
on the battlefield
is not as easy as it sounds;
there's always a secret sauce,
otherwise, the world would overflow
with Googles and Amazons
and Apples and Nepal
would be as prosperous
as Switzerland.
So my mother chops
the chicken breasts,
and I resolve to stop
thinking so much
and start eating whatever
she puts on my plate.

Even the apron, I eat.
I cut it with my trusty knife,
scoop it all up with my spoon,
both of them in love
with each other,
then retire to the living room
to sit in the easy chair,
so helplessly in love
with my ass.

LOST ILLUSIONS

She painted cows as if they were chickens.

Artists can paint whatever they want.

I went to visit her in her studio
after I took my grandmother
to Lake Pontchartrain to see if we'd caught
any crabs in the crab traps
hanging off the seawall,
which reminded me of Grand Isle
at the mouth of Barataria Bay
where it meets the Gulf of Mexico,
and Slidell on the other side of the lake
where we dined at one of those fashionable
restaurants facing the little streets
that ran down at right angles
to the beach where that little girl
who hung her head like an animal
being driven reluctant to its stall
was walking in front
of an authoritarian-looking schoolteacher,
in all probability,
one of her relatives.

Finally we got to her studio
and looked at a picture
by Charles Gleyre titled *Lost Illusions*,
but all I could think about were the apple trees
with their circular shadows,

the fields, the dusty roads,
the knapsacks of the travelers,
the spires of the churches in the distant towns.
Then I looked back at *Lost Illusions*.
Silhoutetted against the sky
in the form of a silver sickle,
the boat lay aground, the women in the boat
in various stages of undress
singing the song the bearded man
on the dock could hear even in his sleep.

Sometimes, in the afternoon sky,
the moon would inch its way up,
high enough to be mistaken for a cloud,
furtive, lustreless, suggesting an actress
who stands in the wings
watching the rest of the company
stomp about the stage,
pretending not to see the actor
twirling his moustache,
gliding onto the boulevards,
hangers-on dogging his heels
in hopes of touching his cloak,
and in doing so,
amplified rather than muted
their supplicant natures,
bringing to the surface
precisely what they'd sought to conceal,
a life betrayed by polite disengagements.

I was reminded of that self-portrait
by Jean-Baptiste-Simon Chardin
who sticks his face out

as if challenging you to a duel,
as if to say you can make a new version
of what you love
by renouncing it.
Is that why she painted cows
that looked like chickens?

Then she offered us a strawberry mousse,
which went so well with the Chateau Margaux
and a glass of port.

"It's time to go," whispered my grandmother.

She took my hand
and down the cobblestone steps we went,
out the front gate,
and onto the dusty path
that led back home.

"People are always in a hurry,"
said my grandmother,
"and leave at the moment
they ought to be arriving."

It didn't make sense to me.
Were we leaving too early?
Were we in a hurry?
Should we, just now, be arriving?

So much was on my mind that afternoon,
though all that's left
is a series of paintings:
Van Gogh's *Potato Eaters*,

those peasants laced in darkness,
their fingers stretched out
toward the platter of potatoes,
the woman pouring coffee,
the column behind the table
seeming to hold the building up.
The light from the oil lamp
that hung above the table
was the same light as the light
in *The Money-Changer* by Rembrandt,
the browns and burnt siennas
surrounding that spectacled face
as he holds up a coin
to the light of a candle
projecting its glow against the darkness,
the light bronzing a scrap of leather,
a dagger inlaid with spangles
spreading a patina of gold
on the varnish of an old table
on top of which is nothing
but pinchbeck rubbish.

That night, lying in bed and listening
to the crickets outside my window,
I thought of painted cows
that looked like chickens
and tried to jolt my brain
into comprehension of something
larger than myself.
If I could just learn the meaning of eyes,
I would discover the secret of the universe,
the way one copies the movement
of a shoulder or the tension of a neck

with a few brushstrokes
in order to understand a masterpiece.

And what if the universe didn't have a secret?
What if nothing was hidden
or disguised as something else?
What if in that painting by Bruegel,
Census at Bethlehem, all we can do
is witness it helplessly, grainy and bristling
with brown and white brush strokes
that leap from autumn to early winter,
the frostbound peasants waiting to be counted,
the man kneeling to fix his shoe,
the lady in the apron holding a frying pan
by its long handle,
as crowded figures in brown coats
huddle in the cold before the counting house,
the chickens at the bottom of the painting
looking for seed beneath the snow,
bringing to the surface
what was once concealed.

JACK GRAPES

GOOD PRACTICE

I wrote a poem
yesterday
and then I burned
it good practice
to burn a poem
a day and while
we're at it
burn the pens
and the notebooks
even if they're
empty and don't
forget to set
fire to all the other
tools of your trade—
love, hope, compassion,
regret, grief, loss,
transcendence—
just burn them all
even your head
where all the poems
are stored even
your heart where
all the poems were
born even your feet
where all the poems
settle after a good
day's work
burn it all even your
self

silvery branches
of the night
imaginary waterfalls
drowning in debt
pussytoes
meadowsweets
blindweed
goldenrod
kingscup
speedwell
marvel of peru
queen of the meadows
love in the mist
burn

FLY ZONE AMBIVALENCE

swooned to fly in particular he had more money than nocutur-
anal ambivalence the shoot, the shot, the rainbow effect, and
dead. The next day calamity morsels, cared for, blazed out and
smithereened postal harness, too soon, crunched, a make-up
sandwich his horse. I told it. They fixed it. We caked it. Jammed
up. Torn down. Secret maps of brain power. Sugar can't open
nostril your take out handle of turpentine make-shift war zones,
gluttony, rash-cakes, who pulls around the there it goes medley
of starfish my uncle pre-razor cut in hospitality, foolish errand,
baker's dozen, glitch, formidable, panzer man, dainty scrub,
garden variety toboggen if offered rejected if accepted misdi-
rected gone there back arrived left alone crowd pleaser battal-
ion chief ozone. It was quiet. Mackerals lanced formica tables
and he flossed his brain not noticed until daybreak, rush hour,
carports, tractor-trailers, I mentioned, cartoon whiplash, suffer
the children's hour round-about. Who was picked clean? We all
stood in line. Suffered. Mishandled. Clean-shaven. Afraid to fall.
Despondant. Recalcitrant demigods. And I took action with no
swoons in particular, I was riddled total carcass yes make it two
shot through the throat a peacock. A hen-peck money ozone
in fly zone ambivalence who gets lay it down i'm stopping not
going see there's no here take cover open up stitch in nine paltry
coin purse after rain drops rain shower with kisses her lover her
man her last standing war zone hero.

ALL ALONE SHOE

The world lies at my feet today
as I go out to run my daily errands.
That broken kite, my lord,
did some dog's teeth get hold of it?
It must have come
all the way from Seattle.
How did it end up on my front lawn
torn to pieces?

And there's that shoe I saw
on the side of the freeway,
the San Bernadino Freeway,
to be exact, I saw it as traffic
slowed to a crawl,
then stopped altogether
and I got out
of my car and retrieved it,
all alone shoe amidst ragged tee-shirt
and a yellow tennis ball,
I retrieved it and looked for its mate,
probably close to the Sante Fe exit
a few miles up,
but the cars started moving,
and before I knew it
Sante Fe was in my rear-view mirror
and all I had was that single shoe,
and now, ten years later,
there's its mate,
on my front lawn,

a sign perhaps,
that I should slow down,
or get moving,
who knows which.

Moons of Jupiter.
What they're doing
on my front lawn
is anybody's guess.
Another message perhaps,
that I should heed
before my foot
hits the accelerator.

There's clutter everywhere.
An old carburator.
Torn paperback pulp novel.
Pocket flashlight you buy
in a car wash
next to the air fresheners.
A Lone Ranger mask.
Salami sandwich.
Remnants of Babylon.
The boxing trophy.
A melon.
My father's old photographs.
A red stick.
Jessie, my dog.
American history.
The weeping prophet.
Neither elephant nor sparrow.
Suitcases over the footbridge.
Dolphinz.

Camels written in Greek.
Bottles of glue.
A Pendelton shirt.
One kiss.
Inside and outside,
nothing's worth a penny,
not even a penny.
Miles to go before you sleep,
before you go,
before you lift off,
before you start flapping your arms
how love comes
and you don't know the first thing
about love but it comes at you
and burns away
the soul's country of clutter.

I can look at the moon
only so many times
before it's neither moon
nor not moon.
How deeply can you love
without burning yourself?
Treachery and lust and betrayal
and sugar and wild dreams
and pride and pencil sharpeners
and all those bottles of beer
lying here
on the front lawn
as I step out of my house
and prepare to run my daily errands,
before the world melts
in my hands

JACK GRAPES

and the sky explodes
on my lips
and I am unable
to teach you anything.
Like a blind man,
I put my hands out
in front of me
and expect everything
and am never disappointed.

Pray always with passion.
Make love always with passion.
Eat and drink and dance and play,
Always With passion.
Don't just float there
like a dead fish
in this ocean of God?

— Rumi

Any Style

Who ever anywhere will read these written words?

– James Joyce, *Ulysses*

ANY STYLE

SELECTED NEW POEMS
JACK GRAPES

AN ISLAND IN THE MIDDLE OF A LAKE

I came to Los Angeles 50 years ago
in the fall of 1968
— the same year George Drury Smith founded Beyond Ba-
roque—
to do a pilot for a tv series.
I knew where all the actor-watering holes were
— Jo Allen's, Nicodell's, Hugo's, etc. —
but what about the poet-wateringholes?
Where were they?
This was Los Angeles, you know,
not Paris, where the poets sat in cafes
on the Boul 'Mich or on Blvd. St. Germain
and spouted modern poetry.
It wasn't New York, either,
where the poets hung out in coffee houses
and slouched on park benches
in Washington Square in Greenwhich Village
and spouted modern poetry.
It wasn't Chicago
where poets at the Green Mill
slammed poetry out loud,
and it wasn't even San Francisco
where poets could be found in North Beach
at City Lights Bookstore
or standing on street corners,
reading their poems.

It was as hard to find a poet in Los Angeles
as it was to find Los Angeles in Los Angeles.

I heard there were some poets in Hermosa Beach
hanging out at the Either/Or Bookstore.
Someone spotted a poet
at Small World Books in Santa Monica,
and there was a rumor going around
that two poets were seen
walking along the pier in Long Beach.
I had been corresponding with Bukowski,
but wasn't about to drive over
to his courtyard apartment on De Longpre
and like all his other poet-hangers on
barge in with a six-pack blazing.
I like to keep my distance
with a cigarette dangling.
All my poems at that point
were published under my first name, Marcus.
When I hit L.A., I claimed my public name
and published under Jack.
A few years later, when I ran into the editor
of Vagabond magazine at a writer's convention,
I told him my name was Jack.
"Any relation to Marcus Grapes," he said.
"That's me," I said.
"Oh," he said, "we thought you were dead."
But those first few months in L.A.,
I was looking to find the poets,
where were the poets,
where were all the skinny poets
and their skinny books
spouting out the new underground poetry?
And where the fuck was poetry?
I needed the connection,
I needed to pretend it was Paris in the 20s,

JACK GRAPES

or Greenwhich Village in the 60s.
There was a bookstore just off
Hollywood Boulevard that sold poetry books,
so I took my just-published book of poems
Perchance, in All Your Travels,
Have You Ever Been to Pittsburgh?
and asked the owner if he'd take 5 copies on consignment.
I was hoping I'd run into a poet
among the stacks of "thin" books,
but alas, it was just me
and the handlebarred-mustachioed owner behind the counter.
His name was Red, and I heard he hung out with Bukowski.
But I kept my mouth shut.
I like to keep my distance.
I needed to keep Bukowski as far away as possible.
The bookstore was packed with books, floor to ceiling,
on every counter, on the floor under the tables,
and lots of thin books, but no thin poets.
I became desperate.
I walked the streets of Westwood
in my black beatnick sweatshirt
and asked if anyone wrote poetry,
but was ignored by everyone,
especially the college-dressed
hip-now-and-happening crowd
coming out of the movie theater
next to a pizza joint.
"Poets," I asked, "anyone here a poet?"
I got nothing but blank stares and pitying looks.
Someone put a quarter into my hand
so obligingly I recited one of my poems,
but by the time I got to the big closing line,
they were already across the street
walking into the Hamburger Hamlet.

One day, walking the mean streets of DTLA,
a guy in an alley pulled me over and said,
"Hey, kid, I hear you're looking for poets."
"Yeah," I said, "I'm a poet myself."
"Listen," he said, "there's a poetry reading
today in Topanga Canyon. For a few bucks,
I can give you a map."
"Topanga Canyon," I said, "where's that?"
"Right off PCH," he said.
"PCH?" I said, "sounds like a drug."
"Kid," he said, "don't get smart."
He pulled out a map, showed me the route,
and unable to contain my glee,
I hit the Harbor Freeway,
took the 101 West and turned up PCH
like I was fresh from the creeks and loaded for bear.
A few miles up the twisting turning road on Topanga Canyon,
and there it was, a little theeee-ater carved into the hillside.
I signed up to read, read a few poems, met a few poets,
and kept a look-out in case we'd get busted
by the Secret Police for spreading unauthorized modern poetry.
A tall guy wearing a blue work shirt introduced himself,
said his name was Jim Krusoe,
and that there was a poetry workshop in Venice
that met in a place called Beyond Baroque.
"Beyond Broke," I said, "that sounds perfect."
"No," he said, "Baroque. Like the highly ornate art
that appeared between the Renaissance style
and the Neoclassical style."
"Oh," I said, folding my poems in my back pocket,
"that Baroque."
"Yeah, we meet in a storefront
on West Washington Blvd every Wednesday night,

read poems, get feedback.
About 20 of us.
Why dontcha drop by?"

Twenty poets,
all in one place.
The end of the rainbow.
Twenty struggling, straggling, thin, scrawny poets.
The motherlode.
"Why dontcha drop by?" he repeated.
So I did.
A few days later I gathered up a few poems,
drove down Olympic Boulevard,
and headed west toward the ocean.
Turned out Beyond Baroque
was nothing more than a small
seemingly abandoned store
next to a liquor mart and a bar.
Looking through the plate glass window,
I could see several people
sitting on folding chairs arranged in a circle
on a concrete floor, and a few others
perched on the platform
where mannequins might have stood
when the place was a dress shop
or a retail outlet.
Whatever they were selling before,
now they were giving it away,
giving away poetry for free.
Two poets, John Harris and Joseph Hanson,
were in charge, mostly calling on people to read,
and acting like traffic cops
when the feedback got testy.

I later learned that John owned Papa Bach bookstore,
a block down from the Nu-Art Theater
on Santa Monica Blvd.,
and Joseph Hanson also wrote detective novels
featuring the first gay sleuth, David Brandstetter.
The room was small, not much bigger than my kitchen,
but when the poets read,
it seemed to get larger,
as if the words pushed the walls west
toward the ocean and east
toward the San Diego Freeway.
All the poetry and poets and poetry publications
were either in New York or San Francisco.
We were just an island in the middle of a lake
in the middle of a large desert.
It felt like we were on an L.A. Ghost Ship
re-inventing what modern poetry could be.
The twenty of us.

Once a month, Beyond Baroque invited a poet
from another city to read,
and we twenty straggling struggling poets gathered
to see what the outside world was doing.
They were usually published poets,
bringing their "thin" books to the podium
and reading to us,
hungry for word from other planets.
What were the language poets doing?
What were the confessional poets doing?
What were the neo-narrative poets doing?
What were the minimalist poets doing?
Every Wednesday we drove from Hollywood,
Compton, the South Bay, the Valley,

East Los Angeles, Culver City,
Santa Monica, Calabasas, Ventura, North Hollywood.
We got in our little boats and rowed out to that island
in the middle of that lake
in the middle of this great desert,
and we listened to poetry,
and we fought among ourselves
for our place in this world of poetry,
a world, as John Harris was to say,
that was no bigger than a postage stamp.
Every one of us fought for our place
on that postage stamp,
we argued we tested we complained we corrected
we yelled we threatened we supported we threw fits
we got drunk we tore our poems in half
and thrashed the stale air of poetry
in an effort to make something living breathe
west and east beyond the walls of that small room.
After a year or two, we moved to the back room
of this store front, but it was just as small,
just as cold, just as packed.
The twenty of us grew to forty, and the forty
grew to sixty, some of the original gang moving on,
newcomers jockeying for position
in the center of the circle.
When John Harris and Joseph Hanson moved on,
four of us were appointed to run the workshop,
to act as traffic cops:
James Krusoe,
Francis Dean Smith (Bukwoksi's ex-wife)
Carol Marsh,
and me.
And at some point,

after another few years,
we moved on too,
and others took over.
The Ghost Ship sailed on,
poetry kept going.

During that time, I met a lot of poets,
wrote lots of poems,
argued about poetry, shared wine.
Some nights a mild fight would break out,
some nights a drunk
or stoned street person would wander in,
trying to figure out what was going on
in that little storefront room.
"What's this?" they'd slur.
"Poetry," we said.
"Oh," they shrugged, thought about it for a moment,
then staggered back out.
Some nights someone would take their clothes off
and spout modern poetry.
Some nights Barry Simons would sit bent over,
his bald head bobbing up and down,
as he recited a poem he'd made up on the spot,
a wild kind of stream of consciousness
filling the room with Surreal images.
Tom Waits came in to read "Diamonds on my Windshield."
Exene Cervenca and John Doe read poems
that ended up songs in their L.A. Band "X".
We were a motley crew,
huddled together in that storefront room,
chilly in winter and humid in summer.
But for all the crazy shenanigans,
we were serious poets

serious about poetry.
If you didn't know better,
you'd think our lives were at stake.
If you knew better, you'd know
our lives were at stake.
We weren't playing games or fooling around.
We were out to bring the word, to spread the gospel.
I argued with them, I fought with them, I supported them,
I loved them:
Wanda Coleman, Dennis Ellman, Michael C Ford,
Peter Levitt, Michelle T. Clinton, James Krusoe,
Michael Andrews, Leland Hickman, Bob Flanagan,
Holly Prado, Harry Northup, Eloise Klien Healy,
Kita Shantiris, Dennis Cooper, Doraine Poretz,
Steve Richmond, Curtis Lyle, Kate Braverman,
Ron Koertge, Deena Metzger, John Thomas,
Bill Mohr, and dozens of others
who came for awhile and left.
Bill Mohr published several anthologies of poetry
as part of Momentum Press,
John Harris published Bachy Magazine
that featured many of the L.A. poets,
Michael Andrews and I founded Bombshetler Press,
and so on and so on and so on,
dozens of presses and hundreds of poetry books
and many hundreds of readings and performances
in the small back room
of that small storefront
on West Washington Boulevard.
I forget when exactly,
but Beyond Baroque moved
to what was the old Venice City Hall,
that big while building on Venice Blvd,
next to the old Venice Jail,

that is now SPARC, Social & Public Resource Center.
Most all the poets I know have all come through
Beyond Baroque at some time or other.

Beyond Baroque has been the touchstone
of my life
as a poet in this city
for the last 50 years,
and it's hard for me to imagine
what I would have done
had it not been for the energy
they allowed and the focus they provided
for all the poets in L.A.
We didn't need the Paris cafes
nor the Greenwich Village coffee houses
nor the Chicago south side bars
nor the San Francisco hippies.
We had Beyond Baroque.
All — or most all — of the poetry venues,
cafe readings, workshops, and poetry gatherings
that have sprouted and flourished
in the 50 years since George Drury Smith
founded Beyond Baroque
in that little storefront on West Washington Blvd
trace their beginnings
in some way shape or form
back to that first watering hole for poets,
that small island
in the middle of a lake
in the middle
of this large desert.

Well, it's getting late.
I have to go write a poem . . . .

HOTSPUR

A line that goes nowhere
starts in Spain where bats
through the low trees
make morning needles
in my hair but I'm relent
less about austerity something
you can cry forever and it fails
to absolve you like the unfamiliar
cross on that hill where travelers
like you having found what was
lost and lost what they'd found
dream the distant cries of yokels
looking for a handout right there
where the woman lifts her dress
on a dare and dusts off the park
bench she's been sleeping on
all night and nothing you say
to yourself or anyone can
replace the notion you
had of yourself growing taller
in that chevy bel air with
blue seat covers stopped
at the red light on Earhart
Boulevard at 2 o'clock in
the morning on your
way to see the cajun girl
who promised you
her body as ransom
for the prisoners
you denied the king

THE FIRE NEXT TIME

Fire ain't
what it's
cracked up
to be
but that's
another story.
If I say the door
was open,
I'd be lying,
but that's
how it is
in a poem,
the lying
I mean.
It's all a lie.
Like you think truth's
gonna save you
and it ain't.
Mary's gonna weep
no matter how
you slice it,
Jesus gonna get nailed
and you're gonna warm
your toes
by the fire
when you think
life's all cushy and cozy
only to burst
into flame

when the unseen hand
pokes its finger
into your business
just to see
if your legs curl
from the heat
and if the smoke
from your heart
be white
or black.

A TRUE STORY, IT REALLY HAPPENED

I met a young girl on the beach
and we fell in love instantly
and walked into the ocean
sinking all the way to the bottom
and we walked that way holding hands
all the way to Japan.
When we got there, I was still old
and she was still young
and our love had been eaten away
by a thousand fish
but there was so much of it
we still had plenty love left over
when we walked together up to the little
tiki shack on the beach
and ordered belinni's and drank
them until the sun set
and then we drove off in a convertible
and she stood up and took off
her blouse and bra, and waved at everyone
in their cars on the highway.
Guys driving SUV's waved at her,
her beautiful breasts white marbled skin
jolting them at the wheel as they looked
toward the ocean and couldn't believe their eyes.
Their wives or girlfriends
slapped their heads and yelled,
"Keep your eyes on the road!"
"Maybe you better sit down," I said.
Instead, she stepped out of her skirt

and stood there naked, just waving and waving.
She was beautiful and I was old
but for some reason
she said she loved me
and I tried not to question it,
who would dare question love
when it finds you on the edge of a continent,
I just let her love seep into my bones
deep into my heart
and cried tears of gratitude
that no matter how old you think you are
and no matter how unattractive you think you are
love has a way of finding you,
it tracks you down like a cheetah
and eats you, eats every morsel of you,
licks your bones clean
until nothing but the heart is exposed
and then it eats that too in one big fucking
gulping mouthful.

this is a true story.
it really happened.

BEATS

beats the dead beats
being dead beats
the dying beats
the beat of the heart
without a defective
valve beats the mind
unnecessarily cognitive
beats that other thing
what was it I forget what
it beats it beats the tree
you climbed as a boy
the cracked sidewalk you
tripped over and skinned
beats the knee the face
the elbow the shoulder beats
the blood beats the bones
broken on the cement beats
all the city trash
and hollar for a penny
up the tenement steps
for a 2 cents plain
beats the crossing the ocean
beats the boxing ring beats
the mat you slept on beats
the black forest you came from
beats the skinny school
you ran away from the teachers
with sticks who wacked your hand
the ones who beat you

and shoved you in a closet
and said let's see you get out
of this one beats them all
you're still here breathing
giving your son the words
that ain't that something
that ain't that something
that just about beats all.

GULF OF MEXICO

My father liked being on a boat
in the Gulf of Mexico,
anchored near one of the oil rigs,
pulling up spade fish and red snapper
and swigging from a bottle
of Jim Beam.

Fried chicken, ham sandwiches,
burgers from Bud's Broiler,
the bagels and lox my father brought
and who knows what else
he and the men ate with their beers.

The boat was slimy with fish
blood, the men bare-chested,
yelling out instructions
as the fish dangled from their lines.

The one time I went with him,
I was ten-years old,
and all I could think about was
would he be able to drive the car
all the way home, would he end up
falling down drunk as we walked
to the car carrying the ice-chest
full of the day's catch.

But now, when I think back on it –
God, he musta had a good time!

I'm so glad my father had a good time.
These men were not Jewish –
his drinking buddies from AA –
they had all that gentile good-ole boy
razzmatazz, red-necks for sure
slapping their hands together
and howling at the midday sun.

My father, who never finished 8th grade,
who read Kant and Hegel and Lenin and Marx –
God, he musta had a good time!
I'm so glad my father had a good time.
Maybe it brought back the days of summer
on the lower east side,
during the Great Depression,
when he was in his early 30s,
without a job, without a home, a man
riding the rails like Jack Dempsey,
and like Dempsey, he fought
in the ring for chump change
so he could rent a room for the night.

I want my father to have a good time.
I want my father to taste the salt of this life,
to carouse with the men and spend the night
with a woman he met in a bar,
to come home with no money in his pockets,
just the matchbooks we found
from Gentillich's Bar on Rampart Street
or the Econo Lodge Motel
a mile from the airport.
Live it up, Dad. Hook those fish,
spray that Jim Beam all over your face,

guzzle it down and stagger back
to the shed where the fish are gutted
and puke your guts out in the parking lot
and drive down the Airline Highway,
turn right on Carrollton Avenue,
past Borden's Ice Cream Parlor,
past Jim's Fried Chicken,
past Ping Pang Pong's Chinese Restaurant,
then a left on Fontainebleau Drive,
then slam into the driveway of that two-story brick
colonial home you bought
selling eye-glasses to the country folk
from Houma and Gretna and Bogalusa,
then fling open the front door and charge
up the stairs to the bathroom
and slam the medicine chest cabinet
to smithereens,
to this life,
to this fishing trip
on the Gulf of Mexico
where you're finally
and irrevocably free.

RESUME THE RESUMÉ

Some nights I sleep in my tuxedo.
My fingers untie the bow-tie
in my sleep as if I were
swooning to the tune of "Begin the Beguine."
The pain in my hip goes away,
a rapture divine
of fried chicken in a roadside diner.
A song of tropical splendor
comes from an old jukebox
straight from the 1930s.

Powell and Astaire appear
on a winding staircase.
The threads of my dreams
take me back to the two-lane highway
on the way to Baton Rouge, snaking through
the swamps and cypress trees, swearing
my love would last forever
in that smoky bar where we met
over a bourbon and Coke.

I've seen people die from clutching
gold coins too tightly. I'd rather fling them
from the caboose of a train
crossing the Mississippi River
over the old Slidel Bridge, and there,
tap-dancing on those steel girders,
Eleanor and Fred
dancing at the speed of light and the world

surrounding all of us shrinks
to the size
of a peppercorn.

I join them for a moment, tap-dance
between them, an apparition they hardly expected,
an ember between the fires of their love,
and then, in my tuxedo, I dive into the river,
swim the Australian crawl
like Johnny Weismuller
promising the girl in the bar
never never to part.

SEND IN THE CLOWN

October slides down the gullet,
shadows on the grass spreading like smoke.
Someone walks alone along the sidewalk,
stops to watch me put up Halloween
gravestones and skeletons.
"Come by Halloween night," I say,
"the lights and fog machines will be going,
and the sound effects, really fun and scary."

Bones, bloody arms, sawed-off legs,
clawing hands with long fingernails
scattered on the ground.

Dr. Shivers with his green goggles
moves his animatronic head and says:
"I'm doing an experiment with electrici-
electrici-electrici-ty!"

There's the screeching witch, the man
who lifts his head up as the blood drips
down into the hole where his neck was;
there's disembodied heads
that light up and roll their eyes.
But you know what scares the kids
the most? The clown sitting on a box
of dynamite, shaking, and his jaw
trembles up and down and his head
bobs and his teeth chatter.
Something about clowns.

I played a clown once in a play,
and after awhile, I thought I was going
to go crazy.
One of the animatronic figures
that sits on the front porch
greeting the kids as they trudge
toward the front door for treats
holds his head in his hands,
his red clown hair falling forward,
making the macabre sounds of crying,
then lifts his head to show he's really
laughing hysterically, yet you can't
wipe away the notion that he's crying.
A crying clown, Pagliachi, pretty frightening.
When the kids get to the front door,
I make jokes, like a Borscht Belt comedian,
mimicking a Dracula accent.

Sometimes it overwhelms the kids,
and once in a while, a little girl
will tell me proudly that she was scared
last year, but this year, she's not.

"Good for you," I say. "I'm scared every year."

They're puzzled for a moment.
How can I be the one who is scared?
Then I compliment them on their costume—
all in that Bela Lugosi voice—
and shove the bowl of candy at them--
the bowl with the hand in the middle that grabs
their fingers as they reach for the chocolate—
and for good measure, I let out a yell

that, if the hand didn't work, my voice
does, making some piss in their pants
with fright, especially, the teenage ones,
who think they've got it all covered.

Screams all around.

"Hubris," I tell them. "You're never
too old to be scared.

Then I go back to being the Borsht Belt comic,
joking about their bloody faces or twinkly
ballet slippers. "Oh, you must be a fairy
princess," I say as I hold the bowl of candy
out for them to dip into.

The line of kids stretches down the block.
SUV's pull up and drop off a baker's dozen
in their wonderful costumes.
By 7:30pm I'm exhausted, but carry on,
stealing a few bars of chocolate
like an alcoholic stealing a sip of bourbon.
My back starts to hurt from stooping over,
then rushing back to stand on a stool
so I can thrust my face through the speakeasy
portal of the front door and freeze it
into a hysterical smile, eyes wide open,
so the kids can't tell whether it's a mask
or a real person. They stare at it for a few moments,
transfixed, unable to ring the doorbell.
When they finally do, I scream a chilling
helloooooooo and scare the pants off them.
Then I step down from the stool,

fling open the door, and soothe their frightened
hearts.

"Vell, vat haff we here, a voolf in sheep's clothing,
or are you vearing your Uncle Victor's pajamas?"
Then I slide the bowl toward their eager hands
and say, "Von piece of candy per person;
any von grabbing more vill haff his fingers
torn off by zee hungry hand, ha ha ha ha ha!"

At 9pm sharp, the parade of kids stops,
as if on cue.
One minute the front porch and sidewalk are packed,
and at 9pm, as if a curtain suddenly went down,
the streets and sidewalks are empty.

And I'm exhausted.
But I wait just to make sure, in case a few stragglers
come around the corner.
There's something sad and lonely
about the fog and sound effects
and ghoulish creatures working overtime,

but the show's over, the audience has gone.
So I start unplugging the electrical cords,
bring in the fog machines, turn off the boom boxes
that blare out their creepy sound effects of rattling chains
and ghostly screams and horrific voices telling the kids:
"Beware of this house!"

By 9:30, I can't wait to get into the kitchen, have a beer
and a slice of pizza, when three little girls about eleven
come creeping into the front yard. I hand them a handful of

candy
and send them on their way. But they refuse to leave.
"I'm shutting everything down," I say, "show's over."
They start to head toward the gate when one little girl
turns around and says, "We came to see the face.
Can we see the face?"

I melt. They want to see my face in the speakeasy portal
of the front door. They want to see my face, frozen
in a terrible grimace, so they can ring the doorbell
and get the hell scared out of them. The face, I think to myself,
they came to see the face. My face.

I tell them, okay, but you have to go back to the sidewalk
so I can turn on the lights and turn on the sound effects
and fog machines and then go back inside
and stand on the stool and stick my head in the door.
Okay, they agree, as if the four of us were in a play
together, acting out this ritual only for ourselves,
and I'm the wizard and they're the munchkins.

I turn on the spots, set up the sound effects,
crank up the fog machines, close the door, get on the stool,
stick my head through the portal and freeze my face
in that clownish grin. I stare ahead, as if I were unreal,
but I can see the girls take one careful step after another,
up the walkway, up the steps to the front porch,
then approach the door and stare up at the scary clown face
thrust through the speakeasy portal.

They stand there awhile, not wanting to rush the great
moment. Then one of them reaches out and presses
the doorbell, and I look down at them

and say, "Helloooooooo. Haff you come for kandy?
Kandy to make you sick and rot your teeth
and make some dentist rich?!?!"

Then I fling open the door and thrust the bowl of candy
out as if I were about to stab them with a sword.
The girls are ecstatic.
All night long they've waited for this.
Their hands reach into the bowl,
the hand in the bowl bends forward and grabs their fingers,
the girls shriek and giggle, not believing their good fortune.
Finally, after several attempts, they scoop up handfuls
of candy and race down the steps to the front gate.
At the gate, they turn around and look at me.
"Thank you," they say, just like their parents taught them.

And the clown smiles
and waves them off
into the damp
October night.

TEA FOR TWO

The universe is alone.
We are alone.
Just us and the universe.
Snow illuminates the mountains.
My thoughts lay scattered on the ground.
A useless dispute between Chevy and Buick.
Glares of horror anxious the absurdist barbequist.
Does anyone know where the restroom is?
Over there the universe sulks.
Nobody talks to it.
We'd do the talking, but we're alone, too.
God doesn't fit in the thing he made
or she made or you made or they made or
it made or if it got made at all.
Time for a glass of wine, a fine
Bordeaux or a salty Chianti.
Anything to get the taste of hell out of my mouth.
I wanted a moon with the moon
but God advised otherwise.
The universe is alone.
We are alone.
Just us and the universe.
And God, sulking in the corner.
What a cry baby!
No one to play with, he whimpers.
With a bang, God, I tell him.
Try the bang.
It won't sound like a bang, God says.
Why not, I ask.

I made it all too big, He says.
Yep, I agree, it's certainly that.
What, He asks.
Big, I say.
It's real big, I say.
Your little all alone universe is too big,
no one here to play with,
way way too big.
I made it bigger than a breadbox, God says.
Not by bread alone, I tell him.
That's true, he admits.
You wrote that, I say, jabbing God's chest
with my index finger.
Read what you wrote, I say,
and you won't feel so alone.
Alone, he whimpers.
All alone.
The universe is so alone.
We are so alone.
Just us and the universe.

EAGLES ON THE MOON

You're swallowing snow while I eat fire.
When I am out, you're inside somewhere,
putting words on paper,
looking for your name in a poem.

If you send me your name,
I will put it in this poem
so you'll always know,
no matter where you are,
no matter how lost you feel,
that you've found a place
in the world,
and in this poem,
you'll never be lost.

Even in the desperate hours of sleep,
I imagine you are trying to write a poem
or walking through the rooms of your house
taking up the carpet,
or standing in the kitchen
making zuccini bread.
Between us, eagles take flight, eagles land
on the moon, the moon rises in the east,
the full moon full of all possibilities
but the one possibility
of a city like Paris or Denver
or the country of regret we will face
before we die.

I am dying.
Sometimes, it's a little at a time,
as it should be, as it must be,
because that's the way it is
in this life, no one gets out
alive.

But sometimes, I am dying all at once,
a long fall into my body.
Just a tub of emptiness.
Unable to breathe
life back into my heart.

I look into the mirror and see how old
I've become.
I can't stop it, can't hold it back,
can't change it.
How will anyone love me
when I get old?
I am old already.

And eagles landing on the moon
are not enough
when what's the point
of the moon
if those you love
are not there with you.

I imagine
when I turn away from the mirror,
that I turn away from you,

and walk away,
like the cat that goes
under the house
to die alone,
not to bother anyone.

You'll come looking
for me, I suspect.
But you won't find me.

You'll have to fall into yourself,
just like I did,
fall and fall and fall some more,
without me
to hold you
or to scare you into laughter
when you walk into a room.

What will we regret?
That we walked
towards
each other,
or away?

THE OTHER STORY, THE OTHER NARRATOR

I once was told by my 9th Grade writing teacher to lay my cards
on the table at the beginning of a story and let the story be about
how the hand develops, how the players play, what happens as
a result of the luck of the draw, as they say, and what happens
because one of the players remembered that a Queen of Spades
had already been played and the Jack of Diamonds was the
operative card to bet on. Okay, so here goes. I'm laying the cards
down. Number One, and most important for you to know: The
narrator of this story may look like me and talk like me, but he's
entirely different. If you saw the two of us side by side, you'd
think one of us was born in Clovis, California and the other
was transported here from one of the moons of Pluto, which is
not even considered a planet anymore, but a "proto-planet." So
much for the vagaries of astronomy. The narrator of this story,
as you've probably noticed by now, likes to digress, whereas I
like to get to the point. "Don't eat the lobster," I might say, "it's
tainted." See, up front. No wiggling around or hemming and
hawing, I get to the point and make my point. Said, done, fin-
ished. Eat the sandwich. Let's go. Time to leave. Don't call in the
morning. Let's fuck.

Okay, second card, more of a throwaway than a strategic
move. The narrator likes books but he doesn't read them. I hate
books and read everything. Nothing is unimportant, no face or
anecdote too trivial, no description too tedious, no confession
too salacious or too boring. I want it all. I hate it, it's of no use,
to tell the truth, but I want it. Was Lincoln wearing his top hat
just before he got up to deliver the Address? Who the fuck gives
a fuck! But me? It's a fact of great importance, equal to Caesar's
crossing the Rubicon or Shakespeare's phone number. I have

all those facts and anecdotes in my head, filed away in neat little compartments, ready for retrieval at the drop of Lincoln's (he wasn't, by the way, wearing it) hat. The narrator, he's got so many books he could build a house with them, but has he read any? One, even? Not a one. But he knows the titles and the authors. He loves them, the titles and the authors. Mention Dostoyevsky's *Notes from Underground* and he swoons. Say Proust's *Remembrance of Things Past* and he falls to the floor, foaming at the mouth. Call out Flaubert's *Sentimental Education* and his eyes roll into his head and his head begins to spin. But he hasn't read a single one of them. Me? I've read them all. Go ahead. Say *Across the River and Into the Trees*. Say it. Nothing. I could care less. He has a heart attack and drives his jeep across the river and into the trees. I mean, give me a fucking break. Write down on a slip of paper and slide it over to me *The Great Gatsby*. Read it ten times. Daisy, Daisy, give me your answer do. Holy fucking moly! Who the crap cares about Mr. Big Shot Gatsby, poor old Gatsby, sad old Gatsby, mansion-sized Gatsby. You ever read *Microbe Hunters* by Paul DeKruif. I not only read it three times, I read it backwards, that's right, backwards, page by page, when I was fifteen, the summer before my junior year of highschool. Didn't make a difference. Nothing makes a difference. The books are boring, but I read them, slurp up the words and the facts and the anecdotes and the paragraphs, more and more and more until I drop from exhaustion. See what I mean, we're different, the narrator of this story and me. I know you're gonna think that just because I'm using the first-person pronoun that it's me, but it isn't. He and I, we're different as night and day. "Night and Day," a song by Cole Porter. A porterhouse steak. It was like driving a stake into my heart. A lonely hunter. The night of the. Of things past. And punishment. Huckleberry Dick. Catcher in the Lighthouse. Sound and Solitude a Hundred Years Before the Mast. Under the Invisible Man. David Dalloway. Farewell to Flesh. Don Bovary.

Just to be thorough, the narrator prefers to sleep on the left side of the bed, the side closest to the wall, preferably to a window. Me? I don't care. Sometimes, I sleep with my head where my feet would be, my feet where my head would be. Sometimes I try the other side, then the other side, then the other side, until I forget which is the other side. The side by the window or the side by the closet door. Sometimes I sleep with my head up my ass. It doesn't matter to me one stitch. But when he gets a room for the night in some motel off of Highway 129, and there's no left side to the bed, just two right sides, he checks out and drives another 250 miles until he finds one that does. You'd be amazed how many motels have beds with two left sides, or two right sides. Some have left and right sides, but no middles. I love to sleep in the middle of the bed. But what if there's no middle. Me? I take what's given. I'll sleep on the floor, if necessary. But him, it's left side or nothing, left side against the wall or against the window, but that's it. He drives me crazy sometimes. But I put up with him, with it, I should say. The Light in the Heart of Darkness. Song of Native Son. Farewell to Parade's End. Loving the Age of Innocence.

SONG WITHOUT MUSIC

You're never too old to wake up,
Sleeping late is for the birds,
You're never too old to break up
Holding on freezes the heart
      and it ain't smart to start
      believing the crap they
      shove in your brain
      a refrain of coffee and taxes
      that axes your mind
      like the others who
      close their eyes
      and see nothing.

You're never too old to wake up,
drive out to a cabin in the woods
You're never too old to make up
      when love walks around
      in the chambers of your heart
      pumping unleaded rocket fuel
      as you sit in the corner
      ears plugged
      so you don't hear the fake good news
      breaking your knees
      just the bad good news you're trying
      to sleep through.

You're never too old to wake up,
sleeping late is for the birds.
You're never too old to shake up

You're never too old to rake up
      all the leaves on the front lawn
      of your house with the kids
      trying to look like you
      or your mother or your
      grandfather who slept thru
      the wars and the bullshit
      ole moneybags gave him
      ole moneybags who
      oppressed oppressed oppressed
      oppressed oppressed.

You're never too old to wake up.
And you're never too young to sleep.
Close your eyes little one,
Forget the good news, nothing's really
      happening, it's all blues,
      just a bad dream you seem
      tired of it all just sleep and
      stop listening to this song stop
      listening to this song and
      close your eyes to the lies and sleep.
      Just sleep.
      Just sleep.

You're never too young to sleep.

JACK GRAPES

DAY JOB

I think to write poetry is a day job
The boat I missed when I drove the car
upstream with oodles of bagpipes in the trunk
is a night job too poetry gets done when
you're not working but working
if you know what I mean
too many rivers to cross so you camp on land
with each metaphor harpsichords of rondolets
broken marriages dead grief stricken wrong
turns insults given received porridge
and the land mass you drive over from
New Orleans to Elay from New Orleans
to Montreal from Elay to Seattle from battle
ground Idaho to suicide Cincinnati
where I did a tv show once and talked
afterwards to the quarterback for the Bengals
blond hair no opinions he knew fade out
in the flat and the hook and ladder but
not much else though a day job can sap your
spirit and a night job can whack you out
and no job can stone you like the song says
and poetry, poor poetry, pathetic poetry,
a lopsided lobster on the bottom of the ocean,
paltry poetry, piecemeal poetry,
no one wants to see the poetry you wrote in college,
rather talk tax credits and buffalo wings,
something that puts food on the table,
the table – when all are in bed and the house is quiet –
the table on which you write your bloodthirsty poems.

WHAT'S TO COME

You already know what's to come.
Others have seen it already,
know what's coming.
The prophets laid it out
pretty clearly,
voices in the wilderness.
This pair of glasses they covered
along with the ploughshares
and pruning hooks.
They told you about the glass of milk,
and the pair of scissors
you keep by the bed
and the rock you found by the seashore.
Everything's been foretold.
I cut into stale bread and toasted it
and heard them say, you knew it was
going to be stale, I already told you.
You knew I was going to cut it,
I tell them back, see, I'm doing it
as you speak, watching the knife
slide so close to my thumb.
Shall I slice the flesh right there,
just for you, with this unbeaten sword?

JACK GRAPES

DID YOU BRUSH YOUR TEETH TODAY?

Bart was insistent. A skull for one is a skull for all. But rein-
deer? Never. Love has its extremities, granted, he grumbled,
but at what point does protocol attenuate surveillance? The
crowd nodded their heads uplifted arms twinkle-toed fish.
On a rampage, is what they went on. After that, the city was
never the same. Grand boulevards dwindled into trash-strewn
alleyways. Skyscraping monuments slipped into the degener-
ancy of pot-holes. Marthas became Maxs, Rutherfords became
Rex, Amsterdam, Amos. By nightfall, the mansions of the rich
turned to outhouses for salvation, but no one cared or even
lifted a finger to save them. Bart's power grew, though no one
knew why? Power had to flow somewhere. If not to Bart, to
whom? To Ned, who spent more time with his son than the law
allowed? To Bernice, who was a woman. To Jimmy, who was
only seven years old, and imagine the chaos if a seven-year-old
were allowed to cut grass! The obvious became so obvious, it
was not obvious anymore, but obviously, obviousness no longer
held the key to delusions and hallucinations. By the end of the
week, everyone ran out of can-openers. Lemon tarts became as
scarce as powdered beignets. Dust itself, once anonymous even
in sunlight, gathered fellow traveling molecules of schmutz and
made mountains out of molehills. The city slowly seeped into
sleepless alliteration. Bart went to bed without a pillow, having
eschewed duck feathers for cowhide. Love was never spoken of
again. Eyeballs fell from their sockets and the dwellers of the
city believed that, finally, they could see better than they had
ever seen before. The sunshine of a black hole had finally won.
There was nowhere to turn, and everyone had stopped turning.
Perfection at last was perfect. Bart slept like a baby.

ANY STYLE

Driving west out of El Paso,
the sun coming up behind me,
I look for a diner or roadside café
off the main highway.
Maybe I'll just follow those dust clouds
that cars coming the other way
leave in their wake.
Maybe it'll be
just a scratched formica counter
and a waitress wearing
jeans and a T-shirt.
"Eggs any style," I tell her,
waiting to see if she gets it —
the joke, I mean -- but she doesn't.
"Anything on the side?" she asks.
"Yeah," I say, studying
the menu as if it were
that calculus final I barely passed.
"Yeah, gimme the bacon,
the hash browns,
. . . . you got grits?"
I look up from the menu
and admire her frontage.
After seven hours driving
in the dark, then heaving away
from the sun, the mouth waters
for the old breakfast roadside
standbys: toast, butter,
greasy bacon and eggs.

JACK GRAPES

And frontage.
The urge rises from my toes,
through my stomach and into my chest,
the urge to reach out and touch them,
those well-fed breasts
inside that hefty bra
inside that white T-shirt.
"Yeah," she says, moving the eraser
of the pencil back and forth
behind her ear, "we got grits."
"I'm up for grits," I say,
making the word grits sound
like I'd already eaten a mouthful.
She shifts her weight from one leg
to the other, writes on the pad,
then says it,
— what I came in here for
in the first place,
not the food,
but to hear her say the words:
"Three eggs,
any style,
side a bacon,
side a hash browns,
side a grits."
I almost swoon,
almost lean
across the counter
and place my head
between her breasts,
almost blurt out that I love her,
that I've been loving her
all night long —

loving her as I drove through the darkness
on this two lane highway
filled with nothing
but tractor trailers
and 18-wheelers
and tank trucks and boom trucks
and freight liners and box vans,
two-ton stake trucks
and Scammell ballast tractors,
not to mention the flatbeds
and the pick-ups,
all heading west,
just like me.
I want to tell her
that I love her
right now, here in this diner,
thirty miles west of El Paso,
and will always love her,
love her to my dying day,
love her any style,
side a bacon,
side a hash browns,
side a grits.
But I don't.
The sun's already breaking
the water glasses on the counter,
rousting the silverware,
dashing the flies to the floor
where they languish in the heat.
Five-hundred miles to go
before I hit L.A.,
before I take the big curve
where the I-10 turns north
under the overpass,

and heads up the Pacific Coast Highway,
white beaches to my left,
brown cliffs to my right.
Five-hundred miles to go.
"Yeah," I say, "that should do it,
and gimme an order
of wheat toast, butter, jelly,
jam, marmalade with those
little pieces of citrus fruit
and rind, and coffee,
thick black coffee,
coffee that's been sitting
in the pot for days,
just bring the whole pot,
and sugar, lots of sugar,
and cream, lots of cream."
Then she sticks the pencil
in her hair behind her ear
and looks at me, finally.
"Mr. Poet," she says,
smiling as the sun
begins to creep up
across her face.
"Yep," I say, relaxing
onto the stool
and putting both elbows
on the counter,
"I'm Mr. Poet,
and I got
lots of poems,
any style you want,
side a bacon,
side a hash browns,
side a grits."

ACKNOWLEDGEMENTS

Some of the poems in this book first appeared in the following publications, to whose generous editors grateful acknowledgment is made: *AfterImage, Alcatraz, The Alley Cat Readings, Amalgamated Holding Company, American Book Jam, Angel's Gate Review, As Each Unit Is a Constant, Bachy, Bellingham Review, Beverly Hills Playhouse Newsletter, Beyond Baroque Magazine, Bitterroot, Black Rabbit Press, Blitz, Blue Window, Blue Note, Border, California State Poetry Quarterly, California Quarterly, Chattahoochee Review, Comic Spirit, CQ–Contemporary Quarterly, Chiron Review, Cream City Review, Cultural Weekly, Deepest Valley Review, Earth, Electrum, The Fantastic, Foreign Exchange, 48th Street Press, FRE&D, Gorilla Extract, Gridlock, Gypsy, Japanese American Magazine, The Juice Bar, Kauri, Kaleidescope, Labris, LA Weekly, Lingo, Manic Press, Momentum, My Eyes All out of Breath, New Lantern Club Review, New Orleans Express, The New Orleans Review, Nexus, Olé, Orange County Poetry Review, The Outsider, Pinchpenny, Poetry East, Poetry/LA, Poetry Magazine, PoetMeat, rara avis, Rattle, Rufus, Scree, Shattersheet, Southern Spillway, Stone Cloud, Sycamore Review, Tempest, This Poem Knows You, The Tiresian, Tsunami, Up:jut, Vagabond, Voices, Vol.No., Waves, The Willie, The Word, Wormwood Review, Yellow Fingers, ZYZZYVA,* and the following anthologies: *Anthology of Revolutionary Poetry, Gridlock, The Maverick Poets, Men of Our Time, News from Inside, Nueva Poesia de Los Angeles, Peace Among the Ants, Poetry Loves Poetry.*

PHOTO & ART CREDITS:

Cover photo on *Trees, Coffee and the Eyes of Deer*: Samuel Grapes

Cover art on *Lucky Finds*: Jack Grapes

Cover art on *The Naked Eye*: DeLoss McGraw

Cover design on *The Naked Eye*: Alan Berman

Cover design on *Poems So Far*: Baz Here

Cover art on *and the running form, naked, Blake*: Jack Grapes

Cover art & design on *Breaking Down the Surface of the World*: Judith James

Cover art on *All the Sad Angels*: Arturo Michelena, "Escenas del Circo", 1891

Photo of poet: Baz Here

Photo-Shop cover of *Any Style*: Baz Here

INDEX

JACK GRAPES